Environmental and Nuclear Networks in the Global South

For decades, expert bureaucrats have been moving regularly across borders, from their home institutions to international organizations, and forging collaborative networks with peers. Analyzing over twenty-five years of environmental and nuclear technology projects data for 150 countries, this book provides a comprehensive study of international cooperation among elite bureaucrats in developing states. An empirical study that will interest researchers, undergraduate, and graduate students of political and social sciences, this is the first book to explain the causes of transnational cooperation in the Global South and find a link between domestic level of skills and international cooperation. The author methodically illustrates how state experts with high skills can reap the benefits of international technical cooperation. In contrast, bureaucrats with low skills cannot forge stable collaborative ties with foreign peers and gain little from participating in these transgovernmental networks.

Isabella Alcañiz is Assistant Professor and the Harrison Distinguished Professor in Environmental Politics at the Department of Government and Politics, University of Maryland. Professor Alcañiz grew up in South America and has carried out extensive field research in Latin America and Africa. She has taught at the University of Pennsylvania, the University of Houston, and universities in Argentina and Europe. Her research is published in *World Politics*, the *British Journal of Political Science*, the *Latin American Research Review*, *Latin American Perspectives*, *Revista de Ciencia Pólitica, Desarrollo Económico*, *Water Policy*, and *Environmental Science and Policy*. She received her Ph.D. in Political Science from Northwestern University.

Structural Analysis in the Social Sciences

Mark Granovetter, editor

The series *Structural Analysis in the Social Sciences* presents studies that analyze social behavior and institutions by reference to relations among such concrete social entities as persons, organizations, and nations. Relational analysis contrasts on the one hand with reductionist methodological individualism and on the other with macro-level determinism, whether based on technology, material conditions, economic conflict, adaptive evolution, or functional imperatives. In this more intellectually flexible structural middle ground, analysts situate actors and their relations in a variety of contexts. Since the series began in 1987, its authors have variously focused on small groups, history, culture, politics, kinship, aesthetics, economics, and complex organizations, creatively theorizing how these shape and in turn are shaped by social relations. Their style and methods have ranged widely, from intense, long-term ethnographic observation to highly abstract mathematical models. Their disciplinary affiliations have included history, anthropology, sociology, political science, business, economics, mathematics, and computer science. Some have made explicit use of social network analysis, including many of the cutting-edge and standard works of that approach, whereas others have kept formal analysis in the background and used "networks" as a fruitful orienting metaphor. All have in common a sophisticated and revealing approach that forcefully illuminates our complex social world.

Recent Books in the Series

Philippe Bourgois, *In Search of Respect: Selling Crack in El Barrio* (Second Edition)
Nan Lin, *Social Capital: A Theory of Social Structure and Action*
Robert Franzosi, *From Words to Numbers*
Sean O'Riain, *The Politics of High-Tech Growth*
James Lincoln and Michael Gerlach, *Japan's Network Economy*
Patrick Doreian, Vladimir Batagelj, and Anujka Ferligoj, *Generalized Blockmodeling*
Eiko Ikegami, *Bonds of Civility: Aesthetic Networks and Political Origins of Japanese Culture*
Wouter de Nooy, Andrej Mrvar, and Vladimir Batagelj, *Exploratory Social Network Analysis with Pajek*
Peter Carrington, John Scott, and Stanley Wasserman, *Models and Methods in Social Network Analysis*
Robert C. Feenstra and Gary G. Hamilton, *Emergent Economies, Divergent Paths*
Martin Kilduff and David Krackhardt, *Interpersonal Networks in Organizations*
Ari Adut, *On Scandal: Moral Disturbances in Society, Politics, and Art*
Zeev Maoz, *The Networks of Nations: The Evolution and Structure of International Networks, 1815–2002*
Noah E. Friedkin and Eugene C. Johnsen, *Social Influence Network Theory*
Sean F. Everton, *Disrupting Dark Networks*
Dean Lusher, Johan Koskinen, and Garry Robins, eds., *Exponential Random Graph Models for Social Networks: Theory, Methods, and Applications*
Silvia Domínguez and Betina Hollstein, eds., *Mixed Methods in Studying Social Networks*

Environmental and Nuclear Networks in the Global South

How Skills Shape International Cooperation

ISABELLA ALCAÑIZ
University of Maryland

CAMBRIDGE
UNIVERSITY PRESS

CAMBRIDGE
UNIVERSITY PRESS

32 Avenue of the Americas, New York NY 10013

Cambridge University Press is part of the University of Cambridge.

It furthers the University's mission by disseminating knowledge in the pursuit of education, learning, and research at the highest international levels of excellence.

www.cambridge.org
Information on this title: www.cambridge.org/9781107150119

First published 2016

A catalog record for this publication is available from the British Library.

ISBN 978-1-107-15011-9 Hardback

Contents

List of Figures page vii
List of Tables ix
Preface xi
Acknowledgments xix

1 Why Do Bureaucrats Cooperate? International Inter-Agency Networks in the Global South 1
2 Bureaucrats across Borders 29
3 Skill Formation, Economic Crisis, and Expert Networks in the Nuclear Sectors of Argentina and Brazil 47
4 International Inter-Agency Cooperation in Nuclear Energy, Science, and Technology (NEST) 73
5 Explaining International Inter-Agency Cooperation in Nuclear Energy, Science, and Technology (NEST) 97
6 International Inter-Agency Cooperation in the Protection of the Global Environment 116
7 Explaining International Inter-Agency Cooperation in the Protection of the Environment 139
8 After Austerity 157
9 Conclusion: The Hidden Costs of Low Skills 176

Bibliography 191
Index 203

Figures

4.1 Dendrogram of association between members of the ARCAL network *page* 92
4.2 Dendrogram of association between members of the AFRA network 92
4.3 Dendrogram of association between members of the RCA network 93
4.4 Network of inter-agency collaboration in NEST 94
5.1 Effect of government spending and homophily on participation in collaborative nuclear projects 112
6.1 Collaboration network, thinned by high (frequent) collaborators 135
7.1 Effect of homophily terms: region, inter-country differences in GEF financing, scientific publications, and bureaucratic competence 151
8.1 Growth rates for the world and the regions of the global south, 1961–2009 165
8.2 Share of the total project cost financed by GEF, 1991–2011 168

Tables

1.1 A Theory of Expert Bureaucrats *page* 13
4.1 Policy Area Addressed by the Project by Region 79
4.2 Budget for ARCAL 1983–2004 85
4.3 AFRA Affiliation Matrix 88
4.4 ARCAL Affiliation Matrix 89
4.5 RCA Affiliation Matrix 90
A.4.1 Participating Countries in RCA, AFRA, and ARCAL 96
5.1 Participation in Collaborative Projects in NEST 107
5.2 Joint Collaboration in NEST Projects 110
5.3 Exponential Random Graph Models of Nuclear Cooperation, Valued Network 114
6.1 Projects by Policy Area and Region 123
6.2 Percentages of GEF Financing and Countries' Co-financing by Region 132
6.3 Affiliation Matrix of Collaboration in GEF Projects, Selected Latin American Countries 133
A.6.1 Participating Countries in GEF Grants and Number of Projects 136
7.1 Explaining the Determinants of Collaboration in GEF Projects, Regional Model 148
7.2 Explaining the Determinants of Collaboration on GEF Projects, Full Model 149
8.1 Determinants of Inter-Agency Cooperation in GEF Projects 172

Preface

This book started long ago with the first interviews I conducted with nuclear experts, as part of my dissertation fieldwork. I began researching Nuclear Energy, Science, and Technology (NEST) in order to explain the radical turnaround in nonproliferation policy and strategic scale back adopted jointly by the new civilian governments of Argentina and Brazil in the mid- to late 1980s. After years of building up their nuclear programs and refusing to sign the 1970 Nonproliferation Treaty, these two historic regional rivals began collaborating in NEST. Initially, my assumption was that cooperation in the Southern Cone resulted from democratization: military dictatorships built up the nuclear sector in order to increase their geopolitical standing in the (Cold War) world; once they left power, democrats dismantled the sector. But while perhaps democratic change could explain why civilians in Argentina and Brazil sought greater control over their NEST programs separately, regime transition on its own could not explain why they decided to coordinate their nuclear foreign policy and cooperate in technology development.

In the course of those early interviews at the Argentine National Atomic Energy Commission (CNEA) and the Brazilian National Nuclear Energy Commission (CNEN), state experts on both sides of the border highlighted the close ties that existed between them. In many of these conversations (as well as in later ones with environmental experts), I was told that foreign counterparts often made better allies than their own government. Colleagues abroad experienced similar obstacles: budget cuts, hiring freezes, defunding of projects and programs – they said – and faced the same uphill battle in securing new funding from their political principals. The political leadership, on the other hand, operated within the limits of the bottom line, which in the 1980s and 1990s trended toward losses.

Not surprisingly, nuclear bureaucrats told me time and again that they were able to anticipate when a new wave of spending cuts would be put in place. Sometimes, given a common history and a shared culture, they could even read the cues of an economic downturn in the neighboring country, which in all likelihood anticipated an eventual downturn at home. Unexpectedly, in these early interviews, they reported seeking alternatives outside of the budget. That is, in order to continue Research and Development activities and deepen existing programs, nuclear experts sought external options. These alternatives included increasing participation in international technical organizations, in particular the International Atomic Energy Agency (IAEA) and above all, cooperating with peers on common projects.

Thus, what came out of those first interviews in Argentina and Brazil was that cooperation in NEST was more of an economic story than a political one. Rather than security concerns separating bureaucrats along borders, with political principals bringing them together after democratization (as I had expected), it was shared economic uncertainties that brought state experts together. Indeed, collaboration between the two South American countries was done on the cheap. Most exchanges were paid in kind, whereby the CNEA would pick up the tab when hosting training exercises with CNEN experts, for example, and CNEN would do the same when hosting their Argentine colleagues. As Chapter 3 of this book reveals, projects were devised on a shared, tight budget and many, despite this, remained unfinished because of the lack of funding on both sides of the border.

In the course of my research I discovered a network of cooperation in NEST that expanded beyond the two advanced nuclear producers of South America. In fact, all three regions of the developing world had networks of state experts collaborating on technical projects in NEST, with some of the projects involving inter-regional cooperation. As it turned out, countries of the Global South had been working together in NEST since the late 1970s, in Asia; mid-1980s, in Latin America; and early 1990s, in Africa. Cross-national projects included applications in nuclear medicine and public health, the environment, and radiation safety. Since the 1970s, the IAEA sponsors these regional networks, but as the following chapters show, rather than funding technical projects, the international organization (IO) helps facilitate coordination among participants.

The interviews I conducted with South American experts uncovered clear preferences for transgovernmental cooperation. Bureaucrats preferred to cooperate with peers in agencies that were equal or superior in resources. For example, Argentines sought to join cross-national projects where Brazilians were participants, and vice versa. Projects in human health proposed by the Cuban state agency in NEST (the Agency of Nuclear Energy and Advanced Technologies or AENTA) with a well-known niche expertise in nuclear medicine were more likely to be adopted as many Latin American experts would sign on. My interviews with African nuclear professionals revealed similar preferences. Projects based in the state laboratories of Northern African states were more likely to be chosen than those proposed by less developed agencies in the region.

The cooperation preferences of NEST bureaucrats across the developing world revealed in turn a shared preoccupation in accessing resources abroad, particularly skills. This led me to the literature on the political economy of skills, discussed at length in the following two chapters. While most of the focus of this scholarship is on the effect of skills on international economic competition, many of its key findings proved of great interest to my research project on domestic skills and international cooperation. The fact that employers and states tend to privilege a certain type of worker (e.g., young, employed, and skilled) when offering training opportunities resonated strongly with what state experts in NEST had discussed in their interviews with me. In particular, the IAEA officers that help coordinate cross-national projects, whom I interviewed at the Vienna, Austria, headquarters of the IO, identified the level of program development as a major determinant when asked about transgovernmental cooperation. If skilled workers are more likely to access training in the private sector, is there a similar advantage in the public sector? In other words, is there a demonstrable advantage for expert bureaucrats when it comes to training opportunities?

Thus, this is how the theory of the expert bureaucrat and the book's main hypotheses came to be. First, my research sought to explain cooperation between bureaucrats from two advanced nuclear energy producers. Collaboration between CNEA and CNEN resulted from experts' compensatory strategy to make up for lost resources during the Lost Eighties Decade. This led to the question of whether international inter-agency cooperation was just a bilateral strategy between two close neighbors, or was it a standard strategy for economic survival in policy areas with high and sustained demands for resources? Is cooperation with foreign peers a common strategy of bureaucrats from developing countries or rather a scheme between high-skilled neighbors? To answer these questions and to begin testing my theory of "cooperation for skills" across all of the Global South, I ask whether there is an empirical relationship between government spending and international inter-agency cooperation. That is, does government spending shape cooperation?

Second, both the nuclear and environment state experts I interviewed emphasized the importance of working with foreign partners at a certain level of skills – either equal or superior to them. When partners lack resources and technical expertise, they stated, projects are more likely to take longer or even fail, and more importantly, they get less out of the collaboration. This preference for partner selection challenges common practice by international organizations that sponsor cross-national technical cooperation among developing countries. Typically, IOs attempt to match less-developed agencies with more advanced ones, precisely to transfer know-how and technology from the latter to the former. When I spoke to program officers from the IAEA, the Global Environment Facility (GEF), and the United Nations Environment Programme (UNEP), they stressed the importance of cross-national projects as a way to distribute more effectively scarce resources from better to poorer endowed programs within a region. This seeming contradiction led to my second research question: how do differing levels of skills among potential project participants affect partner selection in international inter-agency cooperation?

The high premium placed on access to new skills by expert bureaucrats, evident from a number of face-to-face interviews, led to the rich literature on the political economy of skills. As I discuss in the following chapters, this scholarship mainly focuses on the connection between level of skills and international competition and how different state models of investment in training and industrial apprenticeship shape the relationship. Within the literature, Becker's Theorem of Human Capital was revealing in particular, as he directly takes on the problem of who pays for the costs of training. In his seminal 1968 book, Becker argues that employers face different incentives to invest in the training of their workforce, depending on whether the skills are specific or general, with the latter ones being more transferable than the former. When employers do not pay for skills, the argument goes, workers will put up with training costs themselves.

This resonated with the situation described by state professionals in my interviews. Often, political principals were unable or unwilling to pay for skill formation and upgrading within the bureaucracy, other than offering limited training for routine tasks. Cuts to training based on Research and Development (R&D) tend to follow more general spending cuts within states. Consequently, I expect bureaucrats to face similar incentives to take skill investment in their own hands as workers in the private sector. As the book shows, I tested this corollary to my theory of the expert bureaucrat by analyzing the type of project by skill content. If bureaucrats are after skills to advance professionally, as I argue in the following chapters, they should be more likely to join projects that provide more general, rather than specific, training.

Finally, an important finding from the literature on the political economy of skills and varieties of capitalism is that there are structural biases regarding the type of worker who is offered training opportunities. Typically, younger and better trained employees are the ones with greater access to skill upgrading. This finding also resonated with my interviews. Both state experts in NEST and environmental protection stressed the importance of a starting threshold of expertise in order to participate in cross-national projects. Furthermore, international program managers from IAEA, GEF, and UNEP, tasked with coordinating these projects, also reported on the challenges of inter-agency cooperation when state professionals have a low level of skills. This led to the central question of the book: how do skills shape international cooperation? To answer, I test all of the above hypotheses across the Global South in the two skill-driven areas of Nuclear Energy, Science, and Technology and Environmental Protection.

The Corollary to "Skills Matter" Is that the State Matters Too

This book is ultimately about the state in the Global South and how its bureaucratic agents develop strategies to weather the ups and downs of its resources. It is as much about the revealed practices and strategies of bureaucrats as it is about the fickleness and unreliability of the state. In the interviews and field research I conducted, this became clear. Bureaucrats developed their strategies and ordered their preferences based on the economic health of the state. In periods of "fat cows," they expanded programs and increased hiring; in periods of "lean cows," they went into survival mode at home but expanded abroad through project participation. The centrality of the state in the development of energy, science, R&D, innovation, and technology across the Global South is clear. Yet, for many genuine reasons (e.g., the rise of non-state actors in domestic and international affairs and the widespread adoption of neoliberal reforms that have reduced and weakened the public sector), recent scholarship in political science has overlooked this centrality.

The book is in no way an apology for the lack of state funding, even though it examines the compensatory strategies bureaucrats pursue when government spending drops. Precisely, the main finding presented here – that prior level of skills determines state agencies access to international technical cooperation – unmistakably indicates how without prior investment there can be no surplus in know-how and technology. If the state does not invest first in human capital, there is not much that IOs and international donors can do to compensate. At the high end of the technological spectrum, skilled bureaucrats benefit overwhelmingly of cooperation opportunities with equal peers and IOs. On the low end, bureaucrats in a low-human capital state are limited in what they can achieve with the compensatory strategies described in this book.

There are many reasons why bureaucrats with initial low level of skills will find it hard – if not impossible – to substitute the lack of funding they face at home with resources pooled across expert networks. While the actual mechanism of this skill handicap is beyond the scope of the book, the field research I conducted revealed some possible causes. Both state experts and program officers from IOs pointed to practical reasons (like the lack of language proficiency, typically English) and deeper ones (such as the lack of basic technical proficiency needed to carry out the basics of a complex project). All of these inhibit the participation of bureaucrats from lesser developed programs in NEST and environmental cross-national projects.

Finally, when it comes to the centrality of the state, even well-trained bureaucrats cannot get around it. As discussed at length in the following chapters, because of the dizzying pace of technological change in the information age, workers (whether in the state or in the private sector) can no longer carry out key tasks without periodic skill upgrades. This in turn requires a constant investment in workers' training (like the "learning by doing model"), which adds costs to the employer's bottom line. Yet as the book shows, until the 2000 commodity boom that enriched the coffers of many developing countries, the state in the Global South historically has been too impoverished or politically unstable to maintain sound investment policies in bureaucratic expertise. Thus, especially for those bureaucrats who acquired high skills at some point in time, transgovernmental cooperation with equal peers has been a viable strategy to keep abreast of technological changes and maintain their market value.

But the strategy is no replacement for state investment. As one Argentine nuclear bureaucrat put it to me, when it comes to substituting skills through regional pooling vis-à-vis state investment it is like "a drop of water in a bucket."

Acknowledgments

This book would not have been possible without its own network of experts and sponsors. I would like to acknowledge first the institutional support provided by the Department of Political Science and the College of Liberal Arts and Social Sciences of the University of Houston; the Joseph H. Lauder Institute of Management and International Studies and the Penn Lauder Center for International Business Education and Research (CIBER) of the University of Pennsylvania; and the Department of Government and Politics and the Environmental Science Policy Program of the University of Maryland. I am grateful to these institutions for their funding of my research and, above all, to the people who proved to be wonderful colleagues throughout the endeavor of writing a book. At Cambridge University Press, I was fortunate to work with Robert Dreesen, senior editor, and two anonymous reviewers who provided excellent suggestions to improve the manuscript.

At the University of Houston (UH), where this book project began taking shape, I benefited from the sharp commentary and friendship of Elizabeth Rigby Gibson, Timothy Hellwig, Noah Kaplan, the late Janet Saltzman Chafetz, Ryan Kennedy, Katherine Howard Barillas, Veronica Caro, and Anadeli Bencomo. To Noah Kaplan I owe a special debt of gratitude as he was the one who first noted that my research was very much a "network story" and introduced me to Social Network Analysis.

My two-year affiliation with the University of Pennsylvania (UPenn) was incredibly productive. I am indebted to Mauro F. Guillén, the Director of the Joseph H. Lauder Institute at UPenn, and the Lauder Institute for awarding me a post-doctoral fellowship and the 2011 Penn Lauder CIBER Faculty Project Grant, and the Mack Center for Technological

Innovation – The Wharton School for two field research grants with Mauro F. Guillén as principal investigator. My fellowship at UPenn was intellectually gratifying, yet the best part of it was that I got to spend quality time with my dearest friend and colleague, Tulia G. Falleti. The logistics of my commute to Philadelphia from the greater Washington DC area would have been impossible without Tulia and Richard Moore's generous help. I am indebted to Tulia in friendship and in scholarship, as she has been an extraordinary sounding board for ideas over the years.

The Department of Government and Politics (GVPT) at the University of Maryland is intellectually challenging and has helped support my research with a generous start-up fund and the 2014–2016 Dr. Horace V. and Wilma E. Harrison Distinguished Professorship. I have benefited from chats about my work with my colleagues at GVPT, especially Joel Simmons, Jennifer Hadden, Ernesto Calvo, Kanisha Bonds, Margaret Pearson, Johanna Birnir, Mark Lichbach, John McCauley, and Shibley Telhami. The GVPT department staff is top notch and has helped me with the logistics of multiple out-of-town conferences where I presented early drafts of this book and my many field research trips since the Fall of 2012. I am indebted especially to Michael Mansfield, Cissy Roberts, Apitchaya "AP" Pimpawathin, and Irwin Morris. Beyond the department, the University of Maryland is a rich and exciting campus with great expertise in social networks and environmental politics. I have benefited greatly from participating in the bi-monthly workshop of the UMD Program for Society and the Environment (PSE) led by Dana Fisher, where I presented an early version of a chapter of the book. The UMD Environmental Science Policy Program (ENSP), co-led by Dr. Wendy Whittemore and of which I am faculty advisor, has helped support my research. The wonderful UMD students in the Graduate Seminars on Democratization and Comparative Institutions, and Environmental Policy Analysis, read and commented on parts or the entirety of my book manuscript. I am very grateful to them.

I am equally grateful to the individuals that spoke to me over the years about transgovernmental cooperation as well as the organizations that allowed me to access their archives. The list is a long one. I talked to national bureaucrats, IO program officers, diplomats, and other policy experts, and I visited universities, government agencies, and think tanks in South, Central, and North America; East and Southern Africa; and Europe. Special thanks go to Laércio Antonio Vinhas of CNEN; Elías Palacios of the Brazilian-Argentine Agency for Accounting and Control of Nuclear Materials (ABACC); Orpet J.M. Peixoto also of ABACC; the late Dr. Emma Pérez Ferreira; Roberto M. Ornstein of CNEA; the late

Ambassador Julio C. Carasales; Ambassador Sebastião do Rego Barros; the Technical Cooperation division of the International Atomic Energy Agency; Margarita Astrálaga, Regional Director of the Regional Office for Latin America and the Caribbean-UNEP as well as the rest of the staff; Mounkaila Goumandakoye, Regional Director of the Regional Office for Africa-UNEP as well as the rest of the staff at UNEP and the Global Environment Facility; the Ngorongoro Conservation Area Authority of Tanzania; the African Wildlife Foundation in Washington DC; the Ministry of Natural Resources and Sustainable Development of Argentina; the Africa Institute of South Africa (AISA) in Pretoria; the Parliamentary Library of South Africa in Cape Town; the University Research Institute of Rio de Janeiro (IUPERJ); the Institute for Technological Research (IPT) of the State of São Paulo; the Fundação Getulio Vargas in Rio de Janeiro; the Argentine National Atomic Energy Commission (CNEA); and the Brazilian National Nuclear Energy Commission (CNEN). Of course, all claims, interpretations, and errors are my own.

As a scholar, I am indebted to a large network of social scientists, which over the years has been a wonderful source of ideas and encouragement. I am fortunate to count many of these scholars as friends: Kathryn Hotchstetler, Andrew Schrank, Ramiro Berardo, Margaret Keck, Ricardo Gutiérrez, Mario Pecheny, Marina Farinetti, Gabriela Delamata, Etel Solingen, Virginia Oliveros, Abraham Newman, Javiera Barandiaran, Matthew Amengual, Julián Gadano, Andrés Malamud, Matías Spektor, Teri Caraway, Michael Bosia, Ben Ross Schneider, and Matthew Carnes. A special mention goes to Charles Munnell, who is not only a dear friend and colleague, but also read the entire manuscript and provided invaluable editing and encouragement.

Finally, I am utterly grateful to my closest friends and family. Vicky Murillo has been a true friend and colleague throughout the years and spending time with her is one of the high points of attending any professional conference or visiting Buenos Aires in the winter. My dear friend Carola María Amanda Rossi Rodriguez was the most fun trip companion that I could ask for and made my time in Pretoria and Johannesburg, South Africa, so much more enjoyable. Alejandra Marchevsky has been a key supporter of this project from the beginning. The book has benefited enormously from her sharp reading of the manuscript and her invitation to present early versions of my research at the Department of Liberal Studies at California State University – Los Angeles. I consider myself incredibly lucky for having Ale as my friend. My family in Argentina has encouraged and supported me throughout the long project of writing this book.

Despite the kilometers that separate us physically, we will always be at geodesic distance with my dad, Carlos Alberto Alcañiz; my mom, Magdalena Vilaplana; my sister, Mariana Alcañiz; and my stepmom, Isabel Pessacq. I am also thankful to my parents-in-law, the late Silvia Bleichmar and Carlos Alberto Schenquerman, who so generously opened their home in Buenos Aires to me. My children, Camilo Calvo-Alcañiz and Violeta Calvo-Alcañiz, are my biggest source of pride and joy. I have been privileged to have them accompany me on some of my research trips and our shared travels to East Africa and Panama will remain the coolest memories of this project. Lastly, my husband, Ernesto Calvo, has been instrumental every step of the way as first editor and audience of this book. He is my extraordinary *compañero*. I dedicate this book to him.

I

Why Do Bureaucrats Cooperate? International Inter-Agency Networks in the Global South

> The primary source of the superiority of bureaucratic administration lies in the role of technical knowledge which, through the development of modern technology and business methods in the production of goods, has become completely indispensable.
>
> Max Weber, *Types of Legitimate Domination*, 1922

No skills, no cooperation. That is the core finding of this book, which seeks to explain international inter-agency cooperation in the Global South. Policymaking has become more complex in the information age, more international and interdependent in a globalized world, and more pressed by the urgency of the problems it attempts to address. Much of international cooperation is unthinkable without a large body of expert bureaucrats greasing and turning the wheels of the government machine. In other words, policymaking has become both more skill dependent and transnational. Yet, while high-level diplomacy and multilateral treaties receive the bulk of scholarly attention, the "behind-the-scene" legwork that expert bureaucrats do on a regular basis has not been properly studied.

Partnerships among bureaucrats can yield extraordinary outcomes. The Kyoto Protocol would not have been possible without the preceding coordinated efforts of state climatologists around the world; the Non Proliferation Treaty (NPT) and the Comprehensive Test Ban Treaty (CTBT) would not have been realized if it had not been for the prior work by nuclear bureaucrats from both nuclear and non-nuclear powers; and world summits on wide-ranging issues, like sustainable development, AIDS, and trade, rest on the pooling of expertise from state agencies and the deployment of scientists on government payrolls. In all of these cases, expert bureaucrats have been the drivers of policy change, rather than mere translators of the preferences of voters and politicians. Expert bureaucrats have raised the salience of policy issues about which they care deeply and have used their know-how as leverage to advance broad policy agendas across borders. More importantly, they have done so together, as expert communities, cooperating with like-minded bureaucrats and professional colleagues embedded in a myriad of peer institutions.

For several decades, expert bureaucrats have been moving regularly across borders, from their home institutions to specialized international organizations, and in the process, forging collaborative networks with peers. While links between bureaucrats and expertise have been well noted by students of bureaucracy (from Weber onward), what has gone surprisingly unnoticed is how inter-agency cooperation has become a critical source of skill upgrading and policy innovation for bureaucrats in the developing world. The purpose of this book is to explain the international cooperative behavior of state experts, who increasingly go outside their national agencies and work with foreign peers on technical projects and programs.

I argue that international inter-agency cooperation results from the need of expert bureaucrats to invest in skill formation and skill upgrading when governments fail to provide sufficient funding for training and Research and Development (R&D). Cooperation increases when governments fail to invest in the skills of their workforce. When the state withdraws, I posit, expert bureaucrats take skill investment in their own hands and cooperate with peers to upgrade their skillset, because career advancement is contingent on maintaining their technical expertise current. Bureaucrats from developing countries, with limited state resources and chronically underfunded and understaffed technical agencies, go outside their national borders to access new resources.

From my theory I derive three testable hypotheses, which will be discussed in greater detail in the following pages. Briefly, I expect the strategy of inter-agency cooperation to be contingent on the bureaucrats' relative expertise (skill level), the level of similarity in program development among partnering agencies (skill homophily), and state investment in the expertise of its workforce (access to domestic resources). The key finding of this book, which carries significant policy implications, is that variations in prior levels of skills across cohorts of expert bureaucrats, state agencies, and countries explain international cooperation by bureaucrats in NEST and environmental protection. Bureaucrats with high skills cooperate more and more effectively as they tend to work with foreign peers at similar levels of development. In contrast, state experts with low levels of skills cooperate less and less effectively, as they pair up with bureaucrats from countries that are similarly poorly endowed and have fewer resources to share.

Skill Updating through Partnerships: An Example

The true dimensions of "El Guaraní," one of the world's largest aquifer systems and reservoirs of fresh water, remained unknown and unmeasured to the voters and policymakers of Argentina, Brazil, Paraguay, and Uruguay, the four Mercosur[1] countries under which it exists. With growing populations and unrelenting demands for water to satisfy agricultural production in the region, stakeholders were increasingly concerned with the potential overuse and the likely contamination of the Guaraní Aquifer System (SAG). As a result, by the early 2000s, state experts from local water agencies faced clear demands to find out how feasible, reliable, and cost-effective the Guaraní was as a sustainable source of drinking water. The race to measure, map, and regulate the access and use of "El Guaraní" thus began. Within a few years, expert bureaucrats would draft timetables, budgets, set operational priorities, and devise government procedures to innovate in the area of environmental policy and water management in all four countries. To deal with such complex environmental policy, bureaucrats endowed with scientific and technical training were required. These skilled civil servants brought to the table research agendas, expert teams, professional goals, as well as a variety of policy interests of their own.

Confronted with major cuts in government spending – triggered in part by the 2001 economic collapse in Argentina – and chronic disinvestment in environmental protection, expert bureaucrats in all four Aquifer countries had few resources to retool their skills, to hire new personnel, to invest in new technology, or to outsource a comprehensive water survey to the private sector. Consequently, answering new environmental demands required creativity to develop new goals within existing budgets. These experts were interested not only in measuring *El Guaraní* but

[1] The Common Market of the South (Mercosur) is an economic and political free trade agreement signed between the countries of Argentina, Brazil, Paraguay, and Uruguay in 1991. It was created with the goals of facilitating free movement of capital, goods, and people among signing partners. Recently, Venezuela also became a full member of Mercosur.

also in increasing the scientific and technical training that would allow them to conduct similar assessments in the future. Skilled bureaucrats are interested not only in achieving policy goals but also in advancing their professional careers.

The solution was to design a cross-national scientific project with the objective of uncovering the technical specifications of *El Guaraní*. Expert bureaucrats from the water agencies of the four countries drafted a proposal, coordinated their policy goals, and jointly applied for a multi-million-dollar grant from the Global Environment Facility (GEF), with the World Bank as implementing agency. Local and state agencies covered half of the total project cost of 27 USD, while the remaining 13.5 million came from international donors, primarily the GEF.

Within a few years, the "Environmental Protection and Sustainable Integrated Management of the Guaraní Aquifer" project provided hard data on the depth and length of the SAG and set the foundation for a 2010 international agreement among the governments of Argentina, Brazil, Paraguay, and Uruguay on a legal framework for co-management. One of the greatest technical challenges of the project was the measurement of the Guaraní in Argentina and Uruguay where the SAG is at its deepest. Experts from these two countries had to dig wells up to 1,000 meters deep (about 3,280 feet). Lacking the skills and technology to do so, Argentine hydrologists called on colleagues at the formerly state-owned national oil company, who lent their drilling machinery and expertise. Argentine expert bureaucrats successfully completed their part of the project and transferred that technology to their neighbors in Uruguay. Thus the project was as much about training as it was about surveying the aquifer. One participant stated that the biggest accomplishment had been the learning process involved throughout the cycle of the project.[2]

The SAG project exemplifies a growing trend in the Global South: experts from state agencies work with foreign peers on large, complex projects in order to address common policy problems. International inter-agency cooperation has become more technical and demanding of local bureaucracies and is thriving in critical policy areas such as environmental protection, nuclear development, and public health.[3] For several

[2] Senior water expert, coordinator of the Guaraní Aquifer System (SAG) project. Interview with the author. City of Paraná, Argentina, July 2013.

[3] In this book, I focus solely on *international* inter-agency cooperation – also known as transgovernmentalism – yet I will posit that my theory of the expert bureaucrat also helps explain domestic inter-agency cooperation and offers theoretical traction to public sector analysts and bureaucracy scholars. Transgovernmental cooperation is defined as

decades now, state agencies from Africa, Asia, and Latin America have collaborated – both intra- and inter-regionally – on climate change, water security, agricultural sustainability, and the fight against AIDS as well as on other epidemics, to mention just a few of jointly tackled problems. Cooperation in these policy arenas is predominantly project based, which means state experts must cross national borders in order to negotiate and implement common goals, assign tasks, and agree on a feasible division of labor. When they choose to participate, bureaucrats and their agencies must commit to share with foreigners scarce and costly resources such as personnel, funding, and skills. These large-scale projects have been described as "more complex and varied than national projects, often involving a great number of actors and composed of many regional and cross-border initiatives on the ground" (Stephenson & Baharani, 2012: 270).

The new cooperative behavior of expert bureaucrats does not fit traditional definitions of public servants. According to the literature, bureaucrats are generally reluctant to share resources and have a documented tendency to be inward oriented (Blais & Dion, 1990; Hoffer, 2013). They are expected to take full advantage of their autonomy from politicians (Huber & Shipan, 2006). Their main goal is to maximize their budgets (Niskanen, 2007)[4] and the only tie that truly matters is the one they forge with their political principal (Bendor & Meirowitz, 2004; Gailmard, 2002; Huber & Shipan, 2002, 2006). As a result, we should expect bureaucrats to resist if agency-appropriated funds are executed outside of their organizations – especially in the developing world, where state research agencies tend to be chronically underfunded and understaffed to begin with (Campion & Shrum, 2004; Schwartzman, 1994; Solingen, 1994). Thus, this kind of cooperation is costly to expert bureaucrats, even if projects are partly funded by external donors such as the Organisation for Economic Co-operation and Development (OECD), or international organizations (IOs) with technical specialization, like the Global Environment Facility (GEF), the World Health Organization (WHO), and the International Atomic Energy Agency (IAEA). Despite the costs, again and again state experts have created partnerships across national and

a set of relations formed by the cross-border "interactions among sub-units of different governments that are not controlled or closely guided by the policies of the cabinets or chief executives of those governments" (Keohane & Nye, 1974: 43).

4 Bureaucrats' sole focus on the budget has been described as the "treadmill phenomenon, inducing bureaucrats to strive for increased budgets until they can turn over the management burdens of a stable higher budget to a new bureaucrat" (Niskanen, 2007: 38).

even regional borders. Over time, these partnerships have forged international networks through which bureaucrats and politicians coordinate policy and agree on solutions to common problems, as exemplified by the international agreement on the Guaraní Aquifer System by Argentina, Brazil, Paraguay, and Uruguay.

Despite the prevalence and policy impact of inter-agency cooperation, and how much it conflicts with standard conceptualizations of bureaucratic behavior, little scholarship has explained its origins or described its implications for achieving common governance goals.[5] This book remedies this oversight by addressing the puzzle of the international behavior of state experts in the Global South. It proposes a demand driven theory of international cooperation, resulting from incentives created in part by shared policy bottlenecks and fiscal scarcity, rather than explicit planning by well-financed government agencies. It offers a new direction in research on the protection of the environment and NEST development as it shines a light on the international sources of state expertise. At its heart, this book is about a rising type of government agent in the Global South as well as in OECD countries – i.e., the expert bureaucrat – with incentives to acquire high skills and invest in her own training when the state does not and who sees professional advantages in the forging of transnational networks.[6]

Question and Argument

What explains the rise of international inter-agency cooperation in areas as diverse as nuclear energy, science, and technology (NEST) and the protection of the global environment – the two policy fields that this book examines? Why do bureaucrats in developing countries, embedded in chronically underfunded domestic institutions and accountable to local

[5] Important exceptions include Raustiala (2002), Slaughter (2004), and Bach and Newman (2014). Furthermore, the literature on Epistemic Communities has also examined the link between state experts and international cooperation. Haas (1989, 1992a, 1992b), Adler (2008), Evangelista (1993, 2002), and Kapstein (1992) are some of the most seminal works in epistemic causality.

[6] While many of the propositions of my theory should be applicable to agencies in the industrial North, the cases that I study in this book are in the Global South. I explain the focus on the developing world in greater detail further in this chapter and the next. For now, suffice it to say that fluctuations in government spending and other potential external shocks to states' investment in bureaucrats' skills are frequent enough in developing countries for state experts to anticipate them and forge strategies to compensate for them.

politicians, collaborate with foreign peers? I argue that bureaucrats in the Global South, accustomed to insufficient and irregular funding, anticipate government spending cuts and develop strategies to compensate for the lack of resources at home. Similar to well-documented market failures in the allocation of skills in the private workforce (Booth & Snower, 1996; Estevez-Abe, Iversen, & Soskice, 2001; Ulph, 1996), the state as an employer also may fail to invest in human capital. When the state withdraws, I argue, bureaucrats in technology-based agencies who depend on their expertise to do their job take skill investment in their own hands.

One way to access new skills and help ensure the survival of research programs and institutional knowledge is to cooperate with foreign peers in cross-national technical projects. Through these projects state experts not only pool resources and share research costs, *critically* they upgrade their existing skillsets. Most bureaucracies have certification processes by which outside training and acquired qualifications are recognized and count toward promotion and raises.[7] Politicians in impoverished states often welcome these external sources of training as inexpensive solutions to the problem of outdated expertise. The rationale of certifying international cooperation as an instance of professional development is explained by a senior director of the National Institute of Public Administration (INAP) of Argentina:

> During the 2001 crisis, due to the budgetary restrictions, the INAP allowed communities of practice[8] as a training tool. Because we have had drainage of resources, we allowed the certification of any number of activities to be considered as contributions to the development of technical and professional competence. These [activities] could be courses within INAP, but if by your own initiative you did them outside you could get them recognized by INAP. The system also accepts participation in working teams and international projects.[9]

International technical cooperation not only sharpens skills, but also increases the professional reputation of participants at home. Cross-national partnerships are highly desirable to bureaucrats because they

[7] Recognition of externally certified training, such as participation in international workshops or projects, is carried out by the National System of the Administrative Profession (SINAPA) in Argentina; the National Institute of Public Administration (INAP) in the Dominican Republic; and the South African Department of Public Service and Administration, to name a few.

[8] The interviewee defined "communities of practice" as "somewhat informal and often virtual professional networks to advance knowledge and innovation." Senior official at INAP. Interview with the author in Buenos Aires, Argentina, January 2014.

[9] Senior official at INAP. Interview with the author in Buenos Aires, Argentina, January 2014.

help expand the size of their professional networks and make them more marketable (Heclo, 1978; Sabatier & Jenkins Smith, 1999; Carpenter 2001; Campion & Shrum, 2004). In state agencies of the Global South, where funding for training and professional development tends to be extremely scarce, international cooperation can have significant impact on a bureaucrat's career (Campion & Shrum, 2004; Herrera, 2010; Slaughter, 2004). Training and renewed proficiencies have an impact on wages and career promotions (Green & Sakamoto, 2001; O'Connell & Jungblut, 2008).[10] Consequently, as I will argue, the search for alternative venues to update skills in order to advance in their professional careers explains the emergence of collaborative international networks of expert bureaucrats.

In this book, I define *skills* as the learned capacities and know-how that bureaucrats use to carry out day-to-day tasks and solve concrete policy problems (Ericsson, 2006). The overall level of skills of bureaucrats constitutes *state expertise* or the knowledge that is acquired within the state by "making costly investments in information" (Gailmard & Patty, 2013: 6) and is critical to sound policy adoption. All bureaucrats in technical agencies are sensitive to skill disparity. For example, professionals working in nuclear policy need to have updated skills in radiation safety, regardless of whether they work in a high-skill agency that manages nuclear power plants, like the South African Nuclear Energy Corporation SOC Limited (NECSA), or a small one, with a narrow focus on nuclear medicine, like the Nicaraguan Laboratory of Physics, Radiation, and Metrology (LAF-RAM), at the National Autonomous University of Managua (UNAN-Managua).[11] Without sharp skills, state experts cannot respond to the demands of common citizens as well as those of local and national politicians. Consequently, bureaucrats have an incentive not only to keep their skills current to advance their careers and long-term professional goals, but also to maintain their market value – often at the intersection of the private, semi-public, and public sectors (Campion & Shrum, 2004; Teodoro, 2011).

[10] There is a strong consensus among labor and skills scholars that "continuing job-related training is also believed to be highly influential in determining both corporate or organizational performance as well as individual earnings and career development" (O'Connell and Jungblut, 2008: 109).

[11] These are the state agencies with national jurisdiction over nuclear policy in South Africa and Nicaragua, respectively. Bureaucrats from these agencies represent their country in cross-national projects in NEST. See www.iaea.org/technicalcooperation/Partnerships/Reg-Coop-Agreements.html.

Increasingly, state experts are members of academic networks or have developed academic careers, in which they forged ties to private sector peers, performed research and teaching responsibilities at public and private universities, and disseminated their work in disciplinary journals (Herrera, 2010; Pielke, 2007). Who are these bureaucrats at the heart of this book? The subject of my theory falls within Daniel Carpenter's definition of "mezzo level" state administrators. That is, the state official who typically serves as "bureau or division chiefs, program planners, and monitors" (Carpenter 2001: 19) as well as scientists, technical personnel, and project managers employed by state agencies. These state actors represent an increasing fraction of the state employee not only in the Global South but in the world at large. They are the life force of agencies like the Environmental Protection Agency (EPA) and the National Aeronautics and Space Administration (NASA) in the United States, the Brazilian Development Bank and the Bureau of Statistics (IBGE), the European Organization for Nuclear Research (CERN), or the National Bureau of Statistics and Geography in Mexico (INEGI). They also make up most of the senior personnel in key ministries of Africa, Asia, and Latin America, such as those of economy, labor, science and technology, and health among others.

While recognizing and controlling for the diversity of bureaucratic institutions in the Global South, the argument of this book is based on a common problem: state funds for research and training are vulnerable to budget cuts, and consequently, fluctuate a great deal (Sarkar, 2012; Schwartzman, 1994; Solingen, 1994). Irregular government funding generates uncertainty throughout the bureaucracy, but it can be particularly disruptive to well-established agencies given that their programs are contingent on the continued ability of the state to hire and train skilled personnel.[12] This is exacerbated by the wave of spending cuts in the aftermath of the foreign debt crisis in the early 1980s and in the wake of

[12] Since the 2008 Great Recession, government spending in R&D and training of state professionals in OECD countries has experienced major cuts too. For example, the termination of the US Space Shuttle Program in 2011 due to the economic crisis led NASA experts to collaborate with their Russian peers for space transportation. Recently, the head of the National Institutes of Health linked recession-triggered budget cuts to the lack of any progress in Ebola virus research. See www.washingtonpost.com/blogs/federal-eye/wp/2014/10/13/nih-director-ebola-vaccine-could-be-ready-if-not-for-budget-austerity/. Nevertheless, bureaucracies in developing countries have a much longer (and less exceptional) history with economic crises triggering austerity measures that directly target funding to science and technology in the state.

the neoliberal reforms implemented in the 1990s throughout the Global South (Frieden, 1991; Harvey, 2005; Huber & Solt, 2004; Kurtz, 2004; Murillo, 2009). For example, in Brazil – a wealthy developing country with a significant science and technology public sector – IMF recommended policies led to "major cuts to the country's science budget – including a block on all new fellowships and research grants" in the late 1990s, with new rounds of cuts in 2011 and 2012 leading to "a 22 percent reduction in the science budget."[13] The adverse effect of fluctuating state funding on skilled civil servants has only worsened in the information age.[14] In fact, over the past two decades, career bureaucrats (and the state agencies they populate) have been caught between two opposing forces that challenge the manner in which policy is carried out. On the one hand, as described above, recurrent economic crisis and ensuing budget cuts lead to fewer available resources and diminished state capacity.[15] On the other, the information age has placed a large premium on highly skilled labor both inside and outside of the bureaucracy (Brown, Green, & Lauder, 2005; Machin, 1996). Indeed, the demand for skilled labor has grown radically over the past few decades, owing to a global "'skill-biased technical change' in the way goods and services are produced in the economy" (Bresnahan, Brynjolfsson, & Hitt, 1999: 1). The need for sharp technical expertise is intensely felt in the state (Danziger & Andersen, 2002).

As a result, bureaucrats are expected to have the necessary expertise to resolve complex problems – such as water pollution, the negative effects of climate change on agricultural production, and energy crises – even under tight budgets. The expectation to deliver comes from political principals, to whom bureaucrats are directly accountable, and civil society, which increasingly demands from its experts solutions to pressing problems. The more demanding social role of expert bureaucrats is not in a vacuum, as:

13 See, respectively, "Brazil forced to cut back science funding" (Kauffman-Zeh, 1998) and "Brazil takes a knife to science funding again" in Royal Society of Chemistry 2014 accessed at www.rsc.org/chemistryworld/News/2012/March/brazil-science-technology-budget-cuts-third.asp.

14 The *Information* or *Knowledge Society* is seen "most obviously in . . . the rapid and accelerating permeation of computerized technologies throughout society, in the increased provision and take-up of education in most social systems, and in the growth of occupations that deal, for the most part, with information (clerks, professionals, instructors and so on). Experiencing such developments, it is not surprising that many observers have come to describe our age in terms of one of its most palpable features: hence, logically, the information society (Webster, 2006: 444).

15 There is a burgeoning literature on how globalization and neoliberalism affects governments' room to maneuver (Alcañiz & Hellwig, 2011; Hellwig, 2014).

> the role of science is changing. Scientists are being asked by policy-makers to contribute more directly to the needs of society. Part of this demand lies in the degree to which the problems that society faces have some close connection to issues of science and technology, for example in areas such as disease, development, terrorism, environmental impacts, adoption of new technologies, and so on. Another reason for such demands is that the resources available to support science and technology are limited.
>
> (Pielke, 2007: 31)

Regardless how scarce resources might be, state experts have a clear incentive to maintain their skills sharp and current. Bureaucrats in agencies in charge of nuclear policy or the protection of the environment need a degree of specialization to carry out the tasks assigned to them. Often, their particular skills are what got them hired in the first place. The more specialized the area in which they work, the greater the impact of skills on job and career advancements (Brown, Green, & Lauder, 2005). So what do bureaucrats do when their budgets get cut and the state reneges on its investment in expertise? If indeed "the practical world of scientists [is one in which they] increasingly face everyday decisions about how to position their careers and research in the context of policy and politics," then we should expect bureaucrats not just to anticipate but also to strategize on how to deal with spending cuts (Pielke, 2007: 8–9). In this book I argue that bureaucrats respond to decreased state funding by networking with foreign peers. International inter-agency cooperation provides state experts and their agencies with the opportunity to pool scarce resources, to attract funds from international donors, and above all, to update their technical skills.

If, as I assert, the incentive to invest in their skillset drives the international behavior of the bureaucrat, then three empirical observations should follow. First, a decrease in government spending should correlate with increased participation of bureaucrats in international inter-agency cooperation. Government cuts signal lean times ahead and cue state experts to seek alternatives to state funding. Activating ties with foreign peers and working together on cross-national projects allow bureaucrats to pool existing resources and better the chances of accessing donor funds. Second, I expect bureaucrats at higher levels of skills to be more willing (and able) to cooperate on cross-national projects with peers. State officials with more expertise face the greatest costs in letting their skills depreciate and the greatest returns – in terms of potential career advancement – in acquiring new knowledge and know-how. Therefore, bureaucrats with higher pre-existing levels of skills should cooperate more with their foreign peers. This prediction mirrors the expectation in the skills literature, given that "there is a substantial body of evidence indicating that in-career training is highly stratified, with the result that those with higher skills or educational attainment are more likely to participate in training" (O'Connell & Jungblut, 2008: 111). Third and finally, if skill upgrading is the primary causal mechanism behind international inter-agency cooperation in NEST and the protection of the environment, the empirical analyses should reveal a strong homophily effect. Homophily refers to the tendency of actors who share similar characteristics to work together, as simply expressed by the adage "birds of a feather, flock together" (McPherson, Smith-Lovin, & Cook, 2001). If bureaucrats' priority is to advance their skills, they will want to seek out partners who have superior training. The rationale for this is that:

> When people acquire skills, they make each other more productive. Since most work is team work, my productivity generally depends on your productivity. The more training you have – on-the-job or off-the-job – the more I can learn from you about doing the job effectively, and the more productively the two of us can interact in production, innovation, distribution, and sales.
>
> (Booth & Snower, 1996: 1)

Consequently, most bureaucrats would prefer to collaborate with foreign peers in advanced programs. However, partner selection goes both ways and experts with superior skills will naturally prefer to work with colleagues from more advanced agencies (or if they are at the top of their field, with their closest peers). As not everyone will be able to get their first preference, I expect a second preference – to collaborate with bureaucrats of equal skill – to result in the dominant strategy. Hence, if skill investment is the driving strategy, we should find empirical evidence of skill homophily within the transgovernmental networks of nuclear and environmental bureaucrats. These three expectations and other hypotheses of this study are discussed in depth and tested in the following chapters. Table 1.1 offers a schematic view of the theory of the expert bureaucrat. It summarizes the argument and the main hypotheses of the book.

This two-by-two table shows two levels of government spending on the *Y*-axis, lower and higher, and two levels of skill endowment on the *X*-axis, also lower and higher. The theory of the expert bureaucrat predicts that state professionals that fall in the upper-right quadrant will be highly motivated to participate in cross-national technical projects and will have the necessary pre-existing skill levels to do so. In contrast, bureaucrats located in the upper-left quadrant – the theory predicts – will be motivated to work with foreign peers, but will be limited significantly by the deficit

TABLE 1.1. *A Theory of Expert Bureaucrats*

		Skill Endowments of Bureaucrats	
		Lower	**Higher**
Government Spending	Lower	Bureaucrats have motive to cooperate (i.e., austerity) but lack the means (i.e., skill).	More cooperation by skilled bureaucrats who are motivated to go abroad by budget cuts at home.
	Higher	Bureaucrats lack the means (i.e., skills) to cooperate and the motive (i.e., austerity).	Skilled bureaucrats have the means to cooperate (i.e., skill) but lack a motive (i.e., austerity).

I thank one anonymous reviewer for this table.

in their skillset to join the knowledge networks of the Global South. State professionals that fall in the bottom row are at high levels of government spending, which will result in them having little incentives to work with professional peers across the border. However, I am intrigued about state agencies located in the bottom-right quadrant, especially those that have been high collaborators in the past. The theory would predict that neither poorly qualified nor well-trained bureaucrats will have clear and strong incentives to seek out international partnerships in order to access new skills and other resources. Yet, if these same state experts have collaborated before with peers across the borders, when government spending increases, do those commitments remain? Is there an inertia-type effect in transgovernmental cooperation, whereby participation in international projects does not fully drop even when domestic budgets get replenished? I explore this scenario both theoretically and empirically in Chapter 8.

The Literature on Skills and the State

The unique contribution of this book is that it asks and answers the question of how skills affect international cooperation. While little scholarly attention has been paid to this problem, the impact of skills on international competition has been studied at length (Booth & Snower, 1996; Mayer & Solga, 2008; Thelen, 2004, 2014). For example, scholars have analyzed how the distribution of training shapes competition and have found evidence that when resources are scarce, workers that are younger, more skilled, and employed benefit overwhelmingly from employer and state investment in skill upgrading (Booth & Snower, 1996; Brown, 2005;

Brown, Green, & Lauder, 2005; Estévez-Abe, 2012; Estevez-Abe, Iversen, & Soskice, 2001; Mayer & Solga, 2008; Thelen, 2014). We also know that the level of skills of the workforce may trigger poaching behavior among competing employers and make them less inclined to invest in employees' general training (Becker, 2009; Streeck, 2012). The effect of different skill levels on economic competition has been examined across countries, and political economists are in strong agreement that "skills have become a highly valued commodity in the new 'knowledge society' and a strategic asset in the economic competition among nations" (Mayer & Solga, 2008: 2).

Yet, states cooperate just as often as they compete. Cooperation across the developing world, in particular, is at an all-time high as a result of democratization, globalization, and the information age (Alcañiz, 2012; World Bank, 2012). These three processes and all they entail have simplified and multiplied the ways in which actors across borders, even across regions, work together. In a world where some of the practical barriers to collaboration have been removed thanks to innovative communication channels, an actor's skillset may be one of the more significant discriminators in cooperation. This is especially true in the developing world, where cooperating countries regularly operate with insufficient budgets. If all participants suffer from a shortage of economic resources, skills (or the lack there of) can be a greater barrier to cooperation than funds. In this book, I test some of the main expectations from the political economy of skills and discover that many of its findings hold for transnational cooperating bureaucrats.

In addition, my argument also draws from, and contributes to, the study of bureaucratic politics. I am interested in how students of bureaucracies understand and explain skill formation and upgrade in the state. The debate on bureaucratic expertise is twofold. One current of thought – prominent in the field of comparative politics – explains variation in the level of bureaucratic expertise among countries as a function of different institutional arrangements (Evans, 1995; Evans, Rueschemeyer, & Skocpol, 1985; Hall, 1989; Maggetti, 2014; Pierson, 1993; Schneider, 1999; Sikkink, 1991; Weber, 1958). The focus on state institutions by this theoretical approach contrasts with the delegation literature, which emphasizes the strategic behavior of political principals who must decide whether to micro-manage or grant autonomy to skilled bureaucrats. For delegation scholars, behavior is more important than institution because what matters is *how* the bureaucrat may use her expertise against the wishes of the political principal, not the origin (or continued source) of that expertise (Huber & Shipan, 2006). State skills, in this tradition, are fixed and exogenous to the study of bureaucratic politics. In other words, bureaucracies either have expertise or not.

This book finds common ground with both theoretical perspectives. On the one hand, it problematizes the critical question of skill formation in the state as *institutionalists* do. Bureaucratic expertise, particularly in the Global South, cannot be assumed away and – while not the focus of this book – the argument presented here begins with the understanding that the ability states have to hire, train, and maintain skilled workers goes hand in hand with the type of institutional investments they are willing to make. On the other hand, as delegation theorists remind us, bureaucrats have agency, regardless of the type of state institution in which they are embedded (McCarty, 2014; Huber & Shipan, 2006; Bendor and Meirowitz, 2004; Huber & Shipan, 2002; Gailmard, 2002). Because of this, the incentives they face and the strategies they develop in order to advance in their careers and improve the terms of delegation should be examined. How have global trends, such as the information revolution, globalization, and – for the third world – the wave of recent democratizations, changed the incentives of state experts to acquire and maintain their technical skills? What explains the international cooperation of so many state experts in the world? The field of bureaucratic politics has been slow to examine the effect of these issues, especially through a comparative method, even though public administrators and state experts have articulated in multiple ways the importance of innovation and international cooperation.[16]

Expert Bureaucrats and Epistemic Communities

The scholarship on epistemic communities was one of the first to note the link between domestic experts and international cooperation (Adler, 1992, 2008; Evangelista, 1993, 2002; Haas, 1989, 1992a, 1992b; Kapstein, 1992). Seminal pieces, such as the 1992 articles by Peter Haas, explain the critical role that technical specialists play in advancing policy (Haas, 1992a, 1992b). Defined as "a network of experts with

[16] For example, the scientific director of the São Paulo Research Foundation (FAPESP) stated: "Since about 2006 we have seen an important increase in international opportunities," says Brito Cruz. These days he spends more than a third of his time "talking to foreign delegates and organizing partnerships – with Germany, the UK, Denmark, Argentina, Portugal, the US." See www.bv.fapesp.br/namidia/noticia/46466/brazil-aims-its-science-have-greater-impact/.

recognized expertise and competence in a particular domain and an authoritative claim to policy-relevant knowledge within that domain," epistemic communities help decision-makers decipher political and scientific uncertainty (Haas, 1992a: 3). The impact of epistemic communities has been observed in technology-intensive policy areas, where the need for authoritative knowledge is greatest. Students of the epistemic approach have written about the influence of different coalitions forged by environmentalists, marine biologists, and atmospheric scientists in the protection of the natural world and by knowledgeable activists, policy experts, and nuclear scientists in the pursuit of nuclear disarmament (Adler, 1992, 2008; Evangelista, 1993, 2002; Haas, 1989, 1992a, 1992b; Kamelarczyk & Smith-Hall, 2014). Critically, members of the coalition hold a common policy goal that is shaped significantly by shared beliefs and ideals (Haas, 1992b).

Two key differences between the theory of the expert bureaucrat and the epistemic approach stand out. First, in this book, the beliefs and principles held by skilled bureaucrats are irrelevant, as the key motivator of their behavior is the incentive to invest in lost or degraded skills. Second, the role of crises differs greatly. In the epistemic literature, crises facilitate access to power and influence. Kapstein explains: "Analysts have asserted that epistemic communities are most likely to influence domestic and international politics during periods of crisis, as public officials, faced with uncertainty, seek experts armed with policy solutions" (Kapstein, 1992: 268). In contrast, my argument reveals how crises – especially economic ones – hinder access to government resources (most notably, skills) and act as exogenous shocks that cue bureaucrats to seek alternatives elsewhere.

Nevertheless, there are similarities. The theory of the expert bureaucrat also links domestic expertise to international cooperation, highlights the potential for coalition-building with foreign peers, and addresses governments and citizens' growing need for *interpreters* of science policy.[17] While the similarities are limited to these three points, I posit that this book tests a key implication of the epistemic paradigm. If experts depend on their skills to influence policy, as this scholarship has shown, it follows that they will have strong incentives to protect their expertise from

[17] Increasingly, state experts must be fluent in the languages of science and politics. Precisely, this same metaphor was used by one of the book interviewees (quoted in the following section) to explain how, as a state manager of NEST, he bridges the political and technical spheres.

degrading. However, akin to delegation theorists, scholars of epistemic communities do not explore how professionals keep their knowledge current and authoritative. Skill updating and upgrading remain outside of the epistemic paradigm.

The present book, I argue, makes a fundamental contribution to the epistemic scholarship as my work helps explain one key way in which epistemic communities may rise and evolve.

Technical vs. Political Skills

Many of the interviews carried out for this book reveal a preoccupation with state corruption and government turnover in the bureaucracy as major obstacles to effective project cooperation. Consequently, a reasonable question to ask is whether the bureaucrats at the heart of this book would be better served investing in political rather than human capital. In other words, if a bureaucrat wants to advance in her career, would she not benefit more by forging ties with key *political* players in her agency rather than forging ties with foreign peers? Is political favor explaining cooperation, in the sense that bureaucrats who are good political operators are "rewarded" with participation in prestigious international projects (as participants get to travel abroad on the state dime)?

I would assert that these two endeavors are not mutually exclusive. In fact, those who secure the domestic adoption of, and participation in, international projects are typically quite savvy in political affairs. This means that they are well aware of the political web of connections and favors in which they are embedded and in which they must negotiate. The state experts interviewed for this book expressed this quite clearly.

Accurate data on bureaucratic corruption are notoriously difficult to obtain and is beyond the scope of this book. Instead, I examine the effect of skills on transgovernmental cooperation from a variety of angles. As I explain below, I use multiple measures of skills that include level of professionalization of the bureaucracy, degree of specialization of state agencies, the pool of scientists in a given country, and skill content of cross-national projects. There is strong evidence that the relationship between professional and political rules is an inverse one, whereby more qualified bureaucracies are less likely to be guided by political principles (Weber, 1958; Sikkink, 1991; Evans, 1995; Schneider, 1999). Conversely, the empirical analyses presented in this book offer robust and significant evidence of a strong correlation between bureaucratic professionalization and international inter-agency cooperation.

If political favor explained cooperation among bureaucrats, I would posit, there should be little or no observed skill effect. The expectation of a "skill effect" in transgovernmental cooperation does not negate the problem of corruption in the Global South (Calvo & Murillo, 2013; Weyland, Madrid, & Hunter, 2010)). Nor does this book conceive of the bureaucrat as an apolitical technocrat. To the contrary, the theory of the expert bureaucrat – who, when the state withdraws, networks with her foreign peers in order to access resources that will advance her career – is predicated on the assumption that this is a strategic agent, with enough political skill to anticipate government cuts, develop strategies to compensate, and finally to navigate both international and local bureaucracies. A senior civil servant from the Brazilian National Commission for Nuclear Energy (CNEN) explains the need mezzo level bureaucrats have for political *and* technical skills when channeling mandates from the government regarding verification and compliance of nonproliferation policies:

> In the nuclear sector there is nothing that is exclusively political or exclusively technical. Nothing is just politics. We usually make a technical-political analysis; everything has at least a political slant. Using the language of soccer, we play the position of midfielders. We hear what *Itamaraty* (the Ministry of External Relations) wants; we transform that into questions to the technicians; the technicians respond technically; and we elaborate the language that the diplomats want to hear. Therefore, we are midfielders.[18]

Why the Developing World?

The central argument of this book focuses on civil servants in technical agencies and the career incentives they have to invest in their professional capital and avoid the depreciation of their skills. In theory, the burden of training and skill upgrading falls on the employer. In practice, bureaucrats in developing countries often share the costs of this training, as research programs are typically underfunded or one of the first items to go when budget cuts are implemented (Solingen, 1994; Schwartzman, 1994; Sarkar, 2012). Historically, as an employer, the developing state has been notoriously unreliable. Even so, governments across the Global South have made very different investments in order to create and preserve bureaucratic expertise (Evans, 1995; Schneider, 2013; Schrank, 2014). Yet variation in the developing world is often overlooked. This

[18] Former director of International Relations of CNEN, Doctor Laercio Vinhas, interview with author in Rio de Janeiro, Brazil, July 2006.

book rectifies this by analyzing how varying levels of bureaucratic expertise, bureaucratic capacity, and government spending in developing countries drive international inter-agency cooperation. To my knowledge, no other study offers such a comprehensive examination of bureaucracies and their international behavior in more than 100 developing states over thirty years of cooperation.

Precisely, the two policy areas that are the focus of this book – nuclear energy, science, and technology (NEST) and environmental protection – are cases in point that help illustrate skill variation in the Global South. For example, even countries with persistent problems of corruption have managed to create "pockets of efficiency," in which a few agencies or office divisions within the bureaucracy are governed by professional norms and a high degree of specialization (Rauch and Evans, 2000). The nuclear energy commission of Argentina, a country with an otherwise troubled bureaucracy, gets high marks on its institutional expertise and capacity (Adler, 1987; Solingen, 1996; Alcañiz, 2000). Another key difference seen across the developing world is the extent of resources that governments can bring to bear on policy problems. For example, government spending and budget appropriations for the protection of the environment will be vastly greater in Brazil than in Tanzania. Furthermore, overall country levels of human capital, particularly in science and engineering, also differ enormously. Consider India, a world leader in exports of pharmaceuticals on the one hand, and Costa Rica, a virtual net importer of industrial and IT goods.

Data on NEST and Environmental Protection

I test my theory in two critical policy areas, nuclear energy, science, and technology (NEST) and environmental protection. These are ideal fields to examine the impact of different levels of human capital and skills on international cooperation for several reasons. First, both are high-technology policy fields, where increasingly STEM-trained (science, technology, engineering, and mathematics) professionals are being hired. While there is no reliable data on the number of bureaucrats with STEM degrees employed in these two state sectors, archival and anecdotal data from my field research indicate a high proportion of technical personnel. Second, these fields are research-intensive, meaning successful policy design, adoption, and implementation needs to be based on scientific knowledge. This in turn requires sustained investment in R&D budgets. Third, both of these fields have been shaped thoroughly by the information age. Because NEST and environmental protection are science based, policymaking in these fields is directly affected by technology change. Further, as the pace of this change has accelerated, so too has the response of nuclear and environmental experts. Fourth, bureaucracies are major players in NEST and Environmental Protection. That is, these are two fields where state-employed experts carry the burden of activity.[19] This is clearly seen in nuclear development, where across the world the state has a virtual (often an actual) monopoly on all related activities. But the state also plays a key role in environmental conservation, remediation, and protection. While the rise of countless nongovernmental organizations (NGOs) in this sector has been a constant for the past twenty odd years (Keck & Sikkink, 1998; Conca, 2005; Hochstetler & Keck, 2007; Hadden, 2015), and these groups have a wealth of resources that they bring to bear (Conca, 2005), it is still the state and its *green* bureaucrats who have the institutional and financial resources to implement policy (Abers & Keck, 2013). However skill-intensive environmental NGOs have become, they cannot compete with the availability of resources of the government, even in impoverished states. In short, outdated expertise in these areas has real-world consequences, as there are few domestic actors who can compensate for the lack of skills in the state.

Yet, there are critical differences between the NEST and environmental areas as well. First, the two sectors have vast differences in the security implications of their endeavors. Most if not all of NEST activities are imbued in security concerns, given the potential risk or threat of radioactivity, mishandling of nuclear materials, and – the greatest fear of all – nuclear proliferation. Given all this, nuclear development is one of the most monitored activities at the state and inter-governmental levels. Domestic and international laws heavily regulate international technology transfers and trade as well as national activities and mandate the adoption of standardized safeguards. The IAEA through its body of nuclear inspectors has a key role in ensuring commitment to nonproliferation by Global South countries.

The security implications of environmental policy are less salient politically, although I would posit that the rapid deterioration of the natural environment and the number of recent climate catastrophes will change this. Still, there is a clear difference whereby most nuclear activity, even

[19] In many of these countries, the activities of expert bureaucrats are complemented often by the work of private contractors. Contractors are outside of the scope of this book, as its primary goal is to explain inter-agency cooperation.

civilian ones, remain securitized to a certain extent. As a general rule, if a policy sector is deemed as one with urgent security implications, the stakes become higher and the resources that the governmental allocates to the sector (which critically include investments in expertise) become richer. A second key difference is the age of the sector. NEST, as an area of state regulation, emerged in the immediate post-world war era. IAEA, for example, was created in 1957. Early adopters of nuclear science in the developing world, like Argentina, Brazil, China, Mexico, and South Korea, have accumulated at present a body of knowledge and expertise generated by several generations of state professionals. In contrast, environmental policy is a relatively new field, and thus the professionalization of environmental bureaucrats is also rather recent. I examine some of the implications of these sectoral differences in Chapter 3.

The data used to test my skill-based theory in the fields of NEST and environmental protection are quite rich. First, I collected qualitative data through field research that spanned four continents and eight countries, where I conducted archival research and in-depth interviews with over forty experts. My research on NEST led me to Buenos Aires, Argentina; Vienna, Austria; Rio de Janeiro, Brazil; and Johannesburg, Cape Town, and Pretoria, South Africa. My research on environmental protection took me to Buenos Aires and Paraná, Argentina; Nairobi, Kenya; Arusha, Tanzania; Ciudad de Panamá, Panamá; and Washington DC. These interviews of key actors in local and international bureaucracies, with firsthand knowledge on inter-agency cooperation, deeply inform the theory, hypotheses, and conclusions presented in this book.

In order to test empirically my theory of the expert bureaucrat, I use two original separate sets of data of cross-national co-sponsored projects in NEST and global environmental protection for all countries of the developing world. The two sets of project data are similar and come from the IAEA and the GEF, who sponsor projects that bring together *bureaucrats* in charge of policy in NEST, on the one hand, and environmental protection, on the other.[20] Applications are wide ranging. NEST projects

[20] Many projects include national (state) universities as participants, in addition to bureaucrats. For example, the SAG project described above was first designed by local state universities, including the Argentine Universidad Nacional del Litoral and Universidad de Buenos Aires; the Brazilian Universidade Federal do Paraná; the Paraguayan Universidad Nacional de Asunción; and in Uruguay, the largest university, Universidad de la República (see Project Appraisal Documents at www.gef.org). National universities make good partners because academic researchers have strong scientific skills needed for project design, and university facilities offer equipment, laboratory, and classroom

contribute to training and problem solving in agriculture, food processing, water, and public health, to name a few. Environmental projects include teams of bureaucrats working on international waters (like the Guaraní project discussed at the beginning of the chapter), climate change, biodiversity, land degradation and deforestation, and ozone layer depletion. On average, projects last two to four years and include at least the participation of four countries (often more). With few exceptions, NEST projects are all regionally based, whereby Latin American, African, and Asian experts only work with their neighbors. In contrast, the GEF data include both regional and global projects; in the latter, experts work with peers extra-region. The NEST data cover close to twenty-five years, from 1984 to 2008. GEF data covers approximately twenty years, from 1991 to 2010. Finally, one key difference is that only the environmental data includes disaggregated figures for funding, indicating how much countries and international donors put up for each project. This allows me to calculate the precise effect of outside funding on project participation. Are developing countries more likely to cooperate if they receive added money from international organizations and other international donors? In Chapters 6 and 7, I answer this question, showing how even though outside funding does increase inter-agency cooperation, it is not the only driver of bureaucratic partnerships.

Thus, in this book I use joint collaboration in NEST and environmental projects as the measure of international inter-agency cooperation. To explain cooperation among bureaucrats in the Global South, I consider a number of important covariates. These include the level of government spending; domestic funds applied to projects; degree of specialization of state agencies; degree of professionalization of national bureaucracies; countries' level of scientific production; skill content of cross-national projects; and a series of measures of homophily between countries. This last group of covariates measures similarities/differences among participating countries along several key dimensions: skill levels in the bureaucracy, overall funding contributions, and national scientific production. Empirical analyses in future chapters show strong evidence for my theory of the expert bureaucrat. That is, bureaucrats use transgovernmental

space. But bureaucrats *always* control the collaborative endeavor and often end up taking over once the university partner has made its contribution. Precisely this happened in the SAG project; once the universities produced the initial survey design of the Guaraní Aquifer, they were removed from the project. Argentine state water expert. Interview with the author in the City of Paraná, Argentina, July 2013.

cooperation in NEST and the protection of the global environment as a way to upgrade critical skills when the state withdraws.

Explaining Cooperation Using the Toolbox of Social Network Analysis (SNA)

The extensive data collection effort described in the previous pages allows me to test in great detail the determinants of inter-agency cooperation in nuclear and environmental projects. I test my skill-based theory of bureaucratic cooperation through a variety of statistical techniques that researchers use to explore relational data. That is, data where decisions to cooperate are not independent from each other but, instead, depend on reciprocal choices made by other agents. This is particularly important when we seek to understand partner selection by expert bureaucrats, where the level of development of the other agencies is an incentive or a deterrent to join in.

Consider, for example, two different projects, one that is sponsored by the Brazilian nuclear agency (CNEN) and another one sponsored by the Peruvian Institute of Nuclear Energy (IPEN). The theory of inter-agency cooperation proposed in this book makes it clear that collaborating in a project with a partner that has a more developed nuclear program, such as Brazil, will provide a higher utility to expert bureaucrats interested in upgrading and updating their skills. Similarly, Brazilian expert bureaucrats will derive more benefits from collaborating with agencies that have personnel with comparable skill levels. Because program similarity (homophily) is an important determinant of cooperation, statistical analyses of bureaucratic cooperation need to account for shared traits among agencies rather than simply focusing on discrete covariates for each of the programs. This is the type of statistical problem where Social Network Analysis has made important contributions to the comparative study of organizations.

The quantitative analyses of international inter-agency cooperation in Chapters 4 through 7 take advantage of recent advances in SNA, including network visualization techniques as well as Exponential Random Graph Models (ERGMs). ERGM is a statistical technique that estimates the probability of observing a collaborative network tie between each pair of agencies. ERGMs allow researchers to include variables that describe agency-specific traits (such as the level of development of the Peruvian Institute of Nuclear Agency) as well as incorporate terms for shared traits (such as differences in financing among potential partners).

In the empirical chapters I describe in further detail the advantages of ERGM for the study of inter-agency cooperation. I also describe a number of specifications that allow me to statistically test the three key hypotheses of this book: first, that declines in government spending increases inter-agency cooperation; second, that higher levels of bureaucratic skills increase cooperation; and, finally, that program homophily increases inter-agency cooperation. The statistical results substantiate my theory, and I find consistent and robust evidence across models and policy area that support the main hypotheses of the book. The empirical analysis complements the extensive archival research, fieldwork, and on-site interviews with expert bureaucrats I conducted in half a dozen countries of the Global South.

Implications and Contributions

How do workers acquire skills? This has been a central and persistent question asked by generations of scholars in comparative politics (international), political economy, and labor economics (Becker, 2009; Booth & Snower, 1996; Brown, 2005; Brown, Green, & Lauder, 2005; Busemeyer & Trampusch, 2012; Estévez-Abe, 2012; Estevez-Abe, Iversen, & Soskice, 2001; Martin, 2012; Mayer & Solga, 2008; Thelen, 2004, 2014; Ulph, 1996). While many Comparative Politics scholars have examined the different types of partnerships the state forges with business for skill investment (Thelen, 2004, 2014; Schneider, 2013; Estevez-Abe, Iversen, & Soskice, 2001), few have looked at skill formation *within* the bureaucracy (Sikkink, 1991; Evans, 1995). To the best of my knowledge, none have asked how expert bureaucrats acquire and *maintain* their skillsets *when the state fails* to make the necessary investment. Yet the question of skill acquisition and upgrading within the bureaucracy is a crucial one, especially in the economies of the Global South where often the state is one of the largest employers. If as human capital theorists posit, workers are differentiated by their varying skillsets, then bureaucracies and the quality of the policy they produce should also hinge on their level of expertise. By testing key findings of the political economy of skills against bureaucratic politics, this book contributes to furthering the two literatures.

My theory of the expert bureaucrat also gives us traction beyond bureaucratic politics and human capital. First, by connecting government spending to transnational cooperation, my theory allows us to discover some of the many international strategies pursued by domestic political actors (such as bureaucrats) as a consequence of state failures. That is, when states withdraw and do not deliver on expected commitments, the international *globalized* domain offers multiple opportunities for local actors to pursue compensatory strategies. Recent scholarship at the intersection of comparative politics and international relations has focused on this phenomenon and produced a wealth of research that examines how "the international" grants coverage and room to maneuver to diverse domestic actors (Alcañiz, 2012; Alcañiz & Hellwig, 2011; Conca, 2006; Hellwig, 2014; Hochstetler, 2002; Keck & Sikkink, 1998; Tarrow, 2005; Von Bülow, 2010).

Second, by linking domestic skill levels to international cooperation, my theory also sheds light on some of the obstacles found in accessing public goods. Inasmuch as transgovernmental projects result in the protection of the global environment and the peaceful use of nuclear power, we can conceive of their yield as public goods. International environmental cooperation helps ensure clean air and water, sustained biodiversity, and less extreme weather. Transgovernmental cooperation in NEST has resulted in greater transparency and renewed commitments to nonproliferation, which in turn help shore up multilateral security across the developing world. Although by definition public goods are non-excludable and thus in theory no one can be denied access to their benefits, researchers have found plenty of examples where access to this class of goods can be more costly for some consumers.[21] As this book shows, skills also inhibit the right to use public goods. That is, low-skilled consumers of technical international cooperation have less access to environmental and nuclear transgovernmental projects than high-skilled consumers. The link between *skills* and *access* is a promising line of research, not just for students of public goods but for those interested in common pooled resources as well. In conjunction with a network perspective, this relationship can help deepen our understanding of natural resources management.

Beyond the theoretical implications discussed above, the study of international inter-agency networks in itself is of significant value. Bureaucratic networks have real-life consequences, well beyond their effects on participants' careers. Networks help solve shared problems, forge

[21] Examples include the costs of internet connection to access public information goods (Cremer & Laffont, 2003); how political marginalization affects access to public goods that mitigate the effects of climate change (Raleigh, 2010); and preference heterogeneity based on ethnic divisions to access public education (Alesina, Baqir, & Easterly, 1997). A similar argument has been made in terms of "network failures" (Schrank & Whitford, 2011).

best practices, and coordinate policy (Bach & Newman, 2010; Raustiala, 2002). In her 2004 book *A New World Order*, Slaughter describes transgovernmental networks as a rising, potentially more democratic alternative to inter-state politics and a critical source of global governance (Slaughter, 2004). She describes their impact:

> What transgovernmental networks can do that traditional international organizations cannot, however, is to counter and engage transnational corporate, civic, and criminal networks. They permit a loose flexible structure that can bring in national officials from a wide range of different countries as needed to address specific problems. They can target problems at their roots, plug loopholes in national jurisdictions, and respond to goods, people, and ideas streaming across borders. Their members can educate, bolster, and regulate one another in essentially the same ways that make private transnational networks so effective. They are indeed the "institutions of globalization" and far better suited to global governance in an age of globalization and information.
>
> (Slaughter, 2004: 264)

My research on networks in NEST and the protection of the global environment finds evidence of similar contributions. Indeed, inter-agency cooperation in these two policy areas increase horizontal governance and inter-state transparency. For example, the Guaraní Aquifer project, discussed at the beginning of this chapter, resulted in the signature of an international treaty in 2010 by the governments of Argentina, Brazil, Paraguay, and Uruguay. In effect, the text of the agreement, which establishes formal guidelines to co-manage the SAG, cites as one of its determinants "the valuable results from the Project for Environmental Protection and Sustainable Development of the Guarani Aquifer System."[22] The treaty creates a Common Information System (SISAG), by which the four states commit to share all data on activities and programs that might affect the sustainability of El Guaraní.[23] Furthermore, the agreement has some teeth in that it can be invoked to halt activities if there is "evidence that the proposed activities or work may cause significant harm in its territory or environment. In such case, the Party that intends to perform the activities or work shall refrain from their initiation or continuation during the length of the consultations and negotiations, which shall be concluded within a maximum term of six months."

[22] Readers can access the full text of the "Project for Environmental and Sustainable Development of the SAG" at www.internationalwaterlaw.org/documents/regionaldocs/Guarani_Aquifer_Agreement-English.pdf.

[23] See www.hidricosargentina.gov.ar/novedad_interna.php?novedad=2528.

The effects of transgovernmental networks on increased regional transparency are even more dramatic in the nuclear case. As I will show in a detailed case study (Chapter 3), peer-to-peer *technical cooperation* between Argentine and Brazilian nuclear state experts led to significant *policy coordination*. Indeed, in the early 1980s, when these countries were experiencing the worst effects of the infamous Foreign Debt Crisis, bureaucrats from the two NEST state agencies began working together on personnel training and radiation technology. As extensive field research will demonstrate, collaborating on projects created trust between the two agencies and increased transparency between the two historic regional rivals. As a direct result of this cooperation process, the governments of Argentina and Brazil began to coordinate their foreign nuclear policy, culminating with the adoption in 1991 of a uniquely supranational system of nuclear safeguards (the Brazilian-Argentine Agency for Accounting and Control of Nuclear Materials or ABACC). Just a few years earlier, members of the international community had concerns the two countries were involved in a potential nuclear arms race against one another (Alcañiz, 2000; Darnton, 2014). Cooperation in the Southern Cone in NEST constitutes one of the few processes of nuclear rollback.[24] The Argentine-Brazilian partnership in NEST later extended to other international security areas as well (Alcañiz, 2012). In both examples, connections made within the bureaucratic network had lasting effects. Consequently, inter-state consultations are greatly facilitated by the pre-existing ties among foreign bureaucrats. This is consistent with findings from the network literature, which offers countless examples of how iterated voluntary horizontal exchanges between actors creates trust among them and increases transparency (Berardo & Scholz, 2010; Scholz, Berardo, & Kile, 2008).

Order of Book

The book is organized as follows. Chapter 2 frames the discussion for the book and expands my theory of the expert bureaucrat. The chapter surveys the literature on skills and bureaucratic expertise. In this chapter I also present the main hypotheses of the book, which are derived from the literature as well as the in-depth interviews I conducted with project participants. Drawing heavily on the interviews I conducted with

[24] South Africa is another case where – for different reasons, mainly racial inequality – the country renounced its strategic nuclear program.

officials from the state nuclear energy agencies in Argentina and Brazil, Chapter 3 offers a case study of Argentine and Brazilian state experts cooperating in NEST projects. The chapter pays close attention to the incentives public servants in research agencies have to take into their own hands the investment of skill upgrading. At the worst of the 1980s economic crisis, nuclear experts in the two countries joined forces to advance stalled research and take up joint training of personnel at lower costs. Inter-agency cooperation in South America resulted in a complete overhaul of the nuclear foreign policy of the two countries and to the creation of a common system of control and accounting for peaceful uses of nuclear energy (namely, the Brazilian-Argentine Agency for Accounting and Control of Nuclear Materials or ABACC).

Chapter 4 describes the larger network of bureaucrats in Latin America, Africa, and Asia cooperating in NEST projects. It also draws from the field research I conducted. It addresses how projects are negotiated, adopted, and implemented by foreign bureaucrats, as well as the facilitating role played by the IAEA. Finally, the chapter uses Social Network Analysis (SNA) techniques to visualize the network of bureaucrats across the three main regions of the Global South that collaborate in NEST projects. Chapter 5 empirically tests my theory against NEST project data. Statistical models support the central argument of the book that when the state withdraws, bureaucrats cooperate with foreign peers to compensate for the loss of resources, especially skills. Chapter 6 describes the networks of environmental bureaucrats who work together on regional and global projects. This chapter draws on my field research, especially numerous hours of interviews with environmental experts. It uses SNA techniques to visualize the network of Latin American, African, and Asian bureaucrats cooperating intra- and inter-region. Chapter 7 empirically tests my theory against GEF project data. Model results support the central argument of the book. Chapter 8 tests the theory of the expert bureaucrat in the context of high government spending. It also uses GEF data to examine the effect on transgovernmental cooperation of the Commodity Boom of the 2000s, which has reversed austerity conditions and increased the growth rates in so many developing and emerging markets. Lastly, Chapter 9 offers the conclusion. Future research and policy implications are also discussed.

2

Bureaucrats across Borders

What explains the international cooperative behavior of expert bureaucrats in the fields of nuclear energy, science, and technology (NEST) and in the protection of the global environment? In this chapter I lay out a theory of inter-agency cooperation that is rooted in the expert bureaucrats' need to maintain their skills current. My theory draws from current advances in the political economy of skills. Yet, whereas this scholarship mostly focuses on the link between skills and economic competition, my theory examines how skills shape cooperation. Furthermore, my theory challenges traditional depictions of civil servants as inward-oriented, budget-maximizing actors, and reveals instead the career incentives that prompt expert bureaucrats to go outside their national agencies and collaborate with peers.

Expert bureaucrats in the areas of science and technology face a very distinct challenge: on the one hand, their jobs increasingly require sharp and current skills; on the other, skills naturally depreciate over time (De Grip & Van Loo, 2002). Similar to workers in the private sector, who have to pay the cost of skill acquisition when the market or employer fails to do so, bureaucrats in high tech areas need to take investment in their own hands when state budgets decline. Different from private sector scientists and researchers, bureaucrats often are constrained by government regulations that may prevent them from seeking outside resources to finance training, equipment, and research operations. In most countries, the state requires prior international agreements to be underwritten by agencies in order to cooperate.[1] Some professionals might be able and

[1] Specialized international organizations (like the International Atomic Energy Agency and the United Nations Environmental Program) greatly facilitate the negotiation and signature of framework treaties that allow technical cooperation between national agencies, as Chapters 4 and 6 will show.

willing to pay to further their own education, for example, by working toward a graduate degree. But given the costs of pursuing private training, expert bureaucrats typically will want to make use of state resources that are available to government employees, and leverage them toward career advancement. State managers are thus incentivized to seek cooperative agreements with foreign agencies.

The causal logic behind the theory of the expert bureaucrat is straightforward. When government budgets decline due to external shocks, state experts should compensate by activating ties with foreign peers and increasing international technical cooperation. The greater the skill endowment of local agencies, the more active they should be in transgovernmental collaborative networks. Further, if partner selection is skill-based, cooperation should reveal a bias toward compatible bureaucratic agencies pairing up. In short, my theory tells us to expect three key empirical observations: (1) an inverse relationship between government spending and international inter-agency cooperation, (2) a positive relationship between overall skill levels and international inter-agency cooperation, and (3) homophily effects, whereby bureaucrats from countries with similar skill levels (and state funding) cooperate together. I explain these expectations with insights from the literatures on skills and bureaucratic politics.

The Formation of Bureaucratic Expertise

Since Weber's early writings on the rise of modern bureaucracy, there has been a rich literature that closely links policy implementation to bureaucratic expertise (Weber, 1958). Yet with few exceptions, existing studies consider state professionals as *off-the-shelf* bureaucrats, whose expertise is exogenously given and who will learn anything else they need to implement policy once they are assigned to their official post. The assumption of exogenously given skills only recently has begun to be challenged, although systematic theories of skill acquisition remain conspicuously absent in the study of modern bureaucracies.

New developments in the study of delegation illustrate this point. While delegation theorists have made significant headway into the determinants of bureaucratic autonomy in contemporary states, by and large, the literature describes skills as exogenously given, whereby bureaucrats are assumed either to have them or not (McCarty, 2014; Huber & Shipan, 2006; Bendor & Meirowitz, 2004; Huber & Shipan, 2002;

Gailmard, 2002). Because the delegation literature is mostly preoccupied with the political control of bureaucratic agents, it "does not problematize the source of bureaucratic expertise and information" (McCarty, 2014: 101). Huber and Shipan's seminal study of bureaucratic autonomy in OECD countries recognizes as much: "Our study rests squarely on the assumption that bureaucrats are Weberian – that they have substantial policy expertise and the capacity to implement policies" (Huber & Shipan, 2002: 12). The authors acknowledge that this is a difficult assumption to generalize, which may hold only in bureaucracies in the industrial North and not in the Global South. More problematic, however, is the unnoticed assumption that bureaucratic expertise and the resources to keep it current hold constant over time.

There are significant anecdotal and statistical data that demonstrate that prior investment in skills is not enough for the bureaucrat to keep up with real-world demands and changing technology (De Grip & Van Loo, 2002).[2] This is exacerbated by state funding for R&D, in-house training, and technical projects that often fluctuates widely, even within short periods of time. In this day and age, given the acceleration of technological changes, which require sustained investment to keep abreast of them, and the complexity of some of the most persistent problems of society (e.g., climate change, water security, and fiscal balance), it is difficult to assume away skill upgrading, whether we consider countries in the industrial North or the Global South.

Indeed, the problem of maintaining state expertise in the face of skill and funding gaps, as well as shifting societal demands, has been fairly salient in recent U.S. political debates. Changes in American public health, a policy sector at the center of Huber and Shipan's *Deliberate Discretion*, illustrate how the need for bureaucratic skills remains anything but constant (Huber & Shipan, 2002). In less than ten years, public health officials in the United States have had to respond to overwhelming challenges where resolution required complex technical skills. American

[2] For recent examples of the former in research-intensive bureaucracies, see reporting in public health and safety in the United States. For the effect of spending cuts on the Ebola crisis of 2014, see www.politifact.com/punditfact/statements/2014/oct/24/stephanie-cutter/stephanie-cutter-ebola-vaccine-research-was-cut-ha/; for the effect of spending cuts on forecasting and preparedness for major weather events, including Superstorm Sandy, see www.nytimes.com/2014/10/31/opinion/our-failing-weather-infrastructure.html?_r=0; and for how "Budget Cuts Reduce Pandemic Influenza Planning and Response Capacity" see http://nacchopreparedness.org/?p=442.

health experts have dealt with global health threats (like the 2009 H1N1 world pandemic and the 2014 Ebola outbreak in West Africa); extreme weather emergencies (like Hurricane Katrina that devastated the city of New Orleans in 2005 and the Superstorm Sandy that destroyed parts of coastal New Jersey and New York in 2012); and the design and implementation of the 2010 Affordable Care Act (commonly known as Obamacare).

If bureaucrats are to meet these extraordinary technical challenges they must have strong skills when hired, but also and more critically, the agencies they work for must ensure that those skills are updated in order to match the evolving complexities they face. Consequently, if the "relative expertise of bureaucrats [is] a central motivation for politicians' delegating policymaking powers to bureaucrats in the first place" – as is the consensus – then explaining skill variation *over time* should matter to delegation theorists as well (Huber & Shipan, 2002: 83).

Endogenous accounts of skill investment in the state have gathered some support among delegation theorists in recent times, although it remains more the exception than the rule (Huber & Shipan, 2006; Gailmard, 2002). Bendor and Meirowitz, for example, expect bureaucrats to invest in skills when the bureaucratic agent realizes that he "keeps authority only if he specializes," given that the political principal might reverse delegation if the cost of specialization is low (Bendor & Meirowitz, 2004: 14). The argument by Bendor and Meirowitz is rooted in perceptions of bureaucratic career advancement that bring together expertise and power and can be linked to Weber's original rationale for skill acquisition in the bureaucracy, as policymaking increasingly relies on technical knowledge (Weber, 1958). Modern bureaucracy, Weber argues, requires candidates to be "selected on the basis of technical qualifications" . . . and a "system of promotion according to seniority or achievement" (Weber, 1958: 220).

Weber's conceptualization of the rational bureaucrat has influenced generations of scholars, who continue to find strong links between the institutional and financial investments states make and the cadre of expert bureaucrats they produce (Carpenter, 2001; Crowe, 2007; Evans, 1995; Evans, Rueschemeyer, & Skocpol, 1985; Hall, 1989; Maggetti, 2014; Pierson, 1993; Schneider, 1999; Sikkink, 1991). Many of them have studied the institutional conditions under which the *Weberian* bureaucrat is likely to emerge and shape complex policy in the developing world, where political favor and rampant corruption are often the norm (Evans, 1995; Schneider, 1999; Sikkink, 1991). In examining the rise of the developmental state in the Global South, scholars have noted the critical role played by state institutions in high-end skill formation, given the limited presence or outright absence of alternative training hubs such as those provided by the private sector (Schneider, 2013).

For example, in her study of developmentalism[3] in Argentina and Brazil, Sikkink examines the ability of the state to train bureaucrats: "In addition to hiring and promotion procedures, the state may use training programs to improve the quality of intellectual talent involved in economic policy making. Training may not only expand technical expertise but also help reshape values toward a common rationality, contribute to the emergence of a shared esprit de corps, and increase the prestige of civil servants" (Sikkink, 1991: 191). However, the author finds that the ability of the state to upgrade the skills of its public servants is highly dependent on past investments of the government in training programs and "the degree of continuity of public officials which would allow them to incorporate their training into their jobs" (Sikkink, 1991: 193). Not all states can manage this. But even dysfunctional bureaucracies may create "pockets of efficiency" where merit-based practices outnumber political favors, resulting in some state bureaus that resemble the Weberian model (Rauch & Evans, 2000).

When looking at technological development in India, South Korea, and Brazil, Peter Evans also links – in a Weberian sense – state structures to state expertise and capacity. Meritocratic hiring and promotion across the bureaucracy are key to explain industrial transformation, but they are not contingent on an insulated state, à *la* Weber. For Evans, only when expert agencies are embedded in key societal relations, will state capacity be at its highest (Evans, 1995). The extent to which bureaucrats have forged this "embedded autonomy" explains the different rates of success across his case studies.

The developmental literature offers two contributions of interest here. First, by showing how uneven skill development is within and across bureaucracies in the developing world, these studies make the case that expertise must be treated endogenously. Second, in stark contrast to Weber's ideal type, the expert bureaucrat in the Global South is reliant on political skills. As Schneider explains in his study of appointive

[3] A politico-economic model popular among the larger economies of the Global South pre-globalization, developmentalism has been defined as the adoption of import substituting industrialization (ISI) through an "expanded involvement of the state in directing the development effort, generally by using some form of indicative planning to channel private initiative into priority areas" (Sikkink, 1991: 4).

bureaucracies in Latin America, "Meritocratic recruitment and promotion are possible in both Weberian and appointive bureaucracies, but depoliticized administration is possible only in the former" Schneider (1999: 292–293). I take up these two points in the following sections.

Skill Depreciation

Thus, scholars and practitioners agree that through merit-based practices and politically insulated institutions, bureaucracies can effectively hire and maintain experts. But is an initial investment in skills by the state enough? Does bureaucratic expertise depreciate over time, requiring periodic investments? Labor economists, who look at the interaction between employers and workers in the private sector, have asked similar questions (De Grip & Van Loo, 2002; Guadalupe, 2007). They find strong evidence of a skills gap between market demands for greater specialization and workers' ability to avoid "rapid skills obsolescence" in both OECD and developing economies.[4] Standard explanations for the rising mismatch between demand and supply of skills emphasize the impact of technology development on a growing number of economic sectors. A recent World Bank report on the education and technology gap in developing countries offers this explanation:

> First, skilled workers are needed to implement new technologies because skilled workers are more adept at dealing with change. Second, the availability of more skilled workers in developed countries has created incentives for firms to develop new technologies that are more skilled intensive. Directed technical change requires an even greater need for speed in the upgrading of education systems in developing countries, as the skill-biased nature of technological change is poised to continue.
>
> (De Ferranti, 2003: 7)[5]

Studies on the quality of labor markets reach the same conclusion: maintaining the value of workers' skills is a significant and necessary investment affecting countries in the industrial North and the Global South (Card & DiNardo, 2002; De Ferranti, 2003; Guadalupe, 2007; Thelen, 2004). In discussing skill acquisition in Germany, a country historically hailed as a top producer of high skills, Thelen notes that a "longstanding

4 William D. Eggers, John Hagel, and Owen Sanderson, "Mind the (Skills) Gap," September 21, 2012, Harvard Business Review Blog at http://blogs.hbr.org/cs/2012/09/mind_the_skills_gap.html.

5 Explaining wage differentials between skilled and unskilled labor as a result of technological changes is known as the Skill-Biased Technical Change (SBTC) hypothesis.

weakness in the German system is the relative underdevelopment of *continuing* vocational education and training" and that while this "is not a new problem, . . . the effects of this deficit may be magnified in the current period. Particularly in rapidly evolving sectors such as information technologies and related industries, ongoing skill development is simply essential to keep pace with production technologies" (Thelen, 2004: 270–271).

Science and Technology in the Developing State

In the Global South, much of the scientific enterprise takes place within the state and is carried out by its experts (De Ferranti, 2003; Schwartzman, 1994; Velho, 2005).[6] Greater technical demands leveled on the state and higher expectations of bureaucratic accountability have raised the premium on skills for civil servants. Governments increasingly need to staff their technical agencies with professionals having advanced credentials, whose work and training often resembles that of academics. These bureaucrats need proper expertise to design and implement policy, as well as to monitor, evaluate, and enforce state regulations of a technical nature. More and more, developing countries have state agencies in policy sectors requiring advanced specialization and expertise – like the Nuclear Energy Programs of South Africa and Algeria (NECSA and COMENA), the Argentine and Brazilian space programs (CONAE and AEB), the Mexican Ministry of Environment and Natural Resources (SEMARNAT), and the public health sector in Uganda (the Uganda AIDS Commission) and Thailand (the Department of Disease Control). But despite the trend toward greater professionalization, bureaucracies in the Global South remain riddled with fluctuating spending and political volatility.[7]

Research facilities in developing countries have been chronically underfunded, and because of this, expert bureaucrats in these countries frequently have to play defense with their budgets (Fan & Rao, 2003). There are many reasons why states allocate insufficient funding to its

[6] Also, see the United Nations Conference on Trade and Development (UNCTAD) 2011 Report on The Least Developed Countries. Accessed at http://unctad.org/en/pages/aldc/Least%20Developed%20Countries/The-Least-Developed-Countries-Report.aspx.

[7] For a report on the state of science and technology investments by country, see the United Nations Educational, Scientific and Cultural Organization (UNESCO) 2010 Science Report accessed at http://unesdoc.unesco.org/images/0018/001899/189958e.pdf. See also (Jordana, Levi-Faur, & i Marín, 2011).

technical agencies: absence of national policies in science and technology, spending cuts triggered by market-oriented reforms, low fiscal capacity, high levels of debt, and recurrent (national and regional) economic crises[8] (Fan & Rao, 2003).[9] Under budget deficits, it is very hard to maintain current values of technical skills, let alone upgrade them. Scientists who work in technical agencies are not just playing catch-up with their skills, often they are trying to revive and move forward their programs. When governments decrease spending, those sectors with higher salaries and investment costs typically face statewide hiring and spending freezes. In such circumstances, starting new R&D projects in government research agencies becomes extremely difficult, and ongoing projects are revised, canceled, or downgraded (Velho, 2005). Commercial agreements with program suppliers, in particular international ones, are also interrupted and the lack of key supplies often results in the total shutdown of projects if there are no domestic alternatives to the imported equipment or technology.[10] Furthermore, reductions in anticipated spending levels frequently result in the cancellation of entire programs since default on contractual obligations in any aspect of the agreement also results in the loss of technology transferred pursuant to that agreement. When budgets are cut, research projects and programs are undermined and considerable scientific capital is lost.[11] This should be particularly pervasive in

[8] In the past thirty years, there have been multiple severe financial breakdowns affecting entire regions of the Global South, including the 1982 Foreign Debt Crisis, the 1994 Mexican *Tequilazo*, the 1997 South East Asian crisis, and Argentina's 2001 sovereign debt default.

[9] See the 2010 UNESCO Science Report at http://unesdoc.unesco.org/images/0018/001899/189958e.pdf.

[10] This is particularly the case for technology-intensive programs in advanced developing countries. For example, for Argentina, Brazil, Mexico, and South Africa, bilateral treaties with advanced nuclear countries were instrumental in developing their nuclear programs. However, these comprehensive agreements (with both commercial and technology transfer aspects) are not always affordable. This affects the possibility of cooperation between North and South. A nuclear bureaucrat from Argentina explains: "Once the commercial aspect of the treaty is over, cooperation stops [...] that happened to us with Germany. Cooperation with Germany was very intense but as soon as the [commercial] relationship was over they were done. The same thing happened with Canada [...] The French were brutally honest with us. They said clearly that they had little interest in cooperation by itself [...] rather they look at it through the dollar or Euro sign." Roberto Ornstein, Director of International Cooperation of the Argentine National Atomic Energy Commission. Interview with the author in Buenos Aires, Argentina, July 2006.

[11] For an account of this in Latin America, see the Second Pugwash Workshop Report on Economic and Social Inequities in Latin America (September 10–12, 2004 Bariloche, Argentina) at: www.pugwash.org/reports/ees/argentina2004/report.htm.

countries that adopted austerity programs in recent decades as these reforms had the effect of dramatically cutting government spending – and consequently, bureaucrats' financial capacity to implement policy and upgrade their expertise (Huber & Solt, 2004; Murillo, 2009; Walton, 2004; Weyland, 2002).

Thus, irregular government spending affects bureaucrats' ability to maintain the value of their skills. This leads to an enduring disparity between the need for new skills and the ability of the state to keep up with demand. It is precisely this skill gap, I argue, that creates distinct incentives for bureaucrats (who rely on their skills to advance their careers) to develop strategies against skill devaluation.

Students of labor in the private sector have examined the problem of skill devaluation and possible strategies to overcome it (Guadalupe, 2007). Many have found that workers are clearly aware of the need to upgrade their specialization.[12] If this is the case, it follows that they will be motivated to attempt to remedy it. In his groundbreaking theory of human capital, Gary Becker maintains that "it is the trainees, not the firms, who bear the cost of general training and profit from the return" (Thelen, 2004: 11). Streeck clarifies this claim: "The thrust of Becker's argument is that the training of workers should be organized in ways that are what economists call *incentive-compatible*, with those who benefit from it bearing the cost" (Streeck, 2012: 324). Similarly, I argue that because expert bureaucrats benefit from keeping their expertise current, they have a clear incentive to invest in updating their skills when the government withdraws its resources.

A Demand-Driven Theory of Inter-Agency Cooperation

To restate, as expert bureaucrats rely on their skills to advance in their careers, they have a preference to stay abreast of market demands for expertise. But one hallmark of the information age is that skills depreciate rapidly. Thus, state experts have an incentive to develop strategies that help slow down or avoid the depreciation of their skills. I focus on one key strategy: networking. Like scientists and academic researchers,

[12] For example, a recent study conducted by the consulting group Accenture found that 55 percent of workers surveyed "report they are under additional pressure to develop additional skills to succeed in their current and future jobs. But only 21 percent say they have acquired new skills through formal, company-provided training during the past five years." Smith, "How Employers Can Help Solve the Skills Gap," *Harvard Business Review* Blog, February 9, 2012.

expert bureaucrats develop ties with peers in other countries, often at the annual assembly meetings of the IO in their policy area.[13] These state experts typically go outside their agencies to stay current; they attend professional meetings in their policy area, present their research, learn of new technologies being developed elsewhere, participate in training seminars and symposia, and become members of professional organizations (Campion & Shrum, 2004).

When their budgets are cut at home, expert bureaucrats activate the ties with professional peers abroad, in order to pool resources and share in the costs of research. This allows them to tap an alternative source of knowledge and know-how at low cost to their employer (the state). There is ample evidence that civil servants forge critical ties with like experts and mentors in order to acquire and maintain appropriate skills to do their job (Abers & Keck, 2013; Alcañiz, 2010; Carpenter, 2001; Heclo, 1978; Sabatier & Jenkins-Smith, 1999; Slaughter, 2002). Professional networks, in contrast to markets and formal organizations, are characterized by non-competitive, reciprocal, and often in-kind exchanges. Many have found inter-agency networks to function as alternative training grounds for bureaucrats from all over the world, even for those who hail from OECD states. For example, Bach and Newman describe one such network (the International Organization of Securities Commissions or IOSCO) as "a voluntary, non-treaty-based body where regulators from more than one hundred jurisdictions share information, develop best practices, and build expertise through organized training programs and peer advising" (Bach & Newman, 2010: 510).

If the argument presented here is correct, then skill-investment strategies like inter-agency networking should be most observable when expert bureaucrats believe their skills are at risk of devaluation. As discussed earlier, I regard the decline of government spending to cue expert bureaucrats to take skill investment in their own hands.[14] Because of the

[13] Interviews with Technical Cooperation Program managers from the International Atomic Energy Agency (Vienna, Austria, 2007) and the United Nations Environmental Program (Nairobi, Kenya, and Panama City, Panama, 2013).

[14] Note that in my theory, the skills held by expert bureaucrats (independent variable) provide an incentive to cooperate (dependent variable). Indeed, the decision to cooperate does not alter the current stock of skills of expert bureaucrats. If anything, it may allow these bureaucrats to increase their skills at a future time. But there is no endogenous effect from the decision to cooperate for the acquisition of skills. In fact, bureaucrats may decide to cooperate but still fail to do it in a way that will eventually be beneficial. Just as overeating during the holidays may explain the decision to join a gym but not necessarily result in a decline in a person's overall weight.

persistent low financial capacity of research sectors and a private economy with limited employment alternatives in developing countries (Solingen, 1994; Schwartzman, 1994; Campion & Shrum, 2004), expert bureaucrats from the Global South must network internationally.[15] Given this, I expect government spending to correlate negatively with international inter-agency cooperation in nuclear energy, science, and technology and environmental protection. This leads to the formulation of the first central hypothesis of this book.

Hypothesis Government Spending: Hypothesis 1: If fear of skill-depreciation drives behavior, we should see bureaucrats pursuing skill-investment cooperative strategies (i.e., participate more in cross-national projects) when government spending declines.

The Political Economy of Skills

The study of skills is today a fertile area of innovation in political economy, with a large body of knowledge arguing that heterogeneity in the skills of workers should induce product differentiation and competition among states (Booth & Snower, 1996; Brown, 2005; Estévez-Abe, 2012; Green & Sakamoto, 2001; Mayer & Solga, 2008; Thelen, 2004, 2014). In an integrated world, one study summarizes, states investment in skill formation at home will determine whether "they can win a competitive advantage in the global 'knowledge wars'... The main policy objective is to outsmart other countries in the development of the nation's human resources" (Brown, 2005: 9). Consequently, the literature has focused on the relationship between skills and competition.

Less attention, however, has been paid to the incentives for cross-national cooperation that are also dependent on skill endowments. Yet in part as a result of enhanced economic interdependence and low communication costs, domestic actors in the private and public sectors are

[15] For example, a 2005 overview of science and technology institutions in Latin America and the Caribbean (LAC) reports that: "In Latin America and Caribbean countries the public sector is still responsible for over 70 percent of R&D funding and performance [...] The research community, for example, struggles for more public research funds and to keep control over how resources are allocated. There is no denying that, as the public sector is the primary sponsor of R&D in LAC, any reduction in government spending has a strong negative effect. Most LAC countries have suffered such effects as the increase in private-sector expenditure on R&D in the region (from 20 percent in 1990 to 36 percent in 2000) did not compensate for the decrease in public R&D funding" (Velho, 2005: 103–105).

increasingly working with peers across borders. Many of the key insights from the political economy of skills hold for workers in the public sector, and as a result are of interest in explaining inter-agency cooperation. For example, past research in skill formation has shown that there are biases in access to training, whereby "those with higher skills or educational attainment are more likely to participate in training" (O'Connell & Jungblut, 2008: 111; Estévez-Abe, Iversen, & Soskice, 2001; Thelen, 2004; Estévez-Abe, 2012). Studies from this field analyzed employers' decisions to invest in employee training and found strong evidence that, when resources are scarce, workers that are more skilled benefit overwhelmingly from employer and state investment in skill upgrading (Estévez-Abe, 2012; Thelen, 2014; Mayer & Solga, 2008; Booth & Snower, 1996). Similarly, the theory of the expert bureaucrat shares the assumption that professionals with greater technical expertise – as determined by the degree of bureaucratic specialization and the size of the country's pool of scientists – will be more active in collaborative networks. This is based on the expectation that the more professional and specialized the employing institution, the stronger the incentive of the employee to keep her skills current, as technology-intensive institutions will put greater technical demands on their workforce. In fact, my theory assumes an initial level of expertise in order for an investment in skill upgrade to pay off. Thus, the second central hypothesis of the book follows.

Hypothesis High Skills: Bureaucrats that have higher pre-existing levels of skills will cooperate more in cross-national projects than bureaucrats with lower level of expertise.

Becker was the first scholar to argue that the employer's incentive to invest in the training of the workforce is contingent on type of skill (Becker, 2009). His human capital theorem begins by distinguishing between *generalist's* and *specialist's* training, whereby the former entails more transferable skills and the latter are specific to the firm in which the worker is employed. Employers, Becker argues, have clear incentives to pay the cost to train and specialize the workforce, but they have little reason to bear the cost of transferable skills, as an investment in this kind of expertise may be easily lost to a competitor (O'Connell & Jungblut, 2008). Because of this, the incentive to invest in general skills is transferred to the worker (Becker, 2009). In other words:

> Specific skills increase productivity more than general skills do, and thus improve workers' wages and job duration. On the other hand, general skills raise the bargaining point of workers, thus both their wages and future utility derived from unemployment. In other words, the trade-off is between improving the workers' prospects within or outside the firm.
>
> (Wasmer, 2006: 816)

Becker's human capital theory makes particular sense in bureaucracies across the Global South, where research agencies typically are understaffed and civil servants are reshuffled after every political adjustment. Under these conditions, a "jack of all trades" strategy can be a winning one to ensure a career in a politicized and ever-changing bureaucracy. Thus, if indeed bureaucrats seek international cooperation in order to invest in their careers, they should prefer projects that offer more general (i.e., marketable) skills. In the empirical chapters of this book, I empirically control for the type of training offered in NEST projects. I expect to see a stronger participation effect in projects that are more intensive in general skills.

Hypothesis Human Capital: Following Becker, expert bureaucrats should be more likely to participate in cross-national projects that offer general training than in those that are more skill specific.

As a key control for my theory of the expert bureaucrat, I test for homophily effects in environmental and NEST collaboration across the Global South. As previously discussed, homophily is the tendency commonly observed in social networks whereby "birds of a feather, flock together" (McPherson, Smith-Lovin, & Cook, 2001; Maoz, 2012; Kinne, 2013; Videras, 2013). Past research reveals homophily to be present in many collaborative networks, similar to the ones studied in this book (Alemán & Calvo, 2013; Kinne, 2013; Maoz, 2012; McPherson, Smith-Lovin, & Cook, 2001; Videras, 2013). If, as I argue, bureaucrats seek to cooperate with foreign peers to access know-how and maximize their skills, we should expect increased collaboration among agencies with similar levels of program development. In other words, bureaucrats should seek out peers who either have superior or equal levels of program development, rather than transfer their skills to peers in programs with lower levels of expertise and capacity.

However, not all bureaucrats will be able to get their first preference to work with peers in advanced programs. Selection goes both ways, and experts in the more advanced program should also want to pair up with better-trained colleagues. As it is impossible to satisfy this preference for all bureaucrats, the logical second preference – to collaborate with experts in agencies with a similar level of program development – should result in a dominant strategy of seeking out real peers. That is, we should observe an increase in the probability of collaboration when programs have similar investment levels, similar scientific development and skill levels, and bureaucracies at comparable levels of competence. I formulate the homophily central hypotheses of the book as follows.

Hypothesis Homophily Agency Specialization: Cooperation will be more likely among two state agencies at comparable levels of specialization and skills.

Hypothesis Homophily Funding: Cooperation will be more likely among two state agencies at comparable levels of funding.

Hypothesis Homophily Bureaucratic Competence: Cooperation will be more likely among two state agencies at comparable levels of overall bureaucratic competence.

Hypothesis Homophily Overall Scientific Development: Cooperation will be more likely among two state agencies from countries at comparable levels of overall scientific development.

Supply Side Theories of Inter-Agency Cooperation and Other Alternative Explanations

There is a long tradition of explaining international inter-agency cooperation using supply-side theories. Students of transgovernmentalism depict the rise of these networks as a result of globalization and its international effect on bureaucratic politics (Bauer, 2006; Biermann & Siebenhüner, 2009; Hicks, Parks, Roberts, & Tierney, 2008; Slaughter, 2004). They find cause in the rising costs of noncooperation, whereby bureaucrats in the same field can no longer afford to ignore policy adoption in other countries (Slaughter, 2004) and highlight how coordination through transgovernmental networks facilitates domestic policy implementation by reducing uncertainty (Keohane & Nye, 1974; Slaughter, 2004).

Since the 1970s, scholars have been tracking these networks and the causes of their ascendancy, revealing an intriguing area of state activity at the intersection of comparative politics and international relations. Keohane and Nye first explained the rise of international inter-agency cooperation or transgovernmentalism as the result of sustained exchanges between autonomous bureaucrats, acting outside of the terms of political delegation.[16] These collaborative networks, according to the authors, develop in a "context of interdependence" under which "subunits of governments are likely to resort to transgovernmental policy coordination or transgovernmental coalition building, making use of existing international organizations to facilitate these relationships" (Keohane & Nye, 1974: 58). In other words, linked economies require some degree of policy coordination and bureaucrats (who frequently need to develop policy with an eye toward external influences) benefit greatly from sharing information with their foreign peers. If economic interdependence leads to transgovernmentalism, then we should expect a rise in international inter-agency cooperation with the globalization of domestic markets.

Indeed, as Slaughter wrote in 2004, "The existence of networks of national officials is not itself new... What is new is the scale, scope, and type of transgovernmental ties" (Slaughter, 2004: 10). Globalization, Slaughter argues, goes hand in hand with transgovernmentalism. "Government networks... are driven by many of the multiple factors that drive the hydra-headed phenomenon of globalization itself, leading to the simple need for national officials of all kinds to communicate and negotiate across borders to do business they could once accomplish solely at home" (Slaughter, 2004: 11). Put differently, transgovernmental networks are primarily information and policy-coordinating structures. Bureaucrats are motivated to collaborate because they need access to policy information, held by their foreign peers, to better develop policy at home.

In his seminal examination of why domestic experts collaborate across borders and forge transnational epistemic communities, Peter M. Haas advances a similar logic: "... as demands for such information arise, networks or communities of specialists capable of producing and providing the information emerge and proliferate" (Haas, 1992b: 4). While theoretically enriching, these works fail to offer empirical evidence of the precise effect of globalization on international inter-agency cooperation.

[16] While Keohane and Nye (1974) were precursors in discussing domestic administrators' *agency* under conditions of bureaucratic autonomy, it is Carpenter who clarifies the distinction between bureaucratic autonomy and discretion many years later. In his words: "Discretion is part of a contractual arrangement between politicians and an agency they establish; a statute may give an agency discretion or leeway to interpret or enforce a law within certain bounds. Bureaucratic autonomy, by contrast, is external to a contract and cannot be captured in a principal-agent relationship" (Carpenter, 2001: 17). The international behavior of bureaucrats at the center of this book undoubtedly falls into the latter category.

Recently, Thurner and Binder sought to remedy this by empirically testing the "interdependence hypothesis" in their study of European transgovernmental networks (Thurner & Binder, 2009). Indeed, the authors find evidence that increased economic connectedness between two states increases the probability of bureaucrats from those countries engaging in transgovernmental ties (Thurner & Binder, 2009). This finding helps shed light on transgovernmental networks, although it is more useful in revealing the conditions under which inter-bureaucracy cooperation is likely to emerge, rather than identifying the precise causal mechanisms driving the phenomenon (Jordana, Levi-Faur, & i Marín, 2011). I formulate the hypothesis to test this alternative explanation below.

Hypothesis Globalization: Expert bureaucrats from states better integrated to the international economy will be more likely to participate in inter-agency cooperation than bureaucrats from less integrated states.

Critically, I empirically control for the role of international actors (and the resources they can bring to bear) in transgovernmental cooperation. Many studies examine the effect of international organizations (IOs) in promoting cooperation among national bureaucrats (Bauer, 2006; Biermann & Siebenhüner, 2009; Hicks, Parks, Roberts, & Tierney, 2008; Slaughter, 2002). To test for this, I empirically control for the possible effects of multilateral grants and loans. An extensive literature examines the conditions under which administrators from the developing world work in partnership with aid agencies and development banks (Chwieroth, 2007, 2010; Kahler, 1992; Vreeland, 2003). As I will show in the following chapters, undeniably, IOs like the International Atomic Energy Agency (IAEA) and the Global Environment Facility (GEF) have the power to influence participation in transnational projects through the institutional and financial assistance they provide, even if minimal. Moreover, GEF was created with the mandate to act as a financial mechanism for five international treaties, including the United Nations Framework Convention on Climate Change and the Convention on Biological Diversity, in order to assist with country implementation.

To test for the international effects of economic resources, such as multilateral aid or loans, and to account for the finding of "a positive relationship between skill upgrading and imported materials, foreign technical assistance, and patent use" (Pavnick, 2000: 7), I formulate the following hypotheses.[17]

[17] This can even involve international pressure to modernize and professionalize the bureaucracy (Schrank, 2009).

Hypothesis Alternative International Source of Skills: The more a country receives in technical grants from IOs, the more likely its bureaucrats will collaborate with foreign peers.

Hypothesis Alternative International Source of Funding: The more a country receives multilateral financing, the more likely its bureaucrats will collaborate with foreign peers.

To test for the specific effect of GEF funding, I desegregate the funding of environmental projects by source – international donor versus national government – and see how this affects the probability of participating in green cross-national project. I expect higher levels of GEF funding to correlate with higher collaboration in environmental regional and global projects.[18] The central hypothesis regarding funding reads in this manner.

Hypotheses IO Financial Power: The more GEF funding available to a country, the more likely its state environmental agency will participate in green cross-national projects.

I also control for a few important domestic-side theories. Recent studies examining the determinants of transgovernmentalism find that key attributes of the domestic policy sector, such as the autonomy of its regulatory body and the relative weight of its industry in relation to the state, lead to cooperation (Andonova, 2014; Bach & Newman, 2014). To test for these alternatives I examine how the overall competence of the bureaucracy (as a proxy for an independent regulator) and the overall degree of environmental regulations (as a measure of state strength over industry) affect the probability of two or more agencies working together on a project. If Bach and Newman's theory holds in inter-agency cooperation in NEST and environmental protection, we should see a positive effect with the first covariate and a negative one with the second (Bach & Newman, 2014). The hypothesis on bureaucratic competence also functions as a central test of the effect of skills on international inter-agency cooperation.

Hypothesis Bureaucratic Competence: The more competent the national bureaucracy is, the more likely its experts will collaborate with foreign peers.

[18] Only the GEF makes available the data on its funding of projects. Thus, the hypothesis testing the financial influence of specialized IOs on international inter-agency cooperation can only be examined for cross-national environmental projects.

Hypothesis Regulations: The more regulations on business in a country, the less likely its environmental state experts will collaborate with foreign peer institutions.

Finally, I test a central derivation of the democratic peace theorem (i.e., democracies are less likely to fight against one another) that expects countries with democratic regimes to pursue inter-state cooperation more than authoritarian regimes. Drawing from numerous studies that posit that countries vary their international behavior contingent on regime type, I formulate the final hypothesis of the book, which will test the alternative explanation of a democratic effect on transgovernmental cooperation (Fredriksson & Gaston, 2000; Mansfield, Milner, & Rosendorff, 2000; Simmons & Hopkins, 2005; Goodliffe & Hawkins, 2006; Alcañiz, 2012).

Hypothesis Democracy: Expert bureaucrats from democratic states will be more active participants in international inter-agency cooperation than bureaucrats from autocracies.

Conclusion

How can we develop a theory that explains the *microfoundations* of international inter-agency cooperation? In this chapter I argued that we must begin by examining the technical demands that bureaucrats face in their jobs and how these demands affect their career incentives. My theory of the expert bureaucrat offers a precise mechanism to explain why state professionals collaborate across borders. Furthermore, my theory allows us to account for the evolution of international cooperation among bureaucrats from developing economies, which is noticeably absent from the literature on transgovernmentalism. What explains these networks of international cooperation, I argue, is the decision by the expert bureaucrat to take investment in skill upgrading in her own hands when the state withdraws. Networking with foreign peers is a key strategy to access needed resources. But not all bureaucrats face the same barriers to access. As I will show empirically in the following chapters, pre-existing levels of expertise determine the ability of a state agency to collaborate with peer institutions.

3

Skill Formation, Economic Crisis, and Expert Networks in the Nuclear Sectors of Argentina and Brazil

In the two previous chapters I have argued that there is a close relationship between skill formation, skill updating, and cooperation. If the need to upgrade existing expertise leads bureaucrats to collaborate across borders, then we must examine how expert bureaucrats acquire skills in the first place. In other words, how do governments create state agencies and recruit expert bureaucrats to run them? This chapter examines the evolution of skill acquisition in two state agencies, the Argentine National Commission for Atomic Energy (CNEA) and the Brazilian National Commission for Nuclear Energy (CNEN). These two cases help illustrate the causal mechanism behind the theory of the expert bureaucrat. From the beginning of the nuclear era in the 1950s and for almost thirty years thereafter, the Argentine and Brazilian governments made sustained and significant domestic investments in nuclear capacity and expertise. However, after a catastrophic economic crisis and democratization compromised the strategic role of the sector in the early 1980s, state support vanished and resources for skill updating faltered.

This chapter will use the examples of the CNEA and the CNEN to show how expert bureaucrats (1) acquire skills within the state, (2) develop vested interests in keeping those skills current, and (3) adapt – when the state withdraws support and government funding fluctuates – through inter-agency and peer-to-peer cooperation. Different from *regular* public servants, who have few incentives to invest in their skills (consider the job patterns of postal employees or administrative personnel that occupy the lower echelons of the bureaucracy), expert bureaucrats seek to acquire skills by following a "learning by doing" model.

Drawing on extended in-depth interviews with key Argentine and Brazilian nuclear bureaucrats and extensive archival work in South America and the International Atomic Energy Agency, this chapter describes how state experts took skill investment in their own hands, partnered with nuclear experts abroad, and facilitated joint training and shared know-how. Finally, this chapter also illustrates the partner-selection mechanisms behind the observed homophily effect in skill-driven, inter-agency cooperation. That is, it explains how expert bureaucrats seek to connect with peers that have similar or higher levels of skills.

State Investment in Skill and Capacity: The Argentine Nuclear Sector (1950–1983)

The first investment in nuclear energy, science, and technology (NEST) in Argentina was as grandiloquent as it was a failure. The President of the country, Juan Domingo Perón, appointed Austrian physicist Ronald Richter (1909–1991) to create an ambitious national program in nuclear energy. Richter vowed to achieve nuclear fusion, an experimental technology to this day, in just two years (1950–1952) (Alcañiz, 2005b). With President Peron's approval, the Austrian scientist oversaw the creation of a research facility on the island of Huemul, located off the Southern Andean city of Bariloche.

Shortly after the creation of the Huemul facility, President Perón publicly announced that the country was on its way to becoming a nuclear power. The new nuclear program of Argentina was so questionable that a report to the U.S. government drafted by the CIA stated that "the possibility of a hoax cannot be discarded" while noting that the announcement was "obviously timed to have the maximum political effect at the opening of the Conference of Western Hemisphere Foreign Ministers."[1] Ultimately, the announcement that Argentina would become a nuclear state in record time using unproven fusion technology was revealed as a hoax, becoming a source of embarrassment for the Argentine president.

After the Richter fiasco, the Perón Administration decided to re-launch the sector under more stringent professional rules. A key objective was to develop state expertise, even though in its initial stage the Argentine nuclear sector was heavily dependent on foreign technology and supplies. As a result, the Bariloche Institute of Physics (later renamed *Instituto*

[1] CIA/SI 109–51 "Argentine Atomic Energy Activities" March 27, 1951.

Balseiro in honor of its first director)[2] was created in 1955 as an institution of higher education offering graduate and post-graduate degrees in nuclear physics and engineering (Alcañiz, 2005b). While *El Balseiro* was a public institution chartered by the National Commission of Atomic Energy (CNEA) and a local state university, it was modeled after the American residential college system, where students live on campus and closely interact with its faculty. Throughout its sixty-year history, the reputation of the Balseiro Institute as a prime generator of nuclear knowledge and skills attracted generations of students from across the country and Latin America. Its location, in the remote Andean province of Rio Negro, was intended to separate this critical source of NEST expertise from the nation's capital and prepare graduates for a career in the nuclear state sector unencumbered by partisan politics.

Since its creation, the National Commission of Atomic Energy (CNEA) became the main recruiter of Balseiro graduates. The agency, created by President Perón in 1950, centralized all research and applied activities in NEST for most of its history. The expert bureaucrats of CNEA adopted a learning-by-doing approach to skill acquisition, which entailed working on large technical projects not unlike the international projects that will be analyzed in later chapters of this book. They also pursued an import substituting strategy to replace progressively foreign know-how with local capabilities. This approach to skill formation was greatly facilitated by the insulation of the CNEA (and the Balseiro Institute) from the political chaos characteristic of Argentine politics in the second half of the twentieth century. Indeed, while the country experienced decades of political turmoil, CNEA remained remarkably stable and insulated.[3] It is telling, for example, that during the seventeen-year tenure (1955–1973) of Admiral Oscar A. Quihillalt, one of only four presidents of the commission prior to 1983, Argentina suffered two coup d'état and had more than six different governments (Adler, 1987). A senior CNEA expert put it this way: "There were no politics in the

[2] José Antonio Balseiro was in a way the first expert bureaucrat of the sector. A local physicist trained in Argentina and England, he was commissioned by President Perón to lead the investigation into Richter's experiments in nuclear fusion. Eventually, he penned a scathing report on the lack of scientific merit of the Huemul Project, as it was known, as well as on the importance of formulating a long-term investment strategy in order to develop nuclear skills in the state (Alcañiz, 2005b).

[3] After the Richter scandal, the newly created CNEA became an exception to the "impossible game" of politics in Argentina, given that it was the only state agency without mandatory affiliation to the Peronist party in the 1950s (O'Donnell, 1978).

Commission. The politics of the country were never replicated within the Commission."[4]

For their first major project, CNEA experts worked on the construction of a small nuclear research reactor, to be used as a training device for local scientists (Adler, 1987). To build the research reactor, Argentina bought the blueprints of the Argonaut (the Argonne Nuclear Assembly for University Training), an American-designed experimental reactor of 100 KW power.[5] While the design was imported from abroad, CNEA engineers built the reactor and produced the nuclear fuel by themselves (Madero & Takacs, 1991; Solingen, 1996; Ornstein & Carasales, 1998). The 1958 Argonaut project was a significant technical coup, as most developing countries typically would have purchased a turnkey reactor, which would have allowed them to bypass the inefficiencies and costs associated with any infant industry. But the expert bureaucrats of CNEA were committed to acquiring skills, more so than they were "after efficiency; instead, they wanted to learn how to build a reactor by themselves."[6] To further the know-how import substitution strategy at the time, CNEA created a special Service of Technical Assistance for Industry (SATI) to assist in the Argonaut project and future endeavors that would increase the share of domestic industrial expertise (Madero & Takacs, 1991).

Argentina inaugurated its first research reactor (the RA-1) in 1958 and that same year exported fuel elements for Argonaut-type reactors to the German company Degussa Leybold (Coll & Radicella, 1998). CNEA continued manufacturing experimental reactors both for teaching and training Argentine scientists and to export to Peru and Algeria (Coll & Radicella, 1998). Next, nuclear experts in the commission tackled a bigger and more ambitious project, the construction of a nuclear power plant. The first step in the process was to conduct a feasibility study

[4] Dr. Jorge A. Coll, former board member of CNEA. Interview with the author in Buenos Aires, Argentina, December 1998. The claim that CNEA was *apolitical* is one that is commonly offered to explain the stability and success of the NEST enterprise in Argentina. I take it to mean that CNEA was removed from the upheaval of *party* politics (as there were few openly Peronist scientists in its midst), but not from political influence, given that under Navy rule the commission reflected intra-military distributive conflicts and deep anti-Peronist attitudes.

[5] For information on the Argonaut, see www.ne.anl.gov/About/reactors/training.shtml. Only after the 1953 Atoms for Peace initiative by the Eisenhower Administration, which called for greater cooperation toward developing countries in the civilian uses of nuclear energy, did the United States began exporting technology (like the Argonaut reactor) to countries that were just beginning to invest in NEST expertise.

[6] See Adler (1987: 296).

to determine site and grid connection. This kind of in-depth assessment was typically contracted to foreign consultants from states with advanced nuclear programs, but CNEA decided to send its own specialists to the field. In 1966 CNEA presented its own report to the government with recommendations on generation capacity (300–500 MW), location (on the Paraná River, just north of the city of Buenos Aires), and service area (the city of Buenos Aires and its metropolitan region) (Madero & Takacs, 1991).

In 1968, the German company, Siemens A.G., won the contract to build Atucha I, a nuclear power plant of 313 MW using natural uranium, of which Argentina had vast reserves, and heavy water (Solingen, 1996). The choice of technology resulted from the bureaucrats' long-term strategy of substituting imported skills with domestic expertise. An alternative plant design would have used enriched uranium and light water, but CNEA had little expertise in enrichment technology and the United States, the largest producer, had significant restrictions on their export (Adler, 1987; Solingen, 1996). To increase domestic participation in construction, nuclear bureaucrats forged key partnerships with local engineering industries. In the end, domestic participation reached 40 percent of the total cost of the Atucha I plant (Madero & Takacs, 1991).

After the construction of Atucha I, Argentine experts embarked on building a second nuclear power plant in Embalse, province of Córdoba. This time, the terms and conditions of the international bid specified that the share of foreign contractors could not exceed 50 percent of the total cost of the project (Madero & Takacs, 1991). Atomic Energy Canadian Limited (AECL) won the bidding, in part because AECL included a generous Technology Transfer Agreement (TTA) in the contract (Madero & Takacs, 1991; Solingen, 1996). The TTA entailed handing over the blueprints of the CANDU (Canada Deuterium Uranium) reactor to CNEA experts, together with all future usage rights at no additional cost. Finally, AECL would invest in the long-term training of local nuclear bureaucrats in Argentina and Canada (Madero & Takacs, 1991).

The construction of Embalse began in 1974, the same year India tested its first nuclear device. As a major supplier of the Indian civilian nuclear program and concerned with unwillingly assisting in the proliferation of atomic weapons in the developing world, the Canadian government quickly reformed its export policy. As a result, the terms of the Argentine-Canadian agreement were revised and some components of the TTA were cut. For example, the supply of heavy water and the technology to produce it locally were canceled. The fallout with Canada left Argentine nuclear bureaucrats feeling that they were victims of a new "scientific colonialism" by the United States and its Western allies.[7]

The expert bureaucrats of CNEA were well aware of the security and political interests underlying the development of nuclear expertise and quickly learned that any investment in NEST skills entailed addressing them:

> Conscious of the limitations of their environment, the Argentine nuclear sector has developed in general a technology free of superficial sophistication and adapted to the possibilities of production and maintenance of the local industry, which is particularly adequate for the requirements and possibilities of many developing countries that lack the necessary logistics for the operative maintenance of highly sophisticated equipment.
>
> (Ornstein, 1998: 93)

Technology transfers from advanced nuclear states to the Global South further deteriorated in the second half of the 1970s. All North-South nuclear exchanges were now shaped by the growing fear that the 1968 Non Proliferation Treaty (NPT), designed to stop more countries from going nuclear, was not enough of a deterrent. Under the Carter Administration, the United States toughened its exports toward the developing world through the 1978 Non-Proliferation Act. All of this affected Argentina, a non-signatory to the NPT. The construction of Embalse was renegotiated with Canada, who would no longer transfer sensitive technology to non-NPT members and even the contract to supply nuclear fuel for Atucha I was revised by Siemens A.G. as a result of demands by the German government (Adler, 1987; Madero & Takacs, 1991).

The expert bureaucrats of CNEA found a committed ally in the military junta that seized power in 1976. By taking on enormous amounts of foreign debt, the de facto government financed the expansion of nuclear skill and capacity. The sector created new programs and forged multiple partnerships with state agents and private industry. For example, the company INVAP (Applied Investigations) was created that same year as a hybrid joint venture between the government of the Rio Negro province and CNEA (Solingen, 1996). INVAP makes reactors and other nuclear instrumentation, and its aerospace division manufactures satellites for

7 Ambassador Julio C. Carasales. Interview with the author in Buenos Aires, Argentina, September 1999.

scientific use (Ornstein & Carasales, 1998).[8] Another key company created under the military regime in 1981 was CONUAR Inc. (Argentine Nuclear Fuel Incorporated Company). CNEA had a third of its share, and provided the necessary technology for fuel production. CONUAR produces nuclear fuel for power plants and research reactors in the country (Madero & Takacs, 1991).

The creation of domestic companies covering key areas of nuclear development aimed at deepening local expertise and reducing dependence on imported technology and knowledge. The president of CNEA at the time, Vice-Admiral Castro Madero, expressed it this way: "We have greatly experienced what it means to depend on other countries for energy sources and it is for this reason that Argentina has defined a (nuclear) policy inclined to be as self-sufficient as possible as a way of guaranteeing the exercise of its sovereign rights."[9]

The Argentine Nuclear Plan of 1979 reflected the goals of expertise and autonomy for the sector. This extremely ambitious scheme had the local company Nucleoeléctrica Argentina SA partner up with the German Kraftwerk Union (KWU Siemens) to build four more nuclear power plants (Solingen, 1996). Of the projected four, the Argentine-German consortium only managed to break grounds on one (Atucha II). This nuclear-electric plant of 700 MGW, initiated in 1980 and set to be inaugurated seven years later, was greatly delayed by the economic crisis and ensuing spending cuts (it finally became operational in 2014). Contract negotiations were arduous and revealed the very difficult international conditions under which Argentina attempted to sign a nuclear TTA. At first, CNEA conceived of a three-party agreement with its former partners, AECL of Canada and KWU of Germany. The Canadians would have responsibilities in nuclear engineering; the Germans, in conventional engineering; and the Argentines would be the industrial architects of the power plants. CNEA experts were particularly interested in the participation of AECL, as the Canadian company held the patent to the CANDU reactor, which employed low-grade enriched uranium (German reactors used enriched uranium technology). In addition, Canada was the sole exporter in the

[8] In 2011 an INVAP-designed and -manufactured satellite for scientific applications (SAC-D) was launched into orbit by the U.S. National Aeronautics and Space Administration (NASA) and the Argentine National Space Activities Commission (CONAE). See www.invap.com.ar/en/aerospace-and-government/products-and-services-aerospacial/satellites.html.

[9] *Clarín* Newspaper, Buenos Aires March 19, 1980.

world of heavy water technology and Argentina wanted to build its own plant. An agreement with Canada would have given CNEA professionals access to critical expertise.[10]

AECL lost their bid, in part because of the tense relationship between the military dictatorship of Argentina and the Canadian government. The contract for Atucha II ended up going to the Germans and Sulzer Brothers of Switzerland won the bid for the heavy water plant (Solingen, 1996). Although CNEA experts preferred the technology option offered by the Canadians, the refusal of Ottawa to approve a nuclear cooperation agreement with Argentina, a non-signatory to the NPT, was insurmountable.

Experts at CNEA aspired to control the whole cycle of nuclear fuel: uranium mining, fuel fabrication, uranium enrichment, fuel reprocessing, and waste disposal (Adler, 1987; Madero & Takacs, 1991; Solingen, 1996). By the late 1970s, under the protection of the military government, a group of CNEA experts tackled the development of uranium enrichment technology. In the past, Argentina bought small quantities of enriched uranium to use in its research reactors from the United States (Solingen, 1996). But once the 1978 Non-Proliferation Act was implemented, U.S. exports of sensitive technology (like enriched uranium) became contingent on whether the importing country had signed the NPT and had all nuclear activities under the comprehensive safeguards sanctioned by the International Atomic Energy Agency (IAEA), something Argentina was not willing to do. While enriched uranium has many nonmilitary uses in NEST, it is also a critical component in making a nuclear weapon; thus, it is considered a dual-use technology and is difficult to buy in the international market.

With the blessing of the military president of CNEA, a small group of experts built a secret uranium enrichment plant by the Southern Andes Mountains in Pilcaniyeu, Province of Rio Negro. The project was kept hidden from the public and most of their CNEA colleagues, who only heard of it once the project was finalized (Madero & Takacs, 1991). A senior nuclear bureaucrat at the time (who would become the first female head of the CNEA just a few years later), remembers her reaction to the news:

> The enrichment thing was a surprise to everyone, even us. I have to confess that at first the physicists were a bit doubtful, because we were not used to secrets. It had been a decision of the Admiral Castro Madero and Conrado Varotto,

[10] The whole negotiation process is best explained by its protagonists in Madero & Takacs (1991: 181–202).

today director of the National Space Activities Commission (CONAE), who loved secrets. With the excuse that if the Americans found out – and this is true – they would shut it down without doubt. As they had tried repeatedly in the past under Castro Madero, I saw it myself: some US representative or senator would come visit to ask directly to close some program. So the old guard of CNEA, we were not happy at all and we demanded an explanation.[11]

The plant was ready to be inaugurated in 1983, the same year Argentina had its first democratic election in seven years. The announcement of the secret Pilcaniyeu plant in December of that year, a delicate operation of nuclear diplomacy, fell to President-Elect Raúl Ricardo Alfonsín (1983–1989) (Adler, 1987). Argentine diplomats were sent to the United States and to the headquarters of IAEA in Vienna, Austria, to reveal – just a few hours before the official press conference in Buenos Aires – what had been achieved in Pilcaniyeu (Madero & Takacs, 1991). Simultaneously, a note from Raúl Alfonsín was delivered in Buenos Aires to the ambassadors of the five veto-wielding countries in the United Nations Security Council (United States, United Kingdom, France, the Soviet Union, and China) with assurances of peaceful objectives regarding the enrichment plant. After the official announcement, CNEA hosted a meeting with all the Latin American ambassadors, and upon his arrival to the country, the general director of IAEA was invited to tour the plant (Madero & Takacs, 1991).

International reaction was more favorable than initially expected; the democratic transition and President Alfonsín's immediate efforts to improve relations with the international nuclear community lessened the political impact of the announcement. As nuclear energy (and other NEST activities) in the country did not require enriched uranium, the mastering of this technology was the ultimate investment by the CNEA in skills.

State Investment in Skill and Capacity: The Brazilian Nuclear Sector (1950–1985)

The initial investment of Brazil in nuclear expertise and capacity differed from that of its neighbor. While Argentina kept all nuclear activities

[11] President of CNEA (1987–1989), Doctor Emma Perez Ferreira. Interview with the author in Buenos Aires, Argentina, March 2001. Dr. Perez Ferreira was not the only senior bureaucrat taken aback by the announcement. Jorge Consentino, the first CNEA president of the democratic era, said that he "found out on the radio of a taxi that Admiral Castro Madero announced that Argentina had developed the complete uranium cycle. They worked on it for five years and nobody knew." *Clarín* Newspaper, Buenos Aires, August 28, 1986.

under the tight control of CNEA, the Brazilian National Commission of Nuclear Energy (CNEN) was established in 1956 to coordinate a number of research institutes that operated autonomously. While for most of its earlier history CNEA was an independent state agency under the jurisdiction of the presidency, CNEN in the 1960s lost its autonomous status and went from being directly under the office of the presidency to becoming part of the Ministry of Mines and Energy (Solingen, 1996; de Andrade & dos Santos, 2013). Furthermore, the all-powerful National Security Council not only dictated policy to CNEN, it often overrode the commission's resolutions, as "the nuclear sector was subject to the whims of the National Security Council (CSN), the Joint Chiefs of Staff (EMFA), and the Ministry of Foreign Relations (MRE)" (de Andrade & dos Santos, 2013: 115). But despite the many differences, Brazilian nuclear experts shared with their Argentine colleagues a similar ambition to invest in technical expertise and institutional capacity.

The Brazilian state in the post-war era was populated by expert bureaucrats committed to developmental goals, which typically involved a substantial investment in technical skills.[12] But nuclear experts in the country had a hard time upholding these principles because of ongoing conflict between nationalists and non-nationalists, as well as restrictions on imports (Adler, 1987; Solingen, 1996; de Andrade & dos Santos, 2013). Nationalists believed that only the state should have a monopoly on nuclear technology if the sector was to grow unfettered from foreign interference (Adler, 1987). The military potential of nuclear development made these beliefs even more entrenched in the sector and although "even the nationalist faction in the nuclear sector clearly favored a developmental policy,"[13] ideological divisions and security stakeholders with veto powers (like the CSN or the EMFA) made impossible a coherent articulation of developmental goals in the sector (Solingen, 1996).

The sector was organized in a number of institutes, each specializing in different aspects of the nuclear cycle, although there was much overlap in

[12] Schneider (1999) defines developmentalism in Brazil through four essential characteristics: a capitalist class dependent on decisions made by the state; a discourse centered on state-led industrialization; exclusion of the majority of the population when adopting and implementing developmental goals; and a vast appointed bureaucracy. For works linking developmentalism and bureaucratic expertise in Brazil, see Sikkink (1991) and Evans (1995).

[13] Senior expert of the Brazilian-Argentine Agency for Accounting and Control of Nuclear Materials (ABACC), Captain Orpet Peixoto. Interview with the author in Rio de Janeiro, Brazil, April 2000.

research. At the forefront was the prominent National Council Research (CNPq),[14] created in 1951 "with the objective of professionalizing careers in science and technology" (de Andrade & dos Santos, 2013: 114). In the post-war era, governments across the globe were founding state agencies to advance science and technological innovation. Even though the mission of the CNPq was to advance knowledge in all scientific fields, nuclear science was particularly dear to council members and clearly had primacy over other disciplines (Solingen, 1996). By law, the council became the guarantor of the state monopoly on nuclear power, in charge of executing the will of the president (and the EMFA) regarding nuclear mining, exports, and science.[15]

The Institute for Atomic Energy (IEA), later renamed Nuclear and Energy Research Institute (IPEN), was another key institution created in the same period by CNEN experts and faculty at the University of São Paulo, where it is located. IEA housed the first Brazilian research reactor designed by the American firm Babcock and Wilcox in 1957 (Solingen, 1996). To this day, IPEN professionals advance research in reactor science and technology, as well as in the complete cycle of nuclear energy, including uranium enrichment and spent fuel (Kassenova, 2014). Another institution of the early nuclear era was the Institute of Radioactive Research in Belo Horizonte. This organization held the second Brazilian research reactor, built in 1960, with another American company, General Dynamics. (Solingen, 1996). All of these state institutions retained significant autonomy to invest in NEST, yet the division of labor and coordination of research activity was led by the expert bureaucrats of CNEN (de Andrade & dos Santos, 2013).

While Brazil effectively established this disaggregated nuclear bureaucracy in the 1950s, the country first began to stake a claim in the field a decade earlier. Given its rich endowment in minerals and a close relationship with the United States fostered during the war, Brazil became an early supplier to the American nuclear program. But Brazilian exports of strategic elements and minerals, like thorium and uranium, raised concerns of future shortages among state professionals who wanted to build an independent *national* program, since the total size of these mineral deposits was unknown at the time (de Andrade & dos Santos, 2013).

[14] The CNPq is known now as the National Council for Scientific and Technological Development.

[15] Law of Brazil N 1.310, January 15, 1951. Accessed at http://centrodememoria.cnpq.br/legis1951.html.

Another source of friction between nationalist and non-nationalist local experts was the lack of reciprocity between Brazil and the United States. Although exports of strategic minerals were flowing from Brazil to the North, the United States – owing to significant restrictions on nuclear cooperation only lifted in 1954[16] – was unable to act as an equal partner for a nascent program in Brazil.

At the beginning of the atomic era, U.S. nuclear policy was highly restrictive. Ruled by the 1946 McMahon Act, it placed an embargo on any technology transfer outside of the United States in an attempt to hinder nuclear proliferation.[17] But over the next few years, the Soviet Union, the United Kingdom, France, and China all had mastered the technology for atomic weapons. Canada (West) Germany, and Japan also became leaders in the development of nuclear energy, but did not pursue a weapons program. In the 1950s, the United States moved away from secrecy toward international cooperation. In 1953 U.S. President Dwight Eisenhower presented before the General Assembly of the United Nations the Atoms for Peace Program, recognizing that "the dread secret, and the fearful engines of atomic might, are not ours alone," he proposed the creation of an international atomic energy agency.[18] The IAEA was to serve as a distributing center for information, knowledge, and research pertaining to nonmilitary fissionable material while functioning as an "acceptable system of world-wide inspection and control."[19] The mission of such international organism was to provide technical cooperation to states embarking on the peaceful exploration and development of nuclear energy. In the years that followed, nuclear agencies multiplied around the world.

Admiral Alvaro Alberto was a leading voice of the nationalist faction and a critical figure in the debate to shape the direction of nuclear development in the country. As a renaissance man of science and first president of the CNPq, the navy officer and engineer was single-handedly responsible for the creation of multiple state agencies: the National Institute for Pure and Applied Mathematics (IMPA), the National Institute of Amazonian Research (INPA), and the Brazilian Institute of Information in

16 See the Atomic Energy Act of 1954 at www.nrc.gov/docs/ML1327/ML13274A489.pdf#page=23.

17 See www.osti.gov/atomicenergyact.pdf.

18 "Atoms for Peace" address given by U.S. President Dwight D. Eisenhower before the General Assembly of the United Nations on Peaceful Uses of Atomic Energy, New York City, December 8, 1953.

19 Ibid.

Science and Technology (IBICT).[20] To achieve his goal of forging "state staff in science, technology, and industry" he remained pragmatic.[21] On the one hand, Alvaro Alberto tried getting support from the United States in setting up a Brazilian nuclear program. For example, he accompanied a contingent of expert bureaucrats from the CNPq to study and train at the Oak Ridge National Laboratory in Tennessee in order to establish a "postgraduate education in nuclear physics at Brazilian Universities."[22] At the same time, the admiral led the charge against non-reciprocal trade with the United States. Voicing the objections of the nationalist faction of scientists and military to the transfer of radioactive material without "specific compensation" Alvaro Alberto proposed a tit-for-tat rule whereby importers of Brazilian strategic minerals had to reciprocate with transfers of nuclear technology and know-how to Brazil (Adler, 1987).

In response to the admiral's proposal, a major piece of nuclear legislation was passed in 1951. This law (1310), which officially created the CNPq, also called for a study to be carried out to learn the extent of mineral reserves; it placed the management of these minerals under state monopoly, and it conditioned their export on direct presidential approval.[23] A few years later, the National Security Council clarified the conditions under which it would allow sales of strategic minerals abroad: "Only after obtaining credible data about the existence, in our country, of substantial deposits of minerals usable in the field of nuclear energy and once convenient stockpiling of treated materials is assured, for our program in this sector, the Government may trade abroad certain quantities of these materials, with the highest degree of treatment available in our industry and exclusively for obtaining specific compensation, instrumental and technical, with a view to the development of the industrial applications of nuclear energy in the country."[24] Council members recommended President Juscelino Kubitschek (1956–1961) cancel some of its mineral sales to the United States, and effectively stopped a shipment of 300 tons of Brazilian thorium oxide which was already *en route* (de Andrade & dos Santos, 2013). The American Ambassador to Brazil

[20] See http://centrodememoria.cnpq.br/alvalb.pdf.

[21] See http://centrodememoria.cnpq.br/alvalb.pdf.

[22] World Wide Chemistry, *International News*, Vol. 30 (8): 810, February 25, 1952.

[23] Law 1310, sanctioned January 15, 1951. See www.cnpq.br/web/guest/lei-1310.

[24] Minutes of the Twentieth Session of the Brazilian National Security Council, Second Brazilian Nuclear Plan, August 30, 1956, History and Public Policy Program Digital Archive National Archive (Brasilia). Obtained and translated by Fundação Getúlio Vargas. http://digitalarchive.wilsoncenter.org/document/116913.

reported back home with alarm that this recommendation was "unquestionably nationalistic in tone" and interpreted it as evidence of plans to develop "Atombras" (similar to the state-owned monopoly, Petrobras).[25]

In effect, the creation of CNEN in 1956 by the CSN can be seen as a step closer to the Petrobras model through increased nationalization and centralization. CNEN was to become coordinator in chief of the sector, in addition to promoting technical, commercial, and professional activities across the field and advising the Ministry of Mining and Energy in the formulation of nuclear policy (Solingen, 1996). Yet, CNEN did not bring about the expected Atombras-centered sector. In contrast to its Argentine counterpart, its "bureaucratic autonomy withered" and the leading state agency in Brazil "played a marginal role in designing the nuclear sector and in negotiating" with key foreign contractors (Solingen, 1996: 34).

CNEN was established amidst an improved international environment resulting from the Atoms for Peace program and the creation of the International Atomic Energy Agency (IAEA). This new climate opened up cooperation from advanced countries to incipient programs. Still, significant restrictions on international technology transfers remained in place, and shaped decisions, strategies, and choice of technology in Brazil. From the late 1950s and well into the mid-1960s, Brazilian nuclear physicists debated what selection of technology would best fit the energy needs of the country and would also be viable given the instability of some international supplies. Summarizing all of this, the CSN stated: "In the international field, the Brazilian program for the production of nuclear energy must take advantage of the scientific and technological experience of all friendly countries, guided only by the criterion of convenience."[26]

The pragmatic principle was not always upheld. A few years after the 1964 military coup, the de facto government of Brazil (which would remain in power until the mid-1980s), moved toward developing nuclear energy. In 1968, under President Costa da Silva, the construction of the country's first nuclear power plant began. It was sited near the city of Rio de Janeiro, with the purpose of serving the densely populated southeast of Brazil. CNEN experts coordinated the international bid for a turnkey plant and awarded the contract to the American company Westinghouse

[25] Ambassador Ellis O. Briggs, in telegram 242 from Rio de Janeiro, Brazil August 31, 1956. See http://history.state.gov/historicaldocuments/frus1955-57v07/d340.

[26] Minutes of the Twentieth Session of the Brazilian National Security Council, Second Brazilian Nuclear Plan. August 30, 1956, History and Public Policy Program Digital Archive National Archive (Brasilia). Obtained and translated by Fundação Getúlio Vargas. http://digitalarchive.wilsoncenter.org/document/116913.

(Solingen, 1996).[27] The share of domestic actors was small: CNEN professionals had licensing responsibilities and Furnas, a subsidiary of the state-owned electric utility company (Electrobras), was in charge of site preparation and some basic public works construction.[28] The plant would generate 600 MW using enriched uranium and light water (Solingen, 1996). Choosing the enrichment option meant that any know-how transferred from the United States to Brazil would be marginal at best given that the former banned the sale of sensitive or dual-use technologies (Adler, 1987). Despite the active participation of the electrical utilities companies, like Electrobras y Furnas, the CNEN leadership was blamed for going with the least beneficial proposal. As the state agency responsible for picking the winning bid, the commission was perceived as caving to pressure from the military government to go with the United States.

Given the increasingly restrictive policy of the United States on the transfer of sensitive technology, the Angra project proved to be a difficult undertaking. In 1973, a year into its construction, the United States Atomic Energy Commission (AEC) revised the contracts for enriched uranium and conditioned the supply of fuel on the international energy market, which was extremely volatile in the aftermath of the recent oil shock (Kassenova, 2014).[29] When India detonated its first nuclear weapon a year later in 1974, U.S. restrictions on nuclear fuel and technology exports became even tighter.[30] This led Brazilians to seek out a new senior partner for their program. In a confidential report to President Ernesto Geisel, the Minister of Foreign Affairs, Azeredo Da Silveira, recommended: "On the question of uranium enrichment, considering the political-diplomatic difficulties associated with a bilateral agreement with the United States due to the fact that we are not signatories to the NPT and the legal restrictions of the US Atomic Energy Commission and the compensation that would be required from us in the field of oil, the most favorable path could be that of contacts with Europe."[31]

27 Also, see the CNEN Report on Safety at www.cnen.gov.br/seguranca/documentos/6NationalReportOfBrazilRev5Final.pdf.

28 See the CNEN Report on Safety at www.cnen.gov.br/seguranca/documentos/6NationalReportOfBrazilRev5Final.pdf.

29 See http://ri.fgv.br/en/node/2037.

30 See http://ri.fgv.br/en/node/2037.

31 "Memorandum, Foreign Minister Azeredo da Silveira, Information for the President of Brazil, 'Uranium Enrichment'" April 02, 1974, History and Public Policy Program Digital Archive, CPDOC Archives, PNB ad 1973.10.05 pp. 100–108. Obtained and translated by Fundação Getúlio Vargas. http://digitalarchive.wilsoncenter.org/document/116875.

Thus, Brazilian nuclear bureaucrats turned to Europe and in 1975 signed a comprehensive nuclear cooperation treaty with the government of West Germany. The agreement served as a framework within which the German KWU (Siemens) and the nuclear sector in Brazil contracted for a significant technology transfer, including uranium enrichment processing, and the construction of eight nuclear power plants over a fifteen-year period (Solingen, 1996). Nuclebras (Brazilian Nuclear Enterprises), the primary government-owned corporation in the sector, took the lead in the joint venture with KWU. In contrast to the partnership with Westinghouse, this time around Brazilian expert bureaucrats planned to take on a sizeable role in the process. To execute the different tasks of the megaproject, several local companies were created, including Nuclen, specializing in reactor engineering, and Nuclep, in charge of manufacturing of heavy components for nuclear reactors (Solingen, 1996).[32] Through its new partnership with Germany, Brazil expected to develop significant human capital in the sector and transfer technology involving the complete nuclear fuel cycle (from uranium conversion to fuel reprocessing).

Critics took aim at the size of the project, finding the number of power plants and their price tag – the initial cost was around 10 billion dollars in 1975 – exorbitant (Wrobel & Redick, 1998; Kassenova, 2014).[33] Another point of contention was the decision to stick to the enriched uranium alternative, as it deepened Brazilian dependency on foreign suppliers, now Germany, in order to power the Angra plants. Furthermore, the German transfer of enrichment technology (contemplated in the agreement) raised the most objections as Brazil ended up receiving the unreliable and ultimately unworkable "jet-nozzle" process (Adler, 1987; Kassenova, 2014). Meanwhile, the U.S. government viewed with great concern the fulfillment of a treaty that contemplated the transfer of enrichment technology to an NPT non-signatory like Brazil. The Carter Administration interpreted the Brazilian interest in enrichment technology as possible evidence of a potential arms race against Argentina (Wrobel & Redick, 1998; Kassenova, 2014). As a result, Vice President Walter Mondale was dispatched to West Germany in 1977 to put pressure on the government in Bonn to revise the TTA enclosed in the mega-deal (Kassenova,

32 CNEN internal undated document.

33 In effect, because of the massive investment needed and a decade-long economic crisis beginning in 1980, of the eight planned power plants, only two were built. Angra II (1275 MW) finally became critical in 2001. Angra III, also with a capacity of 1275 MV, remains under construction and is expected to be finished by 2017 (2013 Sixth National Report of Brazil for the Nuclear Safety Convention).

2014).[34] While U.S. pressure was unable to stop the deal from going forward, it did have two important consequences. First, it forced tougher safeguards into the treaty, which is seen as a decisive factor in the German decision to revoke the transfer of ultracentrifuge enrichment process.[35] Second, it had the unintended effect of uniting the feuding factions across the Brazilian nuclear sector. Brazilian experts were outraged and "nuclear nationalism, always present in Brazil, emerged as a powerful force in the defense of an act that was interpreted as representing simply and plainly the exercise of national sovereignty" (Carasales, 1997: 25).

Citing a toughening international environment that hindered CNEN bureaucrats' access to high skills, the sector created – with the blessing of President João Baptista de Oliveira Figueiredo (1979–1985) – the so-called "autonomous" or "parallel" nuclear program (Adler, 1987; Solingen, 1996; Kassenova, 2014). Whereas all activities under the Brazilian-German agreement were under full-scope IAEA safeguards, the navy-led parallel program remained unfettered from international oversight (Adler, 1987). The intent of the plan was to control the complete fuel cycle, but the real pet project of the "*autonomistas* was to develop a nuclear submarine."[36] A senior CNEN bureaucrat described the rationale of the parallel program as follows:

> Rather than technology transfer, the agreement with Germany was about building the facilities that were manufactured in Germany. It was not an actual transfer of technology. It was like building and operating instead of developing and building. And that was the point. Some people in Brazil understood that we had to have an autonomous program where foreign countries would not pressure directly as to whether we controlled certain technologies. Some institutes were left out of the agreement with Germany, like IPEN, which develops its own technology and several stages of the fuel cycle, like the production of Uranium hexafluoride. After that, other factions, like the navy with the nuclear submarine, thought that we could achieve a technological leap by developing enrichment by centrifuge.[37]

34 *Clarín* Newspaper, February 10, 1977.

35 In the end, Brazil attained the enrichment process more than a decade later and using the gaseous diffusion method instead. The German-Brazilian agreement is held as emblematic of how detrimental U.S. political interference (either direct or indirect) can be regarding technology and development in the periphery. Interviews with senior bureaucrats of CNEN and the Brazilian Ministry of External Relations (*Itamaraty*). Also, see Adler (1987) and Carasales (1997).

36 Senior expert of the Brazilian-Argentine Agency for Accounting and Control of Nuclear Materials (ABACC), Captain Orpet Peixoto. Interview with the author in Rio de Janeiro, Brazil, April 2000.

37 Former Director of International Relations of CNEN, Doctor Laercio Vinhas, interview with author in Rio de Janeiro, Brazil, July 2006.

The Foreign Debt Crisis, Democratization, and Declining Government Spending

As the previous sections show, the development of a nuclear bureaucracy and the acquisition of expertise followed different trajectories in Argentina and Brazil during the first thirty years of the atomic era. From the beginning, Argentina pursued a strategy of progressive substitution of foreign for local know-how, facilitated by sustained investment in the professionalization of its nuclear bureaucrats (Adler, 1987; Solingen, 1996; Ornstein, 1998). Brazil, on the other hand, was less coherent in its adoption of development strategies and relied more heavily on technology transfer agreements from its commercial partners from the industrial North to develop local expertise (Adler, 1987; Solingen, 1996). Nevertheless, by the early 1980s Brazil was quickly catching up to its neighbor thanks in part to the extraordinary technological boost it got from its partnership with Germany.

As a result, Argentina and Brazil entered the 1980s at similar levels of nuclear development. But the extreme political and economic transformation the two countries experienced during this decade, directly threatened the continuity of nuclear expertise in South America. Given the severity of the economic crisis – that led the 1980s to be known as "the lost decade of development" – and the wave of democratization that ensued, maintaining past levels of state investment in nuclear skills became impossible. By 1983, Argentina and Brazil were broke, facing default on their foreign debt, and undergoing deep political reforms after years of military rule. The agencies lost state support, budgets were slashed, and expert bureaucrats in the two countries were left to their own devices during the worst of the crisis (Alcañiz, 2005a; Kassenova, 2014).

The foreign debt crisis that began in August 1982 when Mexico declared moratorium on the service of its external debt, severely disrupted nuclear funding in Argentina and Brazil. The Mexican moratorium sent panic waves through creditors of the region. If Mexico, a country that had massive oil reserves defaulted on its loans, what could be expected of non-oil-producing countries like Argentina and Brazil? International lenders had hitherto seen the right-wing military dictatorships of Latin America as reliable borrowers of the surplus (petro)dollars flooding the system. Now, they saw insolvency. Interest rates went up, as lending money to developing governments became risky business. Creditors pressured borrowers to cancel their debt and investors fled the Region in droves. By the end of 1983, Latin America held half of the total foreign debt of the developing world (Frieden, 1991). The region became a net capital exporter, with more funds (in the form of debt payments) leaving rather than entering Latin America. In 1982 the total service of the debt for the region was equivalent to 66 percent of Latin American exports (Roett, 1983). In the early 1980s GNPs and per capita incomes fell sharply. Recession and inflation also afflicted the Latin American countries. By 1983 Brazil had suffered three years in a row of recession and Argentina had broken world records with its inflation rate: 400 percent (Roett, 1983; Frieden, 1991). Together with Mexico, Argentina and Brazil were the most indebted countries in the region.

The economic crisis deeply transformed the political and economic realities of Latin Americans. First, it ushered in a wave of democratization across the Region. One after the other, military regimes collapsed under the weight of dire economic conditions and new civilian governments took their place. In Argentina, President Alfonsín, a civil rights lawyer during the dictatorship, was committed to the democratization and demilitarization of the state. During his electoral campaign, he had promised to hold the military responsible for their abuses and bring them to justice. Indeed, his administration was one of the few in the Region to fully prosecute the top command of the military Junta. After twenty years of military rule, Brazilians elected their first civilian leader in 1985. The *Junta* had been in power since 1964 and starting in the 1970s had initiated a painstakingly measured process of political liberalization called the *Abertura* that involved local and regional elections (Haggard & Kaufman, 1995). In contrast to the democratic transition in Argentina, where the military left the government in disgrace because of its defeat in the Malvinas/Falklands War, the military in Brazil remained in control of regime change (Haggard & Kaufman, 1995). This despite the massive debt they accumulated while in power (around $90 billion USD by 1984), amassed in part by pursuing mammoth infrastructure projects like the Itaipú dam, which with its price tag of $20 billion USD in the 1970s became the most expensive dam ever built (Da Rosa, 1983).

Nevertheless, the recession, colossal foreign debt payments, and rising inflation prompted the military to finally hold national elections. New President José Sarney,[38] an old ally of the exiting regime, had to deal with

[38] Originally, Tancredo Neves ran for president with José Sarney as his vice president. Neves, an unabashed opponent of the military government, died suddenly after being elected. This left the more military-friendly Sarney as the first civilian president of the democratic era in charge of carrying out a delicate regime transition.

general social unrest under appalling economic conditions. In that sense, he had much in common with president Alfonsín. Furthermore, both governments were under pressure by multilateral financial institutions like the World Bank and the International Monetary Fund (IMF) to cut spending radically in order to continue receiving loans to solve both large state deficits and balance of payment deficits (Frieden, 1991; Haggard & Kaufman, 1995). The austerity programs that were implemented after democratization in Argentina and Brazil had dire effects on the nuclear development, and the budgets of CNEA and CNEN were dramatically cut (Solingen, 1996).

The 1980s inaugurated an era of major budget fluctuations in CNEA, CNEN, and other technical state agencies across the Argentine and Brazilian bureaucracies. The 1990s brought even deeper cuts, as the two countries adopted comprehensive market reforms. Carlos Saúl Menem (1989–1999) in Argentina and Fernando Collor de Mello (1990–1992), Itamar Franco (1992–1995), and Fernando Henrique Cardoso (1995–2002) in Brazil embraced neoliberal reforms. President Menem, who took office in the midst of a hyperinflationary process and with a virtually bankrupt Central Bank, privatized most government-owned corporations and thoroughly deregulated the Argentine economy (Weyland, 2002). Whereas his predecessor had reticently adopted heterodox policies to deal with deteriorating economic conditions, Carlos Menem embraced the orthodoxy of the plans endorsed by the IMF and the U.S. government.[39] In Brazil, the 1990s also brought increased spending cuts and market reforms, albeit not as severe as in Argentina. At the beginning of the decade, President Collor de Mello adopted comprehensive reform to deregulate the economy, which was continued by his successor, Itamar Franco, when the former was impeached for corruption and forced to resign in 1992. But it was President Cardoso who pushed forward an ambitious privatization agenda, managing to sell off companies even in the "most politically sensitive or hard sectors: electricity, telecommunications, mining, and petroleum" (Baker, 2009: 174; Murillo, 2009). Thus, recurring economic crises, the political priorities of the new democratic

[39] President Carlos Menem even tried to privatize the management of Atucha. The unsuccessful plan involved "creating an association among a capitalist partner, an enterprise from the nuclear/electricity sector (if possible, foreign), and a cooperative formed by the technical personnel from the nuclear power plants." Interview with a senior official of the Argentine Nuclear Regulatory Authority (ARN) in Buenos Aires, Argentina, February 2004. Also, see Alcañiz (2005a).

leadership, and harsh austerity measures made state funding for the sector very unreliable.[40]

Expert Bureaucrats, Networks, and Skill Updating

Fluctuating government funding is particularly damaging to research agencies, which rely on sustained investments in skills and technology in order to sustain day-to-day operations and advance knowledge. When the state fails to make these investments, expert bureaucrats anticipate the costs. In Argentina, where market reforms were particularly draconian, nuclear professionals experienced several years of lean budgets. The former head of CNEA described the effect of cuts and austerity on the program:

> There is no investment, we have even lost people. Do you know how costly it is to put together groups with capacity to realize technology, and not even cutting-edge nuclear technology, but at least hi-tech? Generations! Ten years at least, and they just disintegrate with a call to voluntary retirement. It's pathetic. The state in which the department of reactors of CNEA has been left in is pathetic.[41]

Hiring freezes tend to follow spending cuts. When they persist over time, state agencies cannot update their critical skills and as a result, bureaucratic expertise often becomes obsolete and institutional knowledge is lost. Hiring freezes in the information age are especially egregious as research organizations need to hold steady rates of investment in skills in order to remain abreast of technological change. One consequence of hiring freezes in technology-dependent sectors is that they can create an age gap within the workforce, which in turn hampers access to leading-edge technology. A senior official of CNEA discussed the difficulty of preserving existing knowledge in the face of this challenge:

> What happened here was that there was a large group of people who when they entered, *en masse*, were young and they stayed for 30, 40 years in the Commission. But a gap formed where the age curve of the Commission is bimodal and it's rather

[40] This problem is shared by most developing countries. As the former chairman of the Pakistani Atomic Energy Commission put it: "while there is an increasing emphasis on privatization and deregulation, the energy program in the third world is still very much under the public sector and the nuclear sector can thus get the long term commitments it requires subject of course to the availability of the resources with the public sector" (Ishfaq Ahmad 2004 at www.iaea.org).

[41] President of CNEA (1987–1989), Doctor Emma Perez Ferreira. Interview with the author in Buenos Aires, Argentina, March 2001.

funny, at one end, over 75, there is only one – that's me – and at the other end it is even more dramatic, 25, there is just one. The average age is 52, very poorly distributed. Consequently, if someone leaves and wants to pass along knowledge, he can't find anyone because no one was trained. That's why there is an effort to try to save the knowledge that holds the whole capital of the organization.[42]

Not only do expert bureaucrats anticipate spending cuts by their own governments, they may also become aware of cuts happening to peer agencies across the border. A senior manager of CNEN described his interest in events in Argentina using the analogy of a popular Brazilian ad campaign of the 1980s. The "*Efeito Orloff: Eu sou você amanhã*" was a TV commercial for Orloff vodka where a stranger urges a man at a bar to drink only the best brand of vodka in order to avoid a hangover the next morning. When the drinking man asks the stranger why he cares, the latter replies: "I am you, tomorrow." The CNEN expert likened the commercial to how Brazilians take notice of spending cuts and their effects in the neighboring country, especially as Argentina adopted austerity measures before others in the Region (Weyland, 2002).[43]

What do Argentine and Brazilian nuclear experts do when they expect spending cuts that will hinder projects and programs? They find alternative ways through which they can continue investing in skills.

What we do here to maintain the program in times of no money is to invest in personnel training. A master's degree, a doctorate. You spend a lot less. Technical research is much more expensive than thesis research, so we invest in human resources. Technical cooperation through IAEA, many of the projects in which CNEN participates, significantly contributes to the self-reliance and autonomy of the program. It's extremely important. Horizontal cooperation preserves active knowledge.[44]

Despite a history of regional rivalry, Argentine and Brazilian expert bureaucrats began to cooperate on projects and train together at the worst of the economic crisis in the mid-1980s (Carasales, 1997; Alcañiz, 2000; Kassenova, 2014). This was somewhat surprising because the relationship between the two countries had been tense, especially under military rule. A Brazilian military officer explained the difficult relation: "The problems between Argentina and Brazil transcended the nuclear area. There

[42] Former Director of International Relations of CNEA, Capitan Roberto Ornstein. Interview with the author in Buenos Aires, Argentina, July 2006.

[43] Former Director of International Relations of CNEN, Doctor Laercio Vinhas. Interview with the author in Rio de Janeiro, Brazil, June 2006.

[44] Former Director of International Relations of CNEN, Doctor Laercio Vinhas. Interview with the author in Rio de Janeiro, Brazil, June 2006.

were border disputes. Argentina was always Brazil's main threat in the Southern Cone."[45] Diplomatic ties were further strained in the nuclear field, where competition had been particularly stark. For example, when expert bureaucrats of CNEA announced their mastery of the uranium enrichment process in 1983, Brazilian scientists "felt very jealous."[46] Undoubtedly, Brazil's plans to develop a nuclear submarine under the military-led Parallel (unofficial) Nuclear Program, an open secret at the time, concerned Argentina. Competition between the professionals of CNEA and CNEN stemmed more from a competition in knowledge than military objectives. As a top diplomat of Brazil expressed it: "I am not sure there was an arms race going on (between Brazil and Argentina). There was, though, a competition for prestige."[47]

Nuclear experts in Argentina and Brazil easily moved past the difficult history of their governments and embarked on a path of cooperation that continues to this day. Bilateral cooperation entailed working together on complex projects, like plans for a joint fast-breeder reactor, cross-national training of nuclear power plant personnel, and coordinating nuclear foreign policy (Carasales, 1997; Alcañiz, 2000). Bureaucrats in CNEA and CNEN formalized the comprehensive partnership by drafting a series of protocols, which "were mainly initiatives from the two technical agencies (CNEA and CNEN)."[48] The first nuclear protocol adopted between the two countries established common rules for sharing information on radiation safety.[49] The *Protocol for the Immediate Information and Reciprocal Assistance in Case of Nuclear Accidents and Radiological Emergencies* was put to test the next year.[50] A private hospital in Goiania, Brazil, moved to a new location without safely dismantling its old radiotherapy equipment. In 1987, it was discovered that the abandoned equipment

[45] Senior expert of the Brazilian-Argentine Agency for Accounting and Control of Nuclear Materials (ABACC), Captain Orpet Peixoto. Interview with the author in Rio de Janeiro, Brazil, April 2000.

[46] Brazilian Ambassador Sebastião do Rego Barros. Interview with the author in Buenos Aires, Argentina, July 2000.

[47] Brazilian Ambassador Sebastião do Rego Barros. Interview with the author in Buenos Aires, Argentina, July 2000.

[48] Former Director of International Relations of CNEA, Capitan Roberto Ornstein. Interview with the autor in Buenos Aires, Argentina, July 2001.

[49] This protocol was part of the 1986 Integration Act signed in July 1986 by Presidents Alfonsín and Sarney and constitutes the direct precedent of the 1991 Common Market of the South or Mercosur (Alcañiz, 2000).

[50] Argentine and Brazilian nuclear experts like to stress the fact that their safety procedure predated similar protocols put in place by IAEA immediately after the Chernobyl disaster (Carasales, 1997 and Ornstein, 1998).

had been stolen by locals to sell as scrap metal.[51] Within hours of the ghastly discovery, the head of CNEN alerted Emma Perez Ferreira, his counterpart at CNEA, who swiftly dispatched two Argentine specialists in radioactive waste management to the scene.[52] Professionals from the two agencies had grown so close that Dr. Perez Ferreira gave the order to send the CNEA experts to Brazil before being cleared by the Argentine Presidency (the Office of the President of Argentina had to authorize all foreign travel plans for CNEA experts).[53] "I told the president of CNEN: 'I am sending over our specialists' that same afternoon. I called Alfonsín and he approved it. Our people participated in the cleanup of an entire neighborhood, which had to be closed off."[54]

Expert bureaucrats search to upgrade NEST skills in accessible and inexpensive ways is at the heart of the Argentine-Brazilian partnership. With this purpose, professionals from CNEA and CNEN created a program in nuclear energy plant operation and management during the worst of the economic crisis, which continues to this day. It entails cross-national training sessions for experts working in nuclear energy. A CNEN facilitator of the program described it in these terms:

> Argentines train in a simulator here. When nuclear reactors are shut down, they require a lot of people to do maintenance. Our nuclear power plants do not have sufficient technical personnel, so they hire high skill temporary workers. When Atucha and Embalse shut down for maintenance, a contingent of Brazilians go to work. And when Agra shuts down, Argentine technicians come over. They have an open tab, nobody pays, they just exchange in kind. For example, Brazilian technicians from a reprocessing plant were trained in Argentina. They do research together, people go back and forth. Whenever there is any emergency drill in the power plants in Argentina, there is a Brazilian observer.[55]

Technical inter-agency cooperation led to changes in nonproliferation policy in Argentina and Brazil. Transparency and increased accountability, forged by expert bureaucrats working across the border, helped the governments of Argentina and Brazil mend fences. In 1990, Presidents Menem and Collor de Mello met in the city of Foz de Iguazú, Brazil, and

[51] See www-pub.iaea.org/mtcd/publications/pdf/pub815_web.pdf.

[52] President of CNEA (1987–1989), Doctor Emma Perez Ferreira. Interview with the author in Buenos Aires, Argentina, March 2001.

[53] President of CNEA (1987–1989), Doctor Emma Perez Ferreira. Interview with the author in Buenos Aires, Argentina, March 2001.

[54] President of CNEA (1987–1989), Doctor Emma Perez Ferreira. Interview with the author in Buenos Aires, Argentina, March 2001.

[55] Former Director of International Relations of CNEN, Doctor Laercio Vinhas, interview with author in Rio de Janeiro, Brazil 2006.

approved the Common System of Accounting and Control of Nuclear Materials (SCCC). The SCCC introduced a cross-national verification system, by which Argentine inspectors examined the Brazilian nuclear facilities and Brazilian inspectors, those in Argentina (this regime continues to the present). To implement the SCCC, Argentina and Brazil created the Brazilian-Argentine Agency for Accounting and Control of Nuclear Materials (ABACC). This bilateral agency has the power to perform and evaluate inspections; legally represent Argentina and Brazil before third parties in all matters concerning the SCCC; and even sign international agreements on behalf of the two countries (Carasales, 1997; Ornstein & Carasales, 1998; Kassenova, 2014).[56] In 1994, Argentina and Brazil ratified *together* the Treaty for the Prohibition of Nuclear Weapons in Latin America and the Caribbean (known as the Treaty of Tlatelolco) (Carasales 1997). The following year, Argentina finally ratified the Non Proliferation Treaty (NPT). Brazil followed suit in 1998 (Alcañiz, 2012). Undoubtedly, these political agreements would not have been possible without the prior work done by the expert bureaucrats, nor could the verification system of SCCC be carried out without the technical skills of CNEA and CNEN professionals.

Conclusion

I have argued thus far that there is a close relationship between skill formation, skill updating, and inter-agency cooperation. In periods of economic growth, as the state invested in the nuclear sector, government agencies recruited and trained expert personnel to advance strategic and non-strategic research projects. Then, as government investment dried up, expert bureaucrats took skill upgrading and updating into their own hands and increasingly developed cooperation networks. As argued before, if skill updating and upgrading is a critical motivation to cooperate, we need to understand how expert bureaucrats acquire and preserve these skills. In this chapter, I describe how the governments of Argentina and Brazil created expert agencies and recruited expert bureaucrats to advance their strategic goals. I describe in detail the evolution of skill acquisition in two state agencies, the Argentine National Commission for Atomic Energy (CNEA) and the Brazilian National Commission for Nuclear Energy (CNEN), and illustrate the causal mechanism behind my proposed theory of expert bureaucrats' cooperative behavior.

[56] See www.abacc.org.br/?page_id=5&lang=en.

Today, nuclear experts in Argentina and Brazil continue to pool resources, share research costs, and hone critical skills in cooperation. These bureaucrats seek each other out on a variety of bilateral projects, within the framework of the sectoral agreements forged in the 1980s, cooperating on nuclear development and coordinating nonproliferation policy.

The drive to cooperate, however, also explains the incentives to partner up in larger networks, like the Regional Cooperative Arrangement for the Promotion of Nuclear Science and Technology in Latin America and the Caribbean (ARCAL), sponsored by the IAEA. As the next chapter will show, of the seventy-seven ARCAL projects in which Argentina and Brazil participated, they did so together in seventy-four. This homophily effect, I argue, shows how cooperative ties are forged in order to advance expertise. Argentina and Brazil, at similar levels of program development, benefit from pairing much more than if they were to collaborate with a less developed country. At the same time, larger networks multiply, by the number of participating actors, the amount of resources that go in the common pool. The next chapter focuses on these larger networks in NEST, which expert bureaucrats use to substitute skills and expertise that they cannot obtain at home.

4

International Inter-Agency Cooperation in Nuclear Energy, Science, and Technology (NEST)

The previous chapter described the evolution of skill acquisition in the nuclear sectors of Argentina and Brazil. These two case studies fleshed out the causal mechanism behind the theory of the expert bureaucrat. Chapter 3 provided a blueprint for how state experts further their scientific and technological skills while employed in well-funded agencies and how they update and upgrade their expertise when government resources decline. In addition, Chapter 3 showed how expert bureaucrats pool scarce resources and share know-how through inter-agency agreements to substitute for the lack of government investment. The Argentine-Brazilian case exemplified technical cooperation between advanced programs in Nuclear Energy, Science, and Technology (NEST), where skills depreciate rapidly if investment is withheld.

In the present chapter, I describe a collaborative network of nuclear experts from sixty-nine state agencies across the Global South working together on technical projects in NEST over thirty years. These networks of expert bureaucrats are facilitated by the involvement of the International Atomic Energy Agency (IAEA), which provides institutional support to inter-agency cooperation. The benefits stemming from cooperation are plentiful, including skill upgrading and updating and product design and implementation. Projects in NEST have applications in multiple fields, such as human health, radiation safety, water and food security, agricultural development, and the environment. However, not all nuclear agencies are equally equipped to collaborate, as many projects carry significant technical and scientific demands from participants and require high levels of institutional capacity in order to be implemented.

Consequently, the participation of countries in NEST projects varies greatly across the Global South. As this chapter will show, some state agencies are considerably more active in nuclear networks than others. The descriptive data analyzed in the next pages also reveal great variation in agency partnerships; some agencies form steady ties and work together repeatedly while others lack the resources to participate actively and form stable inter-agency relationships. The chapter uses in-depth interviews, extensive archival research, and statistical data on NEST projects to depict the network of expert bureaucrats. It shows how foreign peers come together to design, adopt, and implement complex projects under extremely constricted budgets and how participants gain access to technical skills, scientific knowledge, and best practices. The next pages address key questions about the mechanisms through which expert bureaucrats access new skills in NEST networks. The chapter answers the call to "go beyond heralding the importance of networks as a form of collaborative public management and look inside their operations" (Agranoff, 2006: 56).

Inter-Agency Networks and Barriers to Entry

There is a stark contrast between the widespread expectation of the bureaucrat as a domestic-bound actor and her increasing international behavior. The significant growth of transgovernmental networks formed by collaborating state experts is a remarkable challenge to traditional views of bureaucratic behavior that expect state agents to guard with zeal domestically appropriated funds and resources (Blais & Dion, 1990; Huber & Shipan, 2006; Niskanen, 2007; Hoffer, 2013). Despite such expectations, we currently find international inter-agency cooperation in diverse policy areas and across all regions of the world. Increasingly, transgovernmentalism "captures a strikingly wide array of contemporary cooperation" that includes national regulators sharing information and state scientists working on international projects (Raustiala, 2002: 5).

Examples of inter-agency partnerships in technology-intensive sectors abound, such as the International Space Station (ISS) and the Pierre Auger International Cosmic Ray Observatory in Argentina. In the ISS, there is a division of labor based on the specific areas of expertise of each national space agency. For example, the Canadian Space Agency (CSA) contributes the *mobile servicing system*, which includes the robotic arms

(Canadarm 2) that first assembled the station in space.[1] The Japan Aerospace Exploration Agency (JAXA) is in charge of the largest module of the station, which was designed and built by Japanese scientists.[2] Making up the majority partnership, the United States National Aeronautics and Space Administration (NASA) and the Russian Federal Space Agency (RKA), closely followed by the European Space Agency (ESA), contribute infrastructure, engineering, and the bulk of the personnel on the ground and in space. This type of complex collaborative project requires partners to possess cutting-edge technology, to share proprietary information, to invest significant resources in common goals, and to train jointly their systems to accomplish common required tasks. Entry costs, for participants to join, are exorbitantly high.

Another international inter-agency project in the area of science and technology, with a much larger membership than the ISS, is the Auger Observatory. Located in the Province of Mendoza, Argentina, the observatory was built to study "ultra-high energy cosmic rays, [which are] the most energetic and rarest of particles in the universe."[3] The ambitious venture is funded and managed by over hundred national laboratories, state agencies, and public universities from seventeen countries. Both the ISS and the Auger Observatory are formidable cross-national inter-agency projects that successfully advance common goals by pooling resources. Neither one could be funded independently (nor carried out technically) by any one state. The ISS and the Auger Observatory are examples of projects with high barriers to entry. This means that only state agencies with abundant expertise and a wealth of resources may aspire to join. The higher the barrier to entry, the fewer the number of potential participants will be found in a project.

In contrast to the closed partnerships of the ISS and the Auger Observatory, which demand skills and investments beyond the reach of most countries in the Global South, the collaborative networks analyzed in this book are open *in theory* to all (developing) countries that want to join, regardless of initial level of expertise. Typically facilitated by specialized International Organizations (IOs), these inter-agency networks develop across wide-ranging policy areas, such as environmental protection, human health, and human security. Rather than working on one

[1] See www.asc-csa.gc.ca/fra/default.asp and www.asc-csa.gc.ca/eng/iss/canadarm2/default.asp.

[2] See www.jaxa.jp/about/index_e.html.

[3] See www.auger.org/index.html.

large project like the ISS or the Auger Observatory, state experts within these networks collaborate over time on multiple projects that advance research, pool skills, and develop new practices. Surprisingly, collaborative networks in the Global South have gone largely unnoticed in the extant literature on transgovernmentalism, which focuses overwhelmingly on international inter-agency cooperation among Organisation for Economic Co-operation and Development (OECD) states. Yet, as this book shows, when expert bureaucrats need to update their existing stockpiles of skills under scarce resources, inter-agency cooperation is not only feasible but also a common strategy among developing countries.

Inter-Agency Networks in NEST: Origin and Focus

How do collaborative networks of expert bureaucrats in NEST originate and what type of projects do actors in these networks advance? Over the past four decades, three major networks in NEST developed across the three largest regions of the developing world: the Regional Cooperative Agreement for Research, Development and Training Related to Nuclear Science and Technology for Asia and the Pacific (RCA); the Regional Cooperative Arrangement for the Promotion of Nuclear Science and Technology in Latin America and the Caribbean (ARCAL); and the African Regional Cooperative Agreement for Research, Development and Training Related to Nuclear Science and Technology (AFRA). Participants in AFRA, RCA, and ARCAL are bureaucrats who come from national state institutions with central jurisdiction in NEST.[4] Agencies vary greatly in degree of specialization, availability of resources, and level of skill. They run the gamut, from Nuclear Energy Agencies; Science & Technology Agencies; National Universities; and Ministries of Energy, Mining, the Environment, Industry, Electricity, and Foreign Affairs.[5] Traversing borders, experts work on large technical projects that apply nuclear science and technology to a wide variety of fields, including public health, nuclear medicine, agriculture, and radiation safety. The IAEA sponsors these programs with technical and (some) financial assistance.

[4] For a list of all participants, see Table A.4.1.

[5] All countries, regardless of level of skill and development, have at least one state institution with jurisdiction in NEST policy because all countries use nuclear technology in radiology and medical imaging. Consequently, the state must regulate and enforce the adoption of safeguards in order to ensure the safe use of these techniques and equipment. Thus, state expertise in NEST is needed even in countries that lack a nuclear energy program.

The first network to emerge was the Asian RCA. Created in 1972, initially it only had six participants (India, Indonesia, the Philippines, Singapore, Thailand, and Vietnam).[6] RCA is the only NEST network in the Global South to include nuclear weapons states like India, a founding member, which developed its first nuclear weapon in 1974. With the later addition of China and Pakistan, this network (which like the others, only adopts projects with peaceful applications of NEST) has three out of the world's eight official nuclear weapons states. The RCA network also shows significant intra-regional disparity when it comes to economic development. In addition to the original six, the network has four advanced industrial countries (Japan, Australia, New Zealand, and Korea) that share membership in the OECD.

Latin Americans founded ARCAL in 1984 at a time of great change; just two years after the 1982 foreign debt crisis and at the beginning of the wave of democratization that was to sweep the region throughout the decade. The initiative was originally proposed by the least developed countries of the Andean Group and soon thereafter endorsed by the Southern Cone states.[7] A few years later, the remaining Latin American countries, including the Central American states, Mexico and the Caribbean states of Cuba, the Dominican Republic, and Jamaica, joined the agreement. The central mission of ARCAL was to promote horizontal cooperation, pool regional resources, and deepen know-how in NEST throughout the region.[8]

Finally, expert bureaucrats in Africa created AFRA in 1990 with an initial membership of twenty-six agency countries. With many of the least developed countries of the world in sub-Saharan Africa, not surprisingly, inter-agency cooperation in NEST faces multiple challenges in the Region. This has been noted by the membership. In its 2007 Strategic Action Plan, Procedures and Operational Guidelines, AFRA participants list as

6 At www.rcaro.org/.

7 The Andean Group comprises Bolivia, Columbia, Ecuador, Peru, and Venezuela. Argentina, Brazil, Chile, Paraguay, and Uruguay are known as the Southern Cone states.

8 To give a sense of the early priorities of the network, its first project in 1984 aimed at developing "the scientific and industrial applications of radioisotopes and radiation in the Latin American Region" in order "to prepare projects in the areas of radiation protection, nuclear instrumentation, radioimmunoassay (RIA) techniques in animal reproduction, food irradiation, nuclear analytical techniques, mutation breeding, utilization of research reactors, and RIA of thyroid hormones and isotope techniques in hydrology." This first project reflects a shared interest by Latin American countries to invest in general skills in NEST.

significant hurdles the "limited financial resources required for addressing the tremendous needs of end-users in member states, using technically and developmentally sound nuclear technologies; wide variation in AFRA member states' stages of development in nuclear science and technology, which requires intensive efforts to narrow down the gap and to create conducive environment for regional cooperation; and inadequate qualified and skilled human resources in many member states, which limits the outreach of AFRA projects."[9] At the same time, the benefits of even marginal gains in level of skills can be enormous.

The problems of the African Region are pressing, such as severe insecurity in food and water, and many of the cross-national projects reflect an interest by local experts to access skills that help remedy them. For example, one of the first projects carried out by the network in 1991 was in food preservation, "to assist the countries participating in the AFRA Agreement to promote the introduction of food irradiation technology through training, demonstrations, workshops and information exchange."[10]

Since their emergence, these networks have increased the number of participants and cross-national projects dramatically. At present, regular participants in Asia stand at seventeen countries; in Latin America, twenty; and in Africa, thirty-two. The Asian RCA leads the pack in the number of completed and active projects, with over 130 projects that are under way or finalized; the Latin American ARCAL follows with 119 projects; and in Africa, a region which is quickly catching up, AFRA has currently eighty projects.[11]

Table 4.1 offers a breakdown of projects by area of application and region. By disaggregating by project type, we can see bureaucrats' priorities for training and skill upgrading.

For example, African bureaucrats charged with nuclear policy invest their cooperation efforts in two critical areas: the Environment (24 percent of total AFRA projects) and Human Health (21 percent of total AFRA projects). As Chapters 6 and 7 will show, African countries are high-profile stakeholders in the protection of the environment, thus it is not surprising that NEST bureaucrats in the Region are such active participants in these types of projects. Human Health projects with a focus

9 See the AFRA Strategic Action Plan, Procedures and Operational Guidelines, April 2007 at www.afra-iaea.org.dz/index.php/en/about-afra?showall=&start=1.

10 See http://tc.iaea.org/tcweb/projectinfo/default.asp.

11 See www.iaea.org/technicalcooperation/Partnerships/Reg-Coop-Agreements.html.

TABLE 4.1. *Policy Area Addressed by the Project by Region*

Type of Project	Africa	Asia	LA	Total
Agriculture/Food	1917.27	2112.65	1611.19	5613.37
Energy	21.82	1710.24	32.1	225.25
Environment	2623.64	2213.25	2316.08	7116.95
Human Capital	1715.45	169.64	1812.59	5112.17
Human Health	2320.91	3219.28	4027.97	9522.67
Industry	43.64	84.82	74.9	194.53
Nuclear Safety	1513.64	3521.08	2215.38	7217.18
Nuclear Science	43.64	159.04	149.79	337.88
Total	110100	166100	143100	419100

Note: Some projects are categorized in more than one policy area. Consequently, the number of policy areas is larger than the total number of projects.

mostly on radiology and nuclear medicine are popular across all of the Global South, as they are a source of inexpensive training for doctors and technicians from public hospitals.

NEST bureaucrats from Asia share with their African counterparts a strong preference for Human Health projects, which make up 19 percent of their participation in the RCA network. However, the greatest participation share of RCA bureaucrats is in Nuclear Safety, with 21 percent of Asian projects in this area. This is explained by the great number of nuclear power plants in the region, the highest concentration in a developing region, dispersed across five states: China, India, Pakistan, South Korea, and Japan. Furthermore, China, India, and South Korea continue to invest in the sector, with multiple plants under construction. Finally, as the Region has three nuclear weapons states (China, India, and Pakistan), it makes sense that NEST experts in Asia are preoccupied with Nuclear Safety and choose to invest more heavily in skills in that area.

Latin American expert bureaucrats resemble their RCA colleagues in that they prioritize training in Human Health and Nuclear Safety. ARCAL nuclear medicine and related projects make up 28 percent of the total. Nuclear Safety, the second priority in skills for Latin Americans, constitutes 15 percent of all projects. Closer to Asia than Africa, Latin America has three major nuclear energy producers (Argentina, Brazil, and Mexico) and several intermediate-level state programs in NEST that utilize research reactors (like Chile, Peru, and Uruguay). These two nuclear activities are probably driving the high demand for skills in safety in the Region.

Adoption and Implementation of Projects in NEST

How are projects within these networks designed and implemented? To begin with, expert bureaucrats from state agencies with primary jurisdiction in nuclear policy are the leading participants in NEST projects. Known as *liaisons* between their state agencies and their foreign peers in the network:

> They are commissioners or directors, scientific or technical directors. They have their jobs and are in a high position in their country, but when they work in AFRA, whatever they do here, all their resulting costs are covered by the country itself.[12]

Still, the implementation of complex international projects in NEST requires the participation of an extended group of professionals, in addition to the mezzo level state bureaucrat. An ARCAL expert describes the broader make-up of country participants as actors who "in reality, are the small nuclear communities which developed around the national atomic agencies."[13]

Participants' skills vary within and across countries. A single country, typically one with a well-developed nuclear program, may contribute experts at both ends of the skill spectrum to a project; for example, a nuclear physicist who decides content and goals and a radiation lab technician who assists with implementation. Countries with rudimentary development in NEST tend to cooperate less frequently in the network, and when they do, they contribute fewer and less-qualified professionals to work in cross-national projects.[14] For example, Eritrea, Namibia, and Costa Rica have public health officials as their network liaisons; Cuba, Benin, and Nepal have bureaucrats with expertise in environmental science.[15]

As there is no centralized authority in NEST networks, cross-national projects are negotiated and designed by participants working across borders. An ARCAL coordinator at the National Commission of Atomic Energy (CNEA) in Argentina explains how bureaucrats in domestic NEST institutions promote their own research agendas in the region:

[12] Mokdad Maksoudi, Tunisian Program Manager for AFRA. Interview with the author in Vienna, Austria, June 2007.

[13] María Cecilia Urbina Paredes. Chilean Program Manager of ARCAL. Interview with the author in Vienna, Austria, June 2007.

[14] Interviews with multiple IAEA-TC officers in Vienna, Austria, June 2007.

[15] See www.iaea.org/technicalcooperation/Partnerships/Reg-Coop-Agreements.html.

Each country has certain national priorities within its own (nuclear) institutions and the project ideas come from there... we present these ideas, just like the other countries and if there is a consensus, that is, if there is a minimum of four countries that have presented similar projects in the area, they get together and move forward.[16]

This brainstorming and bargaining process is described by another participant of the Latin American network:

They [participants] would put their proposals together, analyze them... and narrow it down to 20 or 25 ideas. From these ideas they would design their own projects.[17]

Once the projects are decided upon, country coordinators are chosen. Within the AFRA network:

At the level of each project, the Africans will select among themselves, amongst their peers, the best scientist, engineers who will be the scientific project consultant.[18]

On average, projects last around four years and involve at least the same number of countries. Revolutionary advances made in Informational Technology (IT) greatly facilitate the endeavor of having state experts from multiple countries work together long distance. At the same time, the disparity in skills by state professionals across the Global South affects their participation. A representative of the African network explains how gaps in NEST knowledge shape the quality of, and access to, collective training:

There is not a critical mass of new students every year to be trained and to go out because the nuclear sector [in Africa] is very small. Today there are only 6 countries that have this kind of training. Algeria, Morocco, Egypt, Ghana, Nigeria, South Africa. So all these countries can train their people, but they do it in their own way. So, AFRA brought them together. They discuss the needs for developing training in higher education and to harmonize one curriculum for a master degree in nuclear science and technology for Africa. It is not nuclear technology like Europe; Europe has a master degree in nuclear technology for nuclear power, but African countries the majority of them will not accede to

16 César Tate, ARCAL liaison for Argentina at CNEA. Interview with the author in Buenos Aires, Argentina, July 2006.

17 Maria Zednik, ARCAL Regional Coordinator. Interview with the author in Vienna, Austria, June 2007.

18 Mokdad Maksoudi, Tunisian Program Manager for AFRA. Interview with the author in Vienna, Austria, June 2007.

nuclear power so the issue is much more for socioeconomic development, for nuclear power applications.[19]

Given that keeping skills current and staying abreast of technological change is critical to these bureaucrats, significant training time is spent on mastering new techniques through computer simulations or in Research and Development (R&D) activities. Workshops and symposia also help experts keep current on professional developments in their field and often include training sessions on new methods. Project-based networks serve as effective and far-reaching mechanisms of technology transfer by, as one AFRA manager put it, "train(ing) the trainers."[20] A rare inter-regional nuclear project illustrates how. In 1999, nuclear bureaucrats from Argentina, Egypt, Malaysia, Morocco, Pakistan, the Philippines, and Uruguay participated in a pilot program to test the effectiveness of distance learning as a means to train technicians in radioisotope and radiation oncology treatments. Once experts from these countries were fully trained, they were sent back to distribute the acquired information and train their professional peers in their region.[21]

Another project exemplifies homophily cooperation, which I argue results from peer-selections that are based on a similar level of skills. The ARCAL project "Determining Content of Atmospheric Contamination" in the early 2000s (2000–2004) involved participants from the four largest economies of Latin America: Mexico, Brazil, Argentina, and Chile. This project aimed to identify and characterize toxic pollutants present at trace levels in the air of four Latin American cities with the worst levels of pollution during critical periods (Mexico DF, Mexico; São Paulo, Brazil; Santiago, Chile; and Córdoba, Argentina). The main task was to provide advanced training in a nuclear microscopy technique, PIXE (Proton-Induced X-ray Emission). Initially, Mexico had the expertise, as state officials in that country had long used (and mastered) PIXE in assessing air quality in the capital city as well as in the field of archaeology, a discipline with a rich tradition in Mexico and where practitioners had strong skills. Consequently, Mexican experts were in charge of training Argentine, Brazilian, and Chilean bureaucrats in the technique.

19 Mokdad Maksoudi, Tunisian Program Manager for AFRA. Interview with the author in Vienna, Austria, June 2007.

20 Mokdad Maksoudi, Tunisian Program Manager for AFRA. Interview with the author in Vienna, Austria, June 2007.

21 See www-tc.iaea.org/tcweb/projectinfo/default.asp.

Inter-agency networks transform existing state infrastructures, like research centers and laboratories, into regional training hubs. As the AFRA liaison explains:

We have 10 centers in radiotherapy, radiation safety, biotechnology, and instrumentation. All these centers are in different countries, the majority in South Africa of course, but we have two in Egypt, one in Tunisia, one in Morocco, and one in Algeria. These centers provide, training, advisory assistance, some in South Africa provide training to the other centers and to this program. They train people, short term or long term.[22]

Networking bureaucrats design low-budget projects in NEST that they can afford and to which they can commit.[23] As a state expert from the Brazilian CNEN explains:

To develop cooperation projects, there are many things that you might not need a lot of money to do. Nowadays with telecommunications there is exchange of information. Even more so given that people know each other, they can converse and exchange information.[24]

This type of horizontal cooperation is an inexpensive alternative to costly agreements (entailing significant technology transfers) with advanced nuclear countries, like the ones described in Chapter 3. An Argentine expert from CNEA explicates:

As time went by, the budget situation became tighter and we had to resort to multilateral cooperation as a way to continue having presence in, and collaborate with, the countries of Latin America, through programs like ARCAL

[22] Mokdad Maksoudi, Tunisian Program Manager for AFRA. Interview with the author in Vienna, Austria, June 2007.

[23] The problem of commitment is particularly acute in impoverished bureaucracies. For example, Argentina has a standing invitation to participate in cooperative (non-commercial) research projects with the European Atomic Energy Community (EURATOM). A partnership with EURATOM is an extraordinary opportunity to access the latest technology in NEST and train Argentine professionals with highly skilled nuclear scientists. However, cooperation with Europe has been out of reach for Argentine experts, who lack the resources to commit long term to OECD partners. "We could participate if we had the means. You have to be responsible for your own expenses and you have to have available personnel to work full time on this [. . .] there is a very important opportunity in terms of technology but limited resources prevent us from taking advantage of this" Roberto Ornstein, Director of International Cooperation of the Argentine National Atomic Energy Commission. Interview with the author in Buenos Aires, Argentina, July 28, 2006.

[24] Laercio Vinhas, Director of International Cooperation of the Brazilian National Commission of Nuclear Energy, Interview with the author in Rio de Janeiro, Brazil, July 19, 2006.

or other regional projects [...] in a way, they have replaced the source of financing.[25]

With their pooled resources and shared costs, the NEST networks help advance the career of local scientists. As an AFRA liaison remarked: "If you ask me what is my best achievement for AFRA I would tell you that it is empowering scientists [in Africa]."[26]

The International Atomic Energy Agency and Inter-Agency Cooperation in NEST

Networking among developing countries is greatly aided by IOs that can assume, at least in part, the costs of coordination and serve as a forum where professionals meet and discuss similar concerns. The IAEA has been a critical source of technical assistance for developing countries engaged in nuclear science. Resulting from U.S. President Dwight Eisenhower's 1953 Atoms for Peace initiative to the United Nations, where he proposed the creation of an international watchdog to help stop nuclear proliferation as "the dread secret, and the fearful engines of atomic might, are not ours alone," IAEA had a clear mission.[27] The agency was to serve as a distribution center for information, knowledge, and research pertaining to nonmilitary fissionable material while functioning as an "acceptable system of world-wide inspection and control."[28] Thus, the tit-for-tat behind the creation of IAEA was to provide technical cooperation to states interested in developing nuclear energy in exchange for their commitment to refrain from ever pursuing a strategic program.

Like other United Nations agencies, IAEA has a Department of Technical Cooperation (TC) that provides assistance to national programs in non-OECD states through individual-country and region-based projects.

[25] Roberto Ornstein, Director of International Cooperation of the Argentine National Atomic Energy Commission, Interview with the author in Buenos Aires, Argentina, July 28, 2006.

[26] Mokdad Maksoudi, Tunesian Program Manager for AFRA. Interview with the author in Vienna, Austria, June 2007.

[27] "Atoms for Peace" address given by U.S. President Dwight D. Eisenhower before the General Assembly of the United Nations on Peaceful Uses of Atomic Energy, New York City, December 8, 1953.

[28] "Atoms for Peace" address given by U.S. President Dwight D. Eisenhower before the General Assembly of the United Nations on Peaceful Uses of Atomic Energy, New York City, December 8, 1953.

TABLE 4.2. *Budget for ARCAL 1983–2004*

Sourceof Disbursements	Type of Disbursement	US$ Million	Percent of Total Budget
ARCAL Members	In Kind	13	44%
IAEA	Monetary	13	44%
OECD Donations	Monetary	4	12%

Source: ARCAL-IAEA.

TC support concentrates on transaction costs. For example, IAEA facilitates meeting space for network partners during the annual general conference for all member states. In addition, the Agency hosts numerous international conferences and symposia on different applications and techniques of nuclear science and technology. Attendants to these events have an opportunity to meet and do some of the legwork required to move along a cross-national project.[29] IAEA also helps partially fund network projects, but the contributions of the agency are modest. Member states of IAEA pay their dues to TC, but they also finance NEST projects by in kind contributions. Table 4.2 shows the breakdown of the ARCAL budget over twenty years (1983–2004) by type of disbursement (in kind or monetary) and source (participants, IAEA, and outside donors).

IAEA favors members' self-initiative and contributes with nonmonetary assistance. An AFRA bureaucrat explained this:

> AFRA members manage their own projects. They have to decide what to work on and which project they would like as a project on a regional or sub-regional basis. IAEA just supports, but it doesn't manage. It should be managed by the member state.[30]

While funding might be low, the Agency brings to bear other critical resources that support collaborative networks. Like most International Organizations, IAEA has significant ties to other institutional actors,

[29] Interview with CNEA and CNEN bureaucrats (Buenos Aires, Argentina and Rio de Janeiro, Brazil, 2006). Doubling of duties during the annual general assembly meetings of IOs is a typical way in which cooperating bureaucrats from the Global South get face to face time with peers. As Chapter 6 depicts, this also occurs in the area of environmental protection. The annual conference at the world headquarters of the United Nations Environmental Programme (Nairobi, Kenya) serves as a meeting ground for project partners.

[30] Gérard Bischoff, IAEA TC Officer for Africa. Interview with the author in Vienna, Austria, June 2007.

including domestic ones, a wealth of partnerships with other IOs, and political mandates from its country membership. IAEA makes use of this complex ties when assisting cooperating developing countries. Depending on the policy area of the enterprise, IAEA may call on the expertise of other UN agencies. For example, the AFRA project on "Development and Field Evaluation of Animal Feed Supplementation Packages" (AFRA Project II-17 – RAF/5/041), which addressed the severe nutritional deficiencies of livestock feed in many regions of Africa, was carried out by nine African states with the assistance of the Joint FAO (Food and Agricultural Organization)-IAEA program.[31] The partnership of the two UN agencies was created to promote the use of nuclear techniques in food and agriculture and advance research in livestock production.[32]

While IOs facilitate the conditions under which inter-agency networks in NEST develop, they cannot force member states to develop ties with one another given that a key attribute of a network (which clearly separates it from hierarchical organizations, like IOs) is its voluntary nature. Therefore, IOs do not create international inter-agency networks. Rather, as Slaughter explains them:

> Horizontal information networks bring together [bureaucratic actors] to exchange information and to collect and distill best practices. This information exchange can also take place through technical assistance and training programs provided by one country's official to another.
>
> (Slaughter, 2004: 19)

Participating agencies remain autonomous from the IAEA, having "full ownership of the design, formulation, implementation, and monitoring of the cooperative projects."[33]

Visualizing Networks in NEST

The data from AFRA, ARCAL, and RCA allow us to map the relative proximity of different countries and agencies, a critical first step to understand collaboration, partner selection, and homophily trends. Indeed, in the last fifteen years political scientists have devised a very large number of strategies to translate collaborative decisions into conceptual maps that assess proximity among agents (Poole, 2005). From latent variable

[31] See www-naweb.iaea.org/nafa/.

[32] See www-naweb.iaea.org/nafa/aph/public/iaea-tecdoc-1294.pdf.

[33] AFRA Strategic Action Plan, Procedures and Operational Guidelines, April 2007, page 1.

models measuring unobserved dimensions (Treier & Jackman, 2008) to ideal points estimates (Bafumi, Gelman, Park, & Kaplan, 2005) and multidimensional scaling (Poole, 2005), scholars can use information about concurrent decisions to understand how actors connect with one another. Many of these advances have come from social network analysis, with a variety of tools to understand the ties (edges) between individuals (nodes). In the next chapter I conduct statistical analyses that measure the decision by state agencies to cooperate. First, I provide descriptive and visual evidence of cooperation among country agencies.

Consider, for example, each of the state agencies participating in the IAEA-sponsored collaborative programs. These programs provide an opportunity for countries to collaborate with one another. However, the decision to participate in projects is the choice of the country program, which can be explained by specific and shared traits in a number of countries, such as the relative level of development of nuclear programs, the skills of the bureaucrats recruited by these programs, and the pool of resources that are available locally to finance program operations. Brazil, for example, will have more incentives to participate in the network than Paraguay, as the demand for skills among Brazilian nuclear experts is much greater. Similarly, Argentina will have more incentives to participate in a nuclear project that includes Brazil than in a nuclear project that includes Uruguay. Indeed, although both Uruguay and Brazil have similar GDP per capita and are geographically close to Argentina, there are bureaucratic and scientific similarities, in addition to historical ties, which make Brazil a more appealing partner to Argentine experts.

To explore the data, I first measure the number of times that each pair of countries participates *together* in a nuclear project. This is commonly known as an affiliation matrix, with the diagonal vector of a matrix describing the total number of projects in which a country has participated, and the off-diagonal elements describing the number of projects that included each pair of countries.

Consistent with the skill-driven model of cooperation, Tables 4.3, 4.4, and 4.5, provide preliminary evidence that more developed programs are more active participants in nuclear networks. Table 4.3 shows that countries with more developed nuclear programs and larger numbers of skilled bureaucrats are the ones that (1) participate the most in the network and (2) collaborate the most with other programs. We see the North African states, Algeria, Egypt, Morocco, and Tunisia as the most active participants in the network with forty-nine, fifty, fifty, and fifty-two projects, respectively. South Africa, the only nuclear energy producer

TABLE 4.3. *AFRA Affiliation Matrix*

	AGO	BEN	BFA	BWA	CAF	CIV	CMR	DZA	EGY	ERI	ETH	GAB	GHA	KEN	MDG	MLI	MUS	NAM	NER	NGA	SDN	SEN	SLE	TUN	TZA	UGA	ZAF	ZAR	ZMB	ZWE
AGO	5																													
BEN	3	10																												
BFA	3	9	22																											
BWA	3	7	11	14																										
CAF	3	6	7	6	9																									
CIV	3	5	8	5	4	19																								
CMR	3	9	19	13	9	19	45																							
DZA	3	9	18	14	8	19	41	49																						
EGY	3	10	19	14	8	19	42	48	50																					
ERI	3	5	5	4	4	3	5	4	5	5																				
ETH	3	8	16	11	7	16	30	31	33	5	33																			
GAB	3	4	4	3	3	3	4	4	4	3	4	4																		
GHA	3	10	19	14	9	19	43	48	49	5	33	4	50																	
KEN	4	9	20	14	9	17	41	43	44	5	31	4	44	47																
MDG	3	10	18	13	9	15	34	36	36	5	27	4	37	35	37															
MLI	3	8	14	9	8	13	21	22	22	5	18	3	23	23	21	23														
MUS	4	9	18	13	8	17	37	38	40	5	30	4	40	37	32	20	41													
NAM	5	6	11	6	5	13	24	23	24	4	18	4	24	23	20	12	24	28												
NER	3	10	16	13	8	16	31	33	34	5	26	4	34	32	32	19	30	19	34											
NGA	4	8	14	12	5	16	34	38	38	4	23	3	38	33	28	17	32	19	26	39										
SDN	3	9	21	13	8	18	44	43	44	4	31	3	45	43	35	22	38	25	32	35	50									
SEN	3	4	10	6	5	9	17	19	20	4	19	3	20	19	18	13	18	15	17	13	18	20								
SLE	3	6	9	6	6	13	20	20	21	4	20	3	21	19	19	14	19	15	20	16	19	14	21							
TUN	3	10	21	14	9	19	44	48	49	5	33	4	49	46	37	23	40	24	34	37	47	20	21	52						
TZA	5	10	22	14	9	18	44	46	47	5	32	4	47	46	37	23	40	28	34	36	49	20	21	50	54					
UGA	3	9	18	12	8	11	24	25	26	5	23	4	26	27	25	18	24	16	24	18	25	16	16	27	27	27				
ZAF	5	10	18	13	9	15	38	44	45	5	30	4	45	43	34	23	36	22	30	35	41	19	19	45	45	26	48			
ZAR	3	10	16	12	9	19	41	43	44	5	29	4	45	39	34	21	36	23	32	35	41	17	21	44	42	24	41	45		
ZMB	3	10	18	12	9	18	39	44	44	5	31	4	44	41	35	21	38	23	33	34	41	19	21	45	44	24	40	39	45	
ZWE	3	9	18	14	9	11	30	31	32	5	26	4	33	32	27	20	30	18	25	22	31	19	15	33	33	23	31	29	29	33

Source: Own elaboration from IAEA Projects Data.

TABLE 4.4. *ARCAL Affiliation Matrix*

	ARG	BLZ	BOL	BRA	CHL	COL	CRI	CUB	DOM	ECU	ESP	GTM	HND	HTI	JAM	MEX	NIC	PAN	PER	PRY	SLV	URY	VEN
ARG	77																						
BLZ	2	2																					
BOL	39	2	42																				
BRA	74	2	41	77																			
CHL	69	2	38	68	70																		
COL	41	2	32	42	40	43																	
CRI	51	2	34	50	45	32	56																
CUB	63	2	35	62	58	35	46	68															
DOM	21	2	15	19	20	14	19	23	24														
ECU	46	2	33	44	44	35	37	37	13	46													
ESP	2	0	0	1	1	0	0	2	0	1	2												
GTM	42	2	31	43	40	29	41	38	16	32	0	48											
HND	2	2	2	2	2	2	2	2	2	2	0	2	2										
HTI	8	2	5	8	8	5	6	8	7	6	1	6	2	8									
JAM	6	2	6	6	6	6	5	6	4	6	0	5	2	4	6								
MEX	67	2	34	66	63	36	47	59	21	40	1	38	2	8	6	69							
NIC	18	2	16	19	16	16	20	20	11	11	0	16	2	5	4	19	22						
PAN	26	2	20	26	25	19	27	29	13	20	0	25	2	5	4	26	16	30					
PER	58	2	36	59	55	36	42	52	19	39	2	34	2	7	4	54	20	23	62				
PRY	37	2	28	38	35	30	31	30	14	30	1	30	2	8	4	31	14	16	35	39			
SLV	21	2	20	23	19	11	20	23	13	15	1	17	2	6	3	21	12	12	23	17	24		
URY	57	2	29	55	50	32	40	54	22	33	2	32	2	8	4	54	17	22	47	32	20	59	
VEN	44	2	26	43	41	26	34	44	16	29	1	28	2	7	4	44	18	24	41	26	19	40	45

Source: Own elaboration from IAEA Projects Data.

TABLE 4.5. *RCA Affiliation Matrix*

	AUS	BGD	CHN	IDN	IND	JPN	KOR	LBN	LKA	MMR	MNG	MYS	NZL	PAK	PHL	SGP	THA	VNM
AUS	55																	
BGD	53	90																
CHN	55	87	94															
IDN	52	76	77	80														
IND	55	80	85	72	87													
JPN	19	23	25	22	25	25												
KOR	39	66	66	63	60	20	68											
LBN	4	4	4	4	4	1	2	5										
LKA	40	69	69	63	61	20	56	4	70									
MMR	45	60	60	56	61	19	43	4	48	62								
MNG	44	66	67	63	65	18	52	4	55	53	68							
MYS	51	79	79	74	73	21	64	4	65	57	62	82						
NZL	26	33	32	29	33	11	20	4	26	29	27	30	34					
PAK	52	83	85	77	79	23	66	4	67	58	66	77	32	87				
PHL	48	78	79	73	71	22	62	4	67	56	63	75	28	77	80			
SGP	27	40	41	38	36	17	31	4	37	31	32	38	17	39	39	41		
THA	50	82	83	74	77	22	62	4	66	57	64	79	32	80	77	38	87	
VNM	52	85	86	74	82	22	64	4	66	59	67	77	33	81	75	37	84	90

Source: Own elaboration from IAEA Projects Data.

of the region, is also a high collaborator with forty-eight projects in the AFRA network.

Countries with more developed nuclear programs also tend to collaborate more often with one another. For example, Algeria and Egypt have collaborated in forty-eight projects. South Africa has been in forty-three projects with Algeria, forty-four with Egypt, forty-three with Morocco, and forty-four with Tunisia. Another active subgroup where we observe a homophily effect is formed by Zambia, Tanzania, and Kenya. This cluster of countries with low level of skills has participated in a total of forty-five, fifty-four, and forty-seven projects, respectively, of which almost all have been done jointly.

Similar cooperative behavior seems to characterize the ARCAL network. The three nuclear energy producers in the region, Brazil, Argentina, and Mexico participated in seventy-seven, seventy-seven, and sixty-nine projects, respectively. Unexpectedly, Chile, the third most active country with seventy projects under its belt, does not have a nuclear energy program. However, the country has invested in nuclear research since the 1950s, mostly through university programs, and has benefited from its close relation with the two South American nuclear energy producers. After the *coup d'état* against democratically elected president Salvador Allende, the Pinochet dictatorship (1973–1990) gave the military a larger stake in nuclear development by strengthening the Military Center for Nuclear Studies (CENE) and signing cooperative nuclear treaties with the military governments of Argentina (1976) and Brazil (1980).[34] Cuba, a country that by its size and geographical location should be closer to smaller states such as the Dominican Republic (with participation in only twenty-four projects), boasts participation in sixty-eight projects. The high participation of Cuba is partly explained by the many years of Soviet subsidy and to Fidel Castro's investment in advanced health care. Indeed, under Castro's leadership, Cuba has carved its niche as one of the high-tech medical centers of Latin America, including nuclear medicine.

Finally, as discussed earlier, the RCA network is the most uneven of the three, comprising OECD countries like New Zealand, Australia, South Korea, and Japan; nuclear weapons states, as China, India, and Pakistan; and some of the poorest countries in the world, like Bangladesh and Nepal.

[34] See http://ocw.mit.edu/courses/political-science/17-951-nuclear-weapons-in-international-politics-past-present-and-future-spring-2009/projects/MIT17_951S09_abcs.pdf.

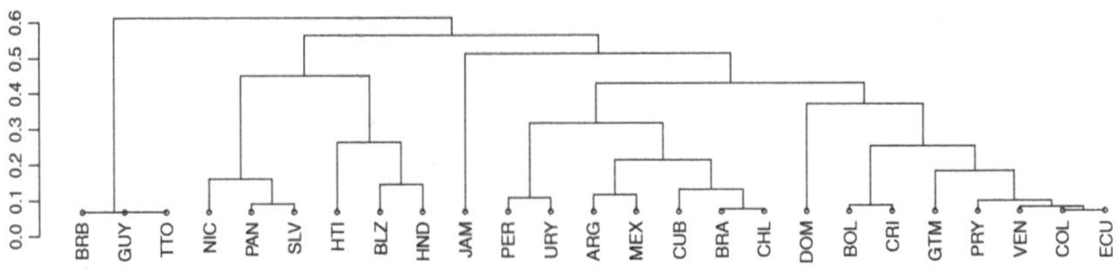

FIGURE 4.1. Dendrogram of association between members of the ARCAL network.
Source: Own elaboration from IAEA Projects Data.

Readers will have noticed already that partner selection in the nuclear network is not as selective as one would expect. The contrast will be noticeable when compared to the networks of environmental cooperation in later chapters. Nuclear projects tend to have a large number of members and are quite dense compared to other scientific networks; consequently, measuring the determinants of partner selection is more difficult.

A first assessment of the level of association between different partners in the NEST network is done through dendrograms. These figures (Figures 4.1, 4.2, and 4.3) summarize the degree of closeness among sets of countries through a technique known as agglomerative clustering. A dendrogram is a tree diagram that visualizes how actors cluster together. Actors "are compared for their 'similarity' or 'distance' from one another, and are grouped together with those to which they are closest or most similar" (Scott, 2000: 129). As a data reduction technique, dendrograms take as input a matrix of differences or similarities and progressively build trees of associations. We can think of these dendrograms as inverted trees, with countries as leaves that are connected to smaller branches, which in turn are connected to larger branches. The farther away the link in the dendrogram, the weaker the association between countries. Conversely, the closer the ties in the dendrogram, the stronger the degree of association between NEST state agencies.

Figure 4.1 describes the degree of association of NEST state agencies in the ARCAL network, which connects the countries of Latin America.

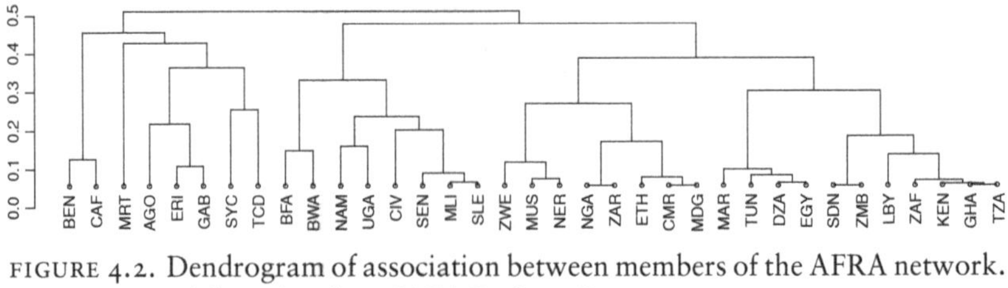

FIGURE 4.2. Dendrogram of association between members of the AFRA network.
Source: Own elaboration from IAEA Projects Data.

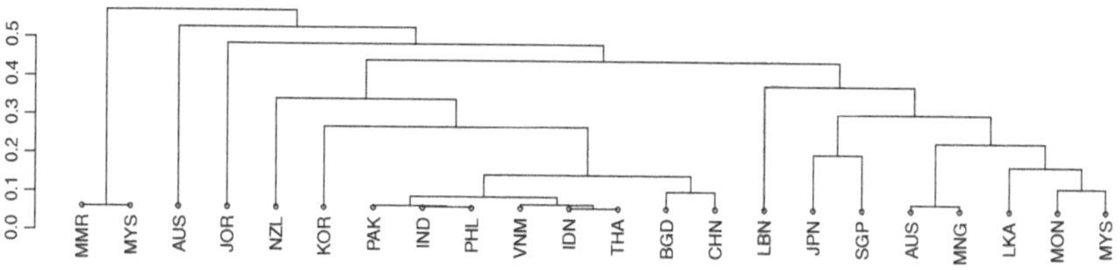

FIGURE 4.3. Dendrogram of association between members of the RCA network.
Source: Own elaboration from IAEA Projects Data.

When looking at the ARCAL network in detail, we find that the most developed programs (which in the affiliation matrix were also the most active project participants) are also tightly connected to each other. Peru and Uruguay, Argentina and Mexico (two of the three nuclear energy producers, who seek out each other in the more technically challenging projects), together with Cuba, Chile, and Brazil are all in a cluster of their own. Chilean nuclear bureaucrats have had historically close ties with the two nuclear giants of the subregion, Argentina and Brazil. However, the relationship with the Brazilian nuclear sector has been smoother as the two countries have no history of geopolitical conflict, as Chile has with Argentina. Cuba is one of the most proactive participants in the network, as explained earlier, partly due to the subsidies it received from the Soviet Union in R&D activities and its niche expertise in nuclear medicine. They are separate from the countries with intermediate programs such as Ecuador, Colombia, or Costa Rica, all of which are also more likely to interact within a separate cluster of lower-level nuclear collaborators. Finally, on the left of the dendrogram, from Barbados to Jamaica, there is a more loosely connected group of smaller countries from Central America and the Caribbean. Not surprisingly, the NEST programs of these states are underdeveloped.

Next, Figure 4.2 describes the degree of association of NEST agencies in the AFRA network. The dendrogram shows more structure on the more developed programs located on the right side of the graph. We can see that the most active agencies in the AFRA network are tightly grouped on the right of the dendrogram (South Africa, Kenya, Ghana, and Tanzania). Also on the right side of the dendrogram, but connected as a separate group, are countries from North Africa such as Egypt, Tunisia, and Morocco. The dendrogram provides evidence that agencies do not only associate by their level of activity in AFRA but also by other connectivity factors that are both regional and program specific. As in Latin America, the smaller and relatively poorer central African countries fall on the left side of the dendrogram, with considerably less structure.

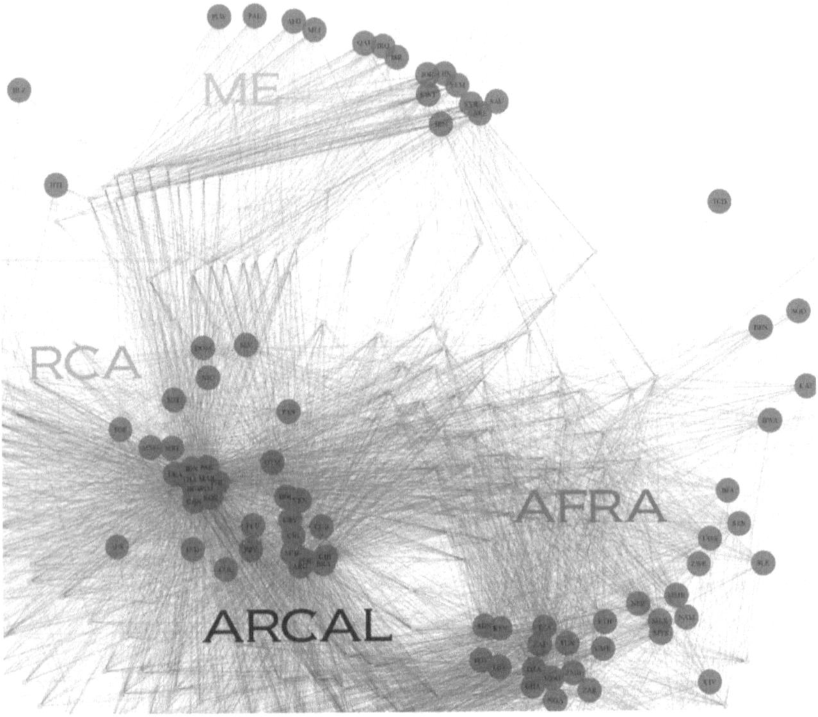

FIGURE 4.4. Network of inter-agency collaboration in NEST.
Note: Bipartite network of project collaboration in NEST projects. Fructerman-Reingold Layout with omitted project labels. Collaborative networks in Asia (RCA), Africa (AFRA), and Latin America (ARCAL). Middle East, Eastern Europe, and donor partners also participate in NEST projects, however marginally, and thus are represented in this network.

Finally, the data from the nuclear network in Asia (RCA) show weaker connectivity, as we can see by the staircase (or piling up) of countries. Interestingly, the two better delimited groups include Pakistan, India, and the Philippines on the one hand, and Vietnam, Indonesia, and Thailand, on the other. The fact that Pakistan and India are clustered together, in spite of historic conflict in all things related to nuclear matters, is of extraordinary interest. Indeed, joint participation as described by the dendrogram can only be explained by the relative similarity (homophily) in program development.

While dendrogram figures provide insight into the degree of association between different countries, what does the *whole* network look like? One characteristic of NEST collaboration networks, which differs from the environmental project data analyzed in Chapters 6 and 7, is its high density. A collective view of the collaborative networks is displayed in the bifurcated network of Figure 4.4, which depicts project-agency ties among countries within and across regions (inter-regional projects in NEST, however, are rare). In Figure 4.4, circles describe countries while the lines reflect the link between national agencies and projects.

Inter-agency networks of NEST projects show closer and more frequent ties among advanced nuclear programs from RCA and ARCAL. Asian programs, relatively more developed, are more closely connected to advanced programs in Latin America than to those of the Middle East and Africa, which are geographically closer.

The descriptive evidence is suggestive, showing that countries with more developed nuclear programs are more closely connected, collaborate more actively, and occupy more central locations in the NEST network. However, the descriptive information provides little insight into the determinants of inter-agency cooperation within the NEST networks of Africa, Latin America, and Asia. In the next chapter I introduce a variety of statistical models to explain international inter-agency cooperation.

Conclusion

This chapter introduced readers to networks forged by the participation of expert bureaucrats from sixty-nine nuclear state agencies in large, complex technical projects in NEST. For over twenty-five years, state experts have worked together across the Global South, assisted in part by the IAEA, which provides institutional support to the collaborative strategy of domestic state agencies. Cooperation among nuclear agencies from Africa, Asia, and Latin America has deepened expertise and spread new knowledge in numerous policy areas beyond nuclear development, such as energy generation, industrial development, medical science, agriculture, radiation safety, etc. This chapter has provided as well preliminary evidence of a link between the skill levels of domestic programs and inter-agency cooperation. Descriptive NEST project data showed that more technically advanced programs are more actively involved in the AFRA, ARCAL, and RCA networks. Finally, it also revealed that skill-rich nuclear programs appear to be more closely connected across regions, superseding geographic proximity and, arguably, historic enmities.

While the descriptive evidence is suggestive, the results are not yet conclusive. In the next chapter I conduct more extensive statistical analyses to test the main hypotheses of this book. I also use Exponential Random Graph Models (ERGM), which allow me to measure the important traits that facilitate cooperation and that explain partner selection in NEST networks.

Appendix

TABLE A.4.1. *Participating Countries in RCA, AFRA, and ARCAL*

RCA		AFRA		ARCAL	
Country Name	Country Code	Country Name	Country Code	Country Name	Country Code
Australia	AUS	Algeria	DZA	Argentina	ARG
Bangladesh	BGD	Angola	AGO	Bolivia	BOL
China	CHN	Benin	BEN	Brazil	BRA
India	IND	Botswana	BWA	Chile	CHL
Indonesia	IDN	Burkina Faso	BFA	Colombia	COL
Japan	JPN	Cameroon	CMR	Costa Rica	CRI
Mongolia	MNG	Central African Republic	CAF	Cuba	CUB
Myanmar	MMR	Democratic Rep of Congo	ZAR	Dominican Republic	DOM
New Zealand	NZL	Egypt	EGY	Ecuador	ECU
Pakistan	PAK	Eritrea	ERI	El Salvador	SLV
Philippines	PHL	Ethiopia	ETH	Guatemala	GTM
Republic of Korea	KOR	Gabon	GAB	Haiti	HTI
Singapore	SGP	Ghana	GHA	Jamaica	JAM
Sri Lanka	LKA	Ivory Coast	CIV	Mexico	MEX
Thailand	THA	Kenya	KEN	Nicaragua	NIC
Vietnam	VNM	Libyan Arab Jamahiriya	LBY	Panama	PAN
Nepal	NEP	Madagascar	MDG	Paraguay	PRY
		Mali	MLI	Peru	PER
		Mauritius	MUS	Uruguay	URY
		Morocco	MAR	Venezuela	VEN
		Namibia	NAM		
		Niger	NER		
		Nigeria	NGA		
		Senegal	SEN		
		Sierra Leone	SLE		
		South Africa	ZAF		
		Sudan	SDN		
		Tunisia	TUN		
		Uganda	UGA		
		United Republic of Tanzania	TZA		
		Zambia	ZMB		
		Zimbabwe	ZWE		

5

Explaining International Inter-Agency Cooperation in Nuclear Energy, Science, and Technology (NEST)

The two previous chapters depicted *how* state experts from agencies in nuclear energy, science, and technology (NEST) work with foreign peers on cross-national, technical projects, forging collaborative networks across the Global South. Interviews with expert bureaucrats and archival research uncovered an image of the state expert that conflicts with standard representations in the literature. Scholars of state politics depict the bureaucrat as inward-oriented professional who forges strategic relationships with political principals to maximize her budget. These beliefs about the bureaucrat's behavior are widespread in the social sciences, leading us to expect that civil servants will guard with zeal the scarce (and often insufficient) funds appropriated for their agencies and invest time and effort in their relationships with political principals that may facilitate greater access to resources.

Yet expert bureaucrats are increasingly outward-oriented, crossing borders to cooperate with foreign peers on large, complex projects that require them to commit funding and other precious resources over a significant amount of time. Further, as described in previous chapters, bureaucrats invest considerable time and effort to forge ties with *external* agents, such as scientists, foreign counterparts, and officials from international organizations. This outward-orientation of expert bureaucrats presents researchers with a puzzle, which has not been properly answered by the existing literature.

In Chapter 2, I laid out a series of hypotheses derived from my skill-driven theory of expert bureaucrats' behavior. These hypotheses explain inter-agency cooperation as a function of the skill-investment strategies adopted by expert bureaucrats when state funding declines.[1] In the present chapter, I offer empirical tests of the central argument of this book. I offer a variety of statistical analyses that provide a definitive answer to the question of *why* expert bureaucrats cross borders to cooperate. These findings support the three main hypotheses of the book: (1) fluctuations in government funding alter the international cooperative behavior of expert bureaucrats; (2) higher skill levels shape international inter-agency cooperation; and (3) skill homophily determines partner-selection among state experts in NEST.[2]

To test my skill-based theory of inter-agency cooperation, I use the cross-national co-sponsorship data described in Chapter 4. These data include all projects in NEST for each of the sixty-nine developing countries between the years 1980 and 2008.[3] The decision to participate in these collaborative projects is voluntary, as described in the previous chapter, and through them agencies can provide cross-national training to their personnel, create new (or maintain existing) regional laboratories, ensure access to new technologies, and develop a common knowledge management system for NEST data. These projects have applications that go beyond nuclear policy and contribute to advancing science and technology in agriculture, industry, public health, nuclear safety, and the protection of the environment.

Using NEST data, I will consider three different yet interrelated decision problems. First, I conceptualize the participation model as an individual agency choice to join NEST projects. That is, I estimate a variety of models that answer the question: *Why does a state agency decide to participate in NEST projects?*[4] I assume that participation may be decided independently from the pool of available partners, and that country agencies may differ in their mean propensity to engage in NEST projects as a

1 In Chapter 7 I test this argument against a large dataset of environmental project data.

2 Conversely, I expect international inter-agency cooperation to stagnate in years of plenty, as expert bureaucrats will have less incentive and time to partake in cross-national projects in NEST. Because of the loss of autonomy that comes with such cooperation, bureaucrats are willing to substitute local resources for foreign ones when budgets decline but are less eager to do so when local resources are plentiful.

3 See Table A.4.1 in Chapter 4 for a complete list of participating countries.

4 In the following empirical analyses, I use "country" and "agency" interchangeably, as only *one* state agency with primary jurisdiction in NEST policy represents the country in these international projects. Thus, for clarity of style, I have elected to forgo the sometimes cumbersome and opaque acronyms of state agencies (e.g., CNEA, for the National Commission of Atomic Energy) and use the name of the corresponding country instead (e.g., Argentina).

function of the resources they have as well as other domestic factors such as regime type or the level of trade openness.

Second, I conceptualize the participation decision as a partner selection problem. That is, I answer the question asked by expert bureaucrats: *Which agency is a suitable partner for my agency?* This second set of models is concerned with the type of traits that make a state agency more attractive as a potential partner. My theory proposes that agencies with bureaucrats that have higher skill levels are more attractive partners than agencies whose bureaucrats have comparatively low skills. If inter-agency collaboration allows bureaucrats to pool scarce resources, access training, and share know-how, partnering up with more skilled agencies provides higher returns to collaboration.

Finally, I conceptualize the participation decision as a network collaboration problem. That is, I answer the question: *What type of collective effort will provide the highest returns to the skills of my agency?* To answer this last question I estimate Exponential Random Graph Models (ERGM) for social network analysis, which allows me to measure cooperation as a decision within the full NEST network. Let me describe in greater detail the empirical roadmap for this chapter.

Modeling the Decision to Cooperate

The theory of inter-agency cooperation by expert bureaucrats purports an observable relationship between government spending and the decision to participate in the NEST network. This observable relationship results from incentives by expert bureaucrats in technology-intensive sectors to find alternatives to state-provided training when government resources falter. As demands to solve technically complex problems increase – e.g., such as climate change or the spread of human epidemics – and as the rate of technological change accelerates, professional development requires steady access to resources, training, and know-how.

Because investment in Research & Development (R&D) is particularly sensitive to the economic cycle, the effect of economic downturns on expert bureaucrats can be devastating. This is particularly relevant in developing economies, where R&D budgets fluctuate greatly and there are fewer private sector alternatives to further training or substitute investment. Consequently, while downturns reduce investment in R&D everywhere, developing countries are particularly sensitive to the deleterious effects of economic crises. Transgovernmental cooperation, whereby similar state agencies pool existing resources at low cost for participants, provides a strategy to upgrade skills and pool scarce resources when budgets decline.

The decision to participate in cross-national collaborative projects – e.g., such as those financed by the International Atomic Energy Agency – provides a window into the link between economic cycles and international bureaucratic networks. Indeed, the data from IAEA described in the previous chapter can be used in three different yet interrelated ways: First, each individual country makes decisions on whether they will embark on international projects to substitute for the lack of resources at home. In other words, we can measure and interpret the decision of each state agency to join the projects sponsored by IAEA. Given the status of the national program, the decision to collaborate provides insight into the needs of individual nuclear programs as well as the expectations bureaucrats have regarding distinct projects in NEST. For example, the data described in the previous chapter shows that NEST projects dealing with the environment are more frequently observed in Africa while nuclear projects dealing with energy supply are favored in Asia. The individual decision to participate connects program goals to other information, such as the type of project, the level of program development, and the type of resources and skills to be substituted.

Second, there is also the problem of partner selection. That is, the decision to collaborate may be explained by the appeal of particular partners that complement the existing resources of an agency, or offers particular sets of skills that could not be accessed without significant investment in new programs and technologies. In this case, the decision to participate is driven by the incentives to participate *with* state agencies that have special traits that contribute and strengthen the program.

Third, we need to account for the effect of the structure of the collaborative network. That is, the entire set of decisions to cooperate creates international inter-agency networks, with different countries taking on different positions across regions. Nuclear programs such as those of Argentina and Brazil have broader incentives to cooperate – i.e., more intense preferences to maintain skills and sustain investment – and are also a more suitable partner for other countries which are more likely to be at the receiving end of skills. From the decision to participate, we can understand the preferences of expert bureaucrats and the effect of economic cycles on program development. However, from the resulting nuclear cooperation networks, we can also learn a great deal about the relative importance of country programs and their linkages with programs at similar levels of development.

Which Skills?

The skill-driven theory of inter-agency cooperation proposed in this book expects that projects with higher potential to transfer skills will elicit more active cooperation. Here, I follow Becker's (1958) distinction between generalist and specialist skills, and argue that we should see general R&D projects dominate the network. Becker asserts that different types of skills entail different investment incentives for employers and employees. That is, employers are willing to pay the cost for specialized (i.e., firm-specific) but not general training, as the latter makes the worker more competitive and therefore more susceptible of being "poached" by competing firms (Thelen, 2004; Becker, 2009; Streeck, 2012). As a result, the worker is left with the choice of making the investment herself. Consequently, expert bureaucrats should favor NEST projects that offer skills that are more transferable, and thus more useful to professional development and career advancements in bureaucracies characterized by flexible approaches to problem-solving rather than rigid specialization. I expect the models presented below to show a positive correlation between participation and NEST projects with training in general skills.

This does not mean that specialization is not valued in the bureaucracies of the Global South. In fact, my theory assumes an initial level of expertise in order for an investment in skill upgrade to pay off. State experts are embedded in government agencies that originally provide the job-specific training to fulfill the job, but tend to withdraw when faced with economic contractions.

As described in Chapters 1 and 2, expert bureaucrats are civil servants with technical credentials who are employed by state institutions in charge of NEST policy. The expectation is, therefore, that the more professional and specialized the employing institution is, the stronger the incentive of the employee to keep her skills current, as technology-intensive institutions will put greater technical demands on their workforce. Thus, in this chapter I also examine the empirical evidence for a correlation between greater specialization and increased inter-agency cooperation.

Model Specification and the Data

Using NEST data, I estimate three separate sets of models that explain international inter-agency cooperation from the three perspectives described earlier: (1) the unilateral decision of a country agency to participate in a project; (2) the decision to select a particular partner (that is, the decision to participate *with* another country among all possible pairs of participating countries); and (3) the probability of observing a participation tie between any two pairs of countries conditional on the full collaborative network. The data provide within and across country variation.

The three different statistical strategies allow me to test the main hypotheses of the book as different decision problems. Consider, for example, the hypothesis that bureaucrats with higher skill are also the ones with the most incentive to collaborate in NEST projects. We should expect agencies with more skilled bureaucrats to participate in the network, as described by the first set of models. We should also anticipate that these agencies will make more appealing partners, as described by the second set of models. Finally, we should also expect bureaucrats with higher level of expertise to take on more central positions in the collaborative network. Therefore, higher levels of skills will generate incentives to participate more actively, to be sought after as a partner more frequently, and to gain greater centrality in the NEST network. Because partners with high skills have a greater propensity to collaborate and are also more likely to seek partners with equal or higher skills, program homophily will evolve in NEST networks. I expect the empirical results to reinforce the qualitative evidence presented in previous chapters. Next, I develop three sets of models that test the hypotheses of the book.

The Models

I estimate three different types of models. First, I estimate **participation models** that measure the likelihood that an agency will join a cross-national project in NEST sponsored by the IAEA. In these models the dependent variable takes the value of one if a country joins each of the NEST projects and zero otherwise. Second, I estimate **dyadic models** that measure the likelihood that a pair of countries will collaborate on a project. In these models the dependent variable takes the value of one if a pair of countries (dyad) joins a NEST project and zero otherwise. Third, I estimate **ERGM** for valued networks,[5] which seeks to explain the number of times that each pair of countries partner up within the collaborative

[5] In social network analysis (SNA), *valued* networks take as the dependent variable the *count* of edges between each pair of nodes. In this case, the dependent variable cooperation in NEST provides information regarding the number of times each pair of countries decides to become partners. Both occasional and frequent collaborators may share an edge (an instance of cooperation), but there is important information in the number of times countries decide to collaborate.

nuclear network. ERGM models for valued networks describe the number of times that pairs of countries cooperate (i.e., count model) while it accounts for network dependency in the data. Using these three different sets of models, this chapter explores the determinants of the decision to participate in transgovernmental projects, the decision to seek out a particular *type* of partner, and the decision to participate within the NEST network.

The Dependent Variables

The three different sets of models require different treatments of the data. In its simplest form, the decision to participate takes the value of one if a country joins a project and zero otherwise. In this case, I use logistic models to analyze the decision by a state nuclear agency to participate in cross-national projects in NEST. In the dyadic models, I estimate not just the decision to participate in a project but more importantly the choice of partners in each project. In this second set of models, the dependent variable takes the value of one if a pair of countries is jointly participating in a project and zero otherwise. This second dataset incorporates information about the degree of similarity among potential partners, i.e., similarities in scientific and technical endowments. Finally, the third set of models takes as dependent variable the affiliation matrix described in the previous chapter, where every cell describes the number of times that each pair of countries collaborated in projects.

Once more, the first set of models measure the decision to join a project, regardless of the decision made by other participants; the second set of models measures the decision to participate with each particular partner, conditional on common traits; and the third set of models describes the structure of collaboration with each partner within the network. The dependent variables of the first and second set of models, consequently, are binary, with the probability of participation – $Pr(Participation = 1|xb)$ – being estimated using a logistic specification for cross-sectional time series data. By contrast, the dependent variable in the third set of models is the valued-network of collaboration, with counts of joint participation for each pair of countries within the network.

I use original co-sponsorship data of cross-national projects in NEST adopted and implemented under regional agreements (ARCAL, AFRA, and RCA) from 1984 to 2008. The data are organized by country, year, and project, allowing for model specifications that control for within- and across-program variation in their decision to participate. For the first set of models, measuring program participation, the data covers 158 projects from Latin America (ARCAL), 119 projects from Africa (AFRA), and 186 projects from Asia (RCA) implemented between 1984 and 2008.[6] Because countries within each region are eligible to participate in these programs, the full dataset includes 4,266 observations in Latin America, 4,403 in Africa, and 6,138 observations in Asia. In all, models are estimated using this large cross-sectional dataset that covers 14,807 total observations across the globe. Given the cross-sectional time series nature of the data, a variety of different models were estimated, including specifications with fixed effects and random effects that control by year and country effects.

For the second set of models that tests for partner selection, I reshaped the participation dataset to create country dyads and measure homophily traits among potential partners. Reshaping the data to form dyadic pairs makes for a very large dataset, with over 498,000 observations. Consequently, models were estimated with clustered errors by dyadic partners (i.e., 3,000+ dyadic partners).

Finally, for the third set of models, the dependent variable is the affiliation matrix that describes the number of times that each country collaborates with another. Each of these alternative specifications yields comparable results while analyzing different aspects of the decision to collaborate.[7]

Independent Variables

The main covariates used to explain the decision to participate are: (i) the percent of **government spending** over total GDP; the (ii) type of skill (**project skill content**) that is promoted by a collaborative project (general or specific); the (iii) level of skills of the national academic community as described by their publication output in scientific journals (**number of scientific publications**);[8] and the (iv) type of state institution, whether

[6] Data also include Middle Eastern and East European countries, but their participation in NEST projects is recent and almost negligible compared to the rate of participation of African, Asian, and Latin American agencies.

[7] Like in Chapter 2, it should be noted that bureaucrats' skills (one of the independent variables of interest) offer *incentives* to pursue international inter-agency cooperation (dependent variable). As the choice to cooperate by state professionals in and of itself does not affect bureaucrats' existing levels of expertise at the time (perhaps in the future, but not at the time of the decision), the choice to cooperate by skilled actors does not entail endogeneity.

[8] The variable "number of scientific publications" is one of the few skill indicators at the country level which is available for most countries in the world.

technical or political (**technical agency**), and whether specialized in nuclear policy (**nuclear agency**). The measure of government spending (or government consumption) as a percent of GDP was obtained from the Penn World Table Version 7.1 and, as discussed above, should have a negative effect on project participation.

To create "Project Skill Content" and to test the human capital theorem, I classified all NEST projects based on the type of training they offer to members. Specifically, I am interested in whether projects help advance participants' skills along the dimensions of general/specific, more/less transferable skills. To get to the skill value for NEST bureaucrats, I consider the content of projects: if participation involves activities that shore up overall capacities and knowledge, they are considered *general*; if they advance training in particular techniques in well-defined policy areas, they are considered *specific*. Given this criterion, a project like ARCAL XCVII, *Improving Analytical Quality through Quality Assurance Training, Proficiency Testing and Certification of Matrix Reference Materials Using Nuclear Analytical and Related Techniques in the Latin American Nuclear Analytical Technique Network*, would be considered *general* in terms of its skills content. On the other hand, a project like ARCAL CVI, *Establishing and Maintaining Fruit Fly Free and Low Prevalence Areas in Central America, Panama and Belize, Using the Sterile Insect Technique*, would be classified as *specific*. The variable takes the value of one if the project transfers general skills and zero otherwise. Given the discussion in Chapter 2 regarding the appeal to expert bureaucrats of accessing more transferable (general) skills, I expect participation to increase in NEST projects that offer general (over special) training.

Engaging in collaboration is more critical for expert bureaucrats with higher skills. To account for the collaboration resulting from higher demands for skills, I consider the number of publications in referred journals of the national scientific community, as collected by the World Development Indicators (WDI) of the World Bank.[9] To measure the effect of the type of bureaucratic institution involved, I created two variables. The first one, technical agency, takes the value of one when the state agency with primary jurisdiction in NEST has a predominantly technical

[9] The World Bank defines the variable Scientific and Technical Journal Articles as "the number of scientific and engineering articles published in the following fields: physics, biology, chemistry, mathematics, clinical medicine, biomedical research, engineering and technology, and earth and space sciences" and is one of the few indicators of the size and quality of national scientific communities that has data for all the countries included in the present study. See http://data.worldbank.org/.

mission (not political), and zero otherwise. The second variable, nuclear agency, takes the value of one when the state agency is specialized in nuclear science and zero otherwise.

A number of controls were also included in the model, such as the **investment** and **consumption** percentages of GDP (World Penn Tables); the **number of** (international) **technical cooperation agreements** signed by the country; the total amount of **multilateral financing** allocated to each country in the year that the project was initiated; the size of the economy of a country as described by its **GDP per capita**; exposure to international trade (**openness**); the total **population**; and the **Polity** IV score with a range of −10 to 10, whereby fully autocratic regimes takes the value of −7 and fully democratic takes the value of 7 or above. The African Region is the baseline.

In the dyadic and network models, in order to measure the extent to which countries with similar levels of technological development are more likely to collaborate, I consider the absolute difference between the number of technical publications of the scientific communities (**difference in total scientific publications**) of each pair of countries $[j, z]$, that is: $ABS(NPublications[j] - NPublications[z])$. As controls, I also consider the absolute **difference in the number of technical cooperation agreements** signed by each pair of countries $[j, z]$, and the **difference in GDP per capita** of each pair of countries. I expect programs with similar scientific communities to be more likely to collaborate as expert bureaucrats seek to pool resources with true peers.

Participation Models: Discussion

Table 5.1 presents the results of the participation models, which estimate the probability that a country will join collaborative projects in NEST. In all three specifications, which include different sets of covariates, the key variables of interest consistently behave as expected. Government consumption is negative and statistically significant, with a 1 percent increase in government spending reducing the odds ratio of participation in NEST projects between 2 percent and 5 percent for every unit of increase in government spending. The effect is both statistically and substantively important. For example, between 1983 and 1989, government spending in Brazil declined by four points, from 19.2 percent of GDP to 14.97 percent, which should result in a 17-percent increase in the odds-ratio of collaborating in ARCAL projects. Separate models for each of the different regions provide further support for the proposed

TABLE 5.1. *Participation in Collaborative Projects in NEST*

	Model A	Model B	Model C
Technical agency	1.259***	0.399	−0.184
	(0.3014)	(0.5039)	(0.4915)
Nuclear agency	0.547**	0.646	0.477
	(0.2374)	(0.4144)	(0.3931)
Government spending (%)	−0.044***	−0.027***	−0.013**
	(0.0058)	(0.0076)	(0.0077)
Investment (%)	0.005	0.02***	0.013**
	(0.0049)	(0.0062)	(0.0065)
Consumption (%)	−0.001	0.007*	0.012***
	(0.0035)	(0.0044)	(0.0046)
Project skill content	0.592***	0.638***	0.593***
	(0.0443)	(0.0506)	(0.0515)
Multilateral financing		0.014	0.024*
		(0.0119)	(0.0129)
Number of scientific publications (LN)		0.264***	0.087
		(0.0558)	(0.0730)
Number of technical cooperation agreements		−0.223***	−0.319***
		(0.0779)	(0.0758)
Asia		−0.793	−1.115**
		(0.4865)	(0.4687)
Latin America		−2.599***	−2.61***
		(0.3633)	(0.3501)
GDP per capita (LN)			0.478***
			(0.1254)
Openness			−0.002
			(0.0019)
Population (LN)			0.374***
			(0.1396)
Polity score			0.005**
			(0.0025)
Constant	−0.941**	2.204	−1.696
	(0.4340)	(1.4722)	(2.1000)
Alpha (LN)	−0.11	0.633**	0.464*
	(0.1695)	(0.2660)	(0.2778)
N	11320	8842	8398
Groups	83	69	66

Note: Cross-sectional time series regression models with random effects by country. Baseline region is Africa. Standard errors in parentheses with confidence levels reported as follows: $^{*}p < 0.1$, $^{**}p < 0.05$, $^{***}p < 0.01$.

hypothesis, with government consumption having larger effects in Asia and more moderate ones in Africa.

Results also show support for a skill-driven theory of cooperation, whereby projects that transfer general skills (*skill content*) significantly increase the likelihood of participation in NEST. As expected, more technical agencies have higher rates of participation in NEST projects. In all models, the variable nuclear agency is positive and significant, showing that sectors that are led by a technical nuclear agency – rather than by other non-nuclear agencies – increase the odds of participation in NEST by approximately 80 percent.

The variables that describe the relative skills of the scientific community also provide support for the hypothesis that more developed nuclear programs are considerably more likely to participate in NEST projects. Each unit of increase in the number (log) of scientific publications increases the odds of participation in cross-national projects by 16 percent and 25 percent, *exp*(.154) and *exp*(.227)

Another important fact is that a variable that increases the availability of domestic resources reduces collaboration in NEST projects. That is the case for a surge in additional resources accrued through international technical cooperation agreements. In addition to these first findings and outside of the expectations derived from my skill-driven theory, there are some interesting results with regards to some of the control variables. Table 5.1 shows that larger, more democratic, and more economically developed countries are more active collaborators in the NEST networks as shown by the population, polity, and GDP per capita variables. However, while the effects of population and GDP per capita are both substantively and statistically significant, the substantive effect of democracy in contrast is rather small.

The first set of models presented in Table 5.1 shows that the decision state agencies make to participate in NEST projects is substantively and statistically shaped by the availability of domestic resources, the level of development of the scientific community, and the type of skill transfer from the different projects. Results are robust to a variety of specifications and remain statistically significant when measures of overall development – i.e., GDP per capita – are included in the equation. Next, I analyze the decision to participate as a partner selection problem, where bureaucrats are not only interested in joining NEST projects but also considering which peer agencies to join in those projects.

Dyadic Models: Discussion

Participation models measure the effect of government spending, skills, and other covariates in the decision to participate in NEST projects. However, they do not explain why some agencies are more sought after as a potential partner. To test for partner selection in nuclear collaboration, Table 5.2 estimates dyadic models that take the value of one if a pair of countries works together in a NEST project and zero otherwise. Different from the previous models, the dyadic specifications incorporate information about the relative similarity/dissimilarity between potential partners. As described earlier, the models include all covariates from Table 5.1 and three new terms that test for homophily with measures of inter-country differences in total number of scientific publications, international technical agreements, and GDP per capita. While these independent variables are based on the difference for each dyad of state agencies, they can be used as inter-country measures of similarities (i.e., homophily) by interpreting them correctly (e.g., the greater the difference between two countries, the less likely they should be willing to cooperate; conversely, the lesser the difference, the more they should seek out each other).

The proposed specifications seek to test not only the effects of government spending and skills on cooperation, but also to test whether scientific communities that are similar (dissimilar) are more (less) likely to cooperate. Again, dyadic models testing for homophily effects ("birds of a feather flock together") are derived from the expectation that foreign bureaucrats who share common traits will benefit from working together.

Table 5.2 presents three models of joint collaboration: a restricted model measuring the effect of government spending (Model A); a "skill" model, testing for the effect of government spending as well as for the relative skill endowment of the expert agency (Model B); and an unrestricted specification which includes also the three similarity/dissimilarity terms. I expect differences in the level of development of the national scientific community (as described by differences in the number of its publications) to reduce cooperation. I also expect differences in the adoption of international technical treaties to reduce cooperation. Finally, I consider differences in GDP per capita as a placebo control, given that it should not affect the level of cooperation.

Overall, models in Table 5.2 are consistent with those presented in Table 5.1. The effect of government spending on joint collaboration is negative and statistically significant, once again supporting expectations of a substitution strategy of international inter-agency cooperation

TABLE 5.2. *Joint Collaboration in NEST Projects*

		Model A	Model B	Model C
Spending	Government spending (%)	−0.056***	−0.029***	−0.018***
		(0.0010)	(0.0012)	(0.0014)
	Investment (%)	0.002***	0.014***	0.014***
		(0.0008)	(0.0011)	(0.0014)
	Consumption (%)	−0.008***	0.008***	0.011***
		(0.0006)	(0.0007)	(0.0009)
	Asia	−0.403***	0.235***	−0.207**
		(0.0571)	(0.0575)	(0.0809)
	Latin America	−0.686***	−0.189***	−0.293***
		(0.0642)	(0.0485)	(0.0572)
Demand for Skills	Technical agency		1.169***	0.744***
			(0.0629)	(0.0827)
	Nuclear Agency		0.207***	0.091
			(0.0481)	(0.0570)
	Project skill content		0.627***	0.777***
			(0.0089)	(0.0107)
	Number of scientific publications (LN)		0.226***	0.129***
			(0.0084)	(0.0141)
Access to Resources	Multilateral financing		0.009***	0.007**
			(0.0020)	(0.0032)
	Number of technical cooperation agreements		−0.103***	−0.183***
			(0.0132)	(0.0159)
	Per capita GDP (LN)			0.289***
				(0.0253)
	Openness			−0.0002
				(0.0004)
	Population (LN)			0.431***
				(0.0249)
	Polity score			0.0076***
				(0.0020)
Homophily	Difference in total scientific publications (LN)			−0.098***
				(0.0098)
	Difference in multilateral financing			0.01***
				(0.0023)
	Difference in per capita GDP			0.004
				(0.0221)
	Difference in technical cooperation agreements			−0.07
				(0.0606)
	Constant	1.019***	−0.933***	−5.216***
		(0.0633)	(0.2368)	(0.3899)

TABLE 5.2. (continued)

	Model A	Model B	Model C
Sigma (u)	0.585***	−0.259***	−0.331***
	(0.0285)	(0.0357)	(0.0422)
Rho	0.353***	0.19***	0.179***
	(0.0065)	(0.0055)	(0.0062)
N	489650	286260	198750
Groups	3058	2244	1676
LogLik	−265488	−163074.09	−113603.42

Note: Cross-sectional time series regression models with random effects by collaborative dyad. Baseline region is Latin America. Standard errors in parentheses with confidence levels reported as follows: $^{*}p < 0.1$, $^{**}p < 0.05$, $^{***}p < 0.01$.

for domestic funding. Every 1 percent increase in government spending decreases the odds of collaboration between −5.4% in Model A to −1.8 in Model C. Countries with technical agencies and/or nuclear agencies are also more likely to cooperate, with the effect being very large and statistically significant for the technical agency and more modest for the nuclear one.

Parameters that describe the demand for skills are large and statistically significant, with projects that transfer general skills being more likely to elicit cooperation and more developed scientific communities being more active partners. Indeed, the total number of scientific publications (LN) of a community increases the odds of cooperation by 25 percent in Model B – i.e. *exp*(.226) – and 14 percent in Model C – i.e., *exp*(.129). Model results for the homophily parameters are in the expected direction, although only the parameter describing differences in the number of scientific publications reaches statistical significance. A one-unit increase in the logged differences in scientific publications between each pair of countries [*i*, *j*] results in a decline of almost 9 percent in the odds of cooperation.[10] By contrast, the variable "difference in technical cooperation agreements" is negative but statistically insignificant. As expected, differences in GDP per capita are of no consequence for cooperative behavior once we control for overall income effects. In all, results of the model strongly confirm expectations in regards to government spending and demands for skills. Model

10 This variable measures the log of the absolute differences in the rate of publications by the scientific community of each country as measured by the World Bank and described in the previous section. The variable describing the difference in the total number of scientific publications of countries [*i*, *j*] is computed as: $DifPub_{[i,j]} = LN(abs(Publications_i - Publications_j))$, with a range of [0,10.95].

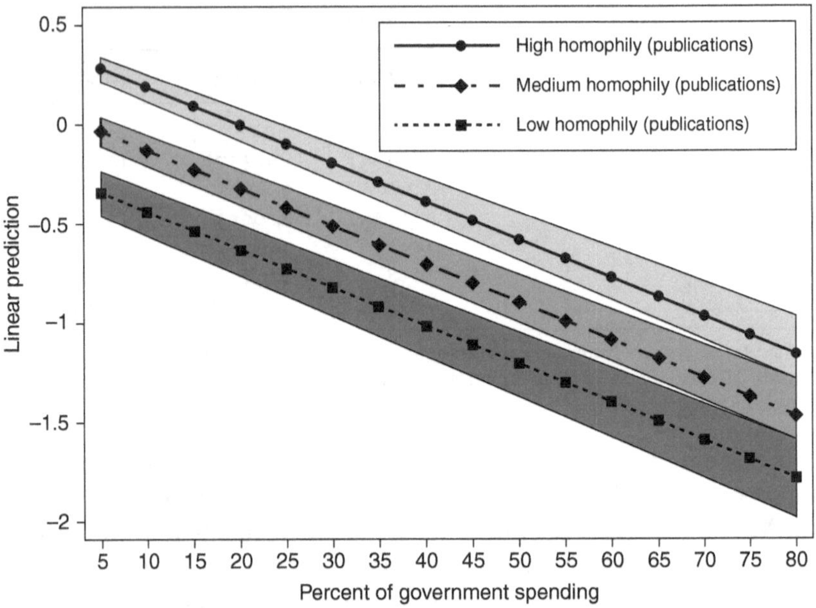

FIGURE 5.1 Effect of government spending and homophily on participation in collaborative nuclear projects.
Note: Plots describe marginal effects of government spending on the decision to participate in cross-national NEST projects with all other covariates set to their means. The different lines reflect differences in inter-agency homophily.

results also show that more populated, wealthier, democratic countries are more likely to cooperate in nuclear projects. The effect is large for populated and wealthier countries and more modest for democratic ones.

Figure 5.1 describes the marginal effect of government spending on program participation for three different levels of homophily (low, medium, and high).[11] As it is possible to observe, the effect of government spending is negative and statistically significant, with joint participation for a pair of countries being more likely when their respective programs are at similar levels of development. At very low levels of government spending (5 percent), the probability of joint participation for countries with very similar scientific communities is roughly

[11] High homophily sets the log of the absolute difference in scientific publications equal to one, medium homophily sets the value of the variable equal to four, and low homophily sets the variable equal to nine.

57 percent i.e., $Pr(1|x) = invlogit(.27) = 0.57$. By contrast, the probability of joint participation when there are significant differences in program homophily is seventeen points lower, roughly 40 percent i.e., $Pr(1|x) = invlogit(-.4) = 0.401$.

Exponential Random Graph Models (ERGM): Discussion

The participation and dyadic models show that declines in government spending, level of program development, and inter-agency homophily are important determinants of program participation. I now measure the extent to which these covariates explain collaboration in the nuclear networks of RCA, ARCAL, and AFRA. The affiliation matrices as well as the network plots were discussed at length in the previous chapter.

To estimate the number of ties between each pair of countries, I take advantage of new developments in social network analysis and estimate ERGM for valued networks. These models allow researchers to describe the number of edges (collaborative instances) between each pair of countries as a function of covariates and by taking into account network structure.

Table 5.3 describes the result of the ERGM for valued networks, explaining the number of times that each pair of countries collaborated as a function of the covariates used in the dyadic model. The underlying Poisson distribution of the valued ERGM allows readers to interpret the coefficients as logged units of change in the number of times that each pair of country collaborates. For example, Model C in Table 5.3 shows that each percent increase in government spending results in a −0.9 percent decline in the number of instances of collaboration between countries e.g., $\exp(-0.01009) = 0.98996$.

As in previous models, we consistently observe that higher levels of skills, positive coefficients for the number of scientific publications, technical and nuclear state agencies are associated with higher collaboration. A 1 percent increase in the total number of scientific publications results in an 8.3 percent increase in the probability of cooperation. Similarly, a program led by a nuclear state agency increases the number of collaborative instances by 25.8 percent.

Homophily estimates also strongly support the proposed theory, with larger differences in the number of publications of a pair of agencies reducing the number of instances of collaboration. The effects are large, with every unit of increase in dissimilarity yielding reductions from 9.5 percent in model A to 3.3 percent in model C. Larger differences in the overall GDP per capita level also result in large and significant

TABLE 5.3. *Exponential Random Graph Models of Nuclear Cooperation, Valued Network*

		Model A	Model B	Model C
Spending	Government spending (%)		−0.00835***	−0.01009***
			(0.0003)	(0.0003)
	GDP per capita (LN)			−0.13964***
				(0.0032)
Demand for Skills	Number of scientific publications (LN)	0.05094***	0.10269***	0.08528***
		(0.0020)	(0.0010)	(0.0016)
	Technical agency			0.08481***
				(0.0084)
	Nuclear agency			0.23411***
				(0.0068)
	Multilateral financing			0.04413***
				(0.0017)
	Number of technical cooperation agreements			0.01362
				(0.0024)
Homophily	Difference in total scientific publications (LN)	−0.10248***	−0.05319***	−0.03355***
		(0.0020)	(0.0018)	(0.0021)
	Difference in GDP per capita		−0.15594***	−0.12440***
			(0.0041)	(0.0041)
	Same region (ARCAL)	0.02805	0.26991***	0.37712***
		(0.0174)	(0.0129)	(0.0125)
	Same region (AFRA)	0.02756*	0.39781***	0.29493***
		(0.0111)	(0.0094)	(0.0121)
	Same region (RCA)	−0.01250	0.10752***	0.17385***
		(0.0110)	(0.0107)	(0.0118)
	Sum (constant)	−0.00835***	−0.00835***	−0.00835***
		(0.0003)	(0.0003)	(0.0003)
	DF	4278	4278	4278
	BIC	−163454	−168838	−174424
	AIC	−163492	−168889	−174507

Note: ERGM estimates of collaboration in valued-network, with a Poisson distribution. Models estimated using CRAN ergm.count in R 3.0.2.

declines in the number of instances of collaboration. In all, the more the programs diverge from each other, the less they collaborate. Finally, mix-and-match results show that, once we control for all covariates, the network of collaboration is denser in Latin America (ARCAL) and sparser in Asia (RCA).[12]

[12] Data and alternative specifications can be requested from the author.

Conclusion

As shown in this book so far, expert bureaucrats in the Global South are networking in new and resourceful ways to cope with widespread government spending cuts, which tend to affect disproportionately R&D budgets. Inter-agency cooperation has enabled the implementation of projects that tend to be low in costs but high on innovation.

Analyses in this chapter lend support for the hypotheses that inter-agency cooperation provides expert bureaucrats with mechanisms to update and upgrade their skills when state resources falter. First, this chapter shows that when government spending decreases expert bureaucrats intensify international cooperation with peers. Second, model results show that more specialized programs in countries with higher skill endowments are more likely to collaborate and that bureaucrats favor projects that provide general skills, which offer the highest returns for a career in the bureaucracy. Finally, collaboration is more likely to develop between true peer programs with similar levels of development (i.e., homophily). The quantitative analyses in this chapter are consistent with the qualitative evidence drawn from numerous interviews with expert bureaucrats. The statistical results provide ample support to the archival research and elite interviews, showing that access to international resources to substitute for declining budgets has a significant impact on the behavior of expert agencies in NEST.

6

International Inter-Agency Cooperation in the Protection of the Global Environment

The previous three chapters examined the effects of skills on international inter-agency cooperation in the field of Nuclear Energy, Science, and Technology (NEST). The present chapter, as well as the next two, will test my theory of the expert bureaucrat in the field of global environmental protection. I will describe the largest network of cooperation in environmental policy forged by state agencies across the Global South. Similar to cooperation in NEST, environmental experts in Africa, Asia, and Latin America work together with regional and global peers on complex projects in Biodiversity, Climate Change, Chemicals, International Waters, Land Degradation, Sustainable Forest Management, and Ozone Layer Depletion. Drawing from three different sources of data – in-depth interviews with expert bureaucrats, archival research, and twenty years of project data from the Global Environment Facility – this chapter explains how state experts work with foreign peers to design, adopt, and implement complex projects under extremely constricted budgets and how, by participating in these projects, they gain access to new skills, knowledge, and best practices.

The chapter also addresses vital questions about the structure and organization of international inter-agency cooperation in the protection of the global environment. It examines the role played by International Organizations (IOs), specifically the Global Environment Facility (GEF) and the United Nations Environmental Program (UNEP), in facilitating cooperation in this area. Different from the International Atomic Energy Agency, the GEF was established as a financial mechanism to help implement the most important multilateral treaties in the protection of the global environment, like the United Nations Framework Convention on

Climate Change (UNFCCC), and to help adopt mitigation and adaptation policies. This second, critical mission of the GEF is fulfilled by partially funding large technical projects through grants at the individual country, region, and global levels.

Through its regional and global grants program, the GEF helps fund international cooperation. Consequently, this chapter and the following one will analyze how donor money shapes inter-agency cooperation. As the GEF data on funding is disaggregated by source (i.e., GEF grant and country contribution), I can measure the incentive effect of donor aid on project participation and whether it lessens the effect of skills on international cooperation. This will help me test with precision whether outside funding helps drive expert bureaucrats' search for skills.

Comparing Environmental and NEST Networks

As noted in previous chapters, there are differences between the environmental and NEST sectors. In particular, domestic environmental agencies across the Global South have access to a donor (namely, the GEF) that allocates resources that help subsidize cooperation on environmental projects. In contrast to IAEA, GEF has disbursed billions of dollars through its grants program to countries of the Global South and emerging markets. Furthermore, as the present chapter will show, the networks forged by environmental and NEST bureaucrats differ in their density, whereas the GEF network is less dense than the nuclear one. I posit that this difference results from varying costs of skill upgrading across sectors, because the type of state investment required to ensure cutting-edge expertise in NEST is much higher than the required investment in the environmental sector.[1] State agencies with high-end expertise in NEST are fewer and rarer across the Global South, and consequently, I expect them to be sought by a larger number of partners. Further, because my theory predicts advanced agencies to be more sensitive to declines in funding, I expect them to be more active participants in the NEST network. Given all this, I anticipate NEST bureaucrats to forge very dense networks.

Acquiring skills for environmental protection is a less taxing enterprise. The demands of environmental projects are also more diverse, as there

[1] To get a sense of the cost disparity between the two sectors, think of the type of equipment and technology required to furnish a laboratory in NEST, especially at the high end of the skill spectrum (e.g., a nuclear reactor or a particle accelerator) in addition to costly security protections which need to be updated on a regular basis. In contrast, most of the training environmental scientists undergo does not require expensive equipment or significant investments in safeguards.

are many different niche areas of expertise across environmental sciences (such as climatology, hydrology, forestry, and biology). Given the higher variation in the expertise required for the protection of the environment, as well as the differences in how skills concentrate across agencies, I expect environmental networks to be less dense. Greater diversity in the specialization of green agencies across the Global South should lead to fewer dominant players and, consequently, fewer recurrent partnerships.

Finally, the two policy areas also differ in the timing of their institutional evolution. In contrast to the development of bureaucratic capacity in NEST, the expansion of state capacity in environmental policy is more recent and strongly driven by the need of government to respond to direct societal demands.[2] In short, "the environmental movement and subsequent social change created the demand for environmental expertise to *grow rapidly* and provided a basis for new elite of risk professionals" (Evetts, Mieg, & Felt, 2006: 120).[3] Accordingly, I offer next a brief description of the evolution of the Argentine state environmental agency as an example of rapid institutional expansion, and the incentives its experts face to form networks outside Argentina in order to access additional resources and skills. The chapter continues with a profile of the GEF and an in-depth description of the network of bureaucrats working on cross-national projects for the protection of the global environment.

Incentives to Cooperate in the Protection of the Environment

International inter-agency cooperation in the protection of the global environment has grown exponentially in recent years.[4] This fact is not completely surprising since a persistent characteristic of environmental crises, seen over the past two decades, is that few are contained neatly within national jurisdictions. Indeed, the most salient environmental challenges go well beyond national boundaries: the effects of pollution in shared rivers and waterways, climate change, deforestation, and the deterioration of biodiversity to name a few, rarely stop at political borders. Given how many environmental problems affect more than one country, international cooperation to minimize the degradation of the natural world is key – especially among neighbors (Ostrom, 2008; Agrawal,

[2] There are some exceptions, particularly in the area of forestry, whereby the government of some countries like India and the United States attempted to develop state capacity before the existence of nuclear power. See Agrawal (2005) and Carpenter (2001).

[3] Italics are mine.

[4] This regulatory expansion can be seen across policy areas (Jordana, Levi-Faur, & i Marín, 2011).

2014). At the same time, few policy areas possess greater incentives to pass on remediation costs to others (Hoel, 1992; Neumayer, 2001).[5] Despite considerable challenges, international cooperation for the protection of the global environment is on the rise (Rohrschneider & Dalton, 2002; Bauer, 2006; Hicks, Parks, Roberts, & Tierney, 2008). Since the 1992 Earth Summit, increases in cooperation have been particularly noteworthy among environmental agencies in the developing world.[6] International cooperation, however, is not without costs to the bureaucrat and her agency. It requires investing scarce resources in organizational adaptation and change, reduces policy discretion, and entails negotiating *inter-agency* the allocation of shared resources.

Still, domestic bureaucrats, preoccupied with policy discretion and budgetary independence, often forfeit policy autonomy and internalize coordination costs to further cooperation with foreign peers. One reason for this stems from the rapid expansion of functions and responsibilities environmental state agencies have taken on in recent years. Originally created as small administrative divisions with limited policy jurisdictions, environmental agencies have developed into complex organizations that carry out a multitude of activities (e.g., regulation, monitoring, enforcement, evaluation, and research) and hold stakes in numerous policy domains. Nowadays, national environmental agencies may oversee policy in areas that transcend the management and protection of the natural world, such as public health, food security, and the rights of indigenous peoples. Over time, the expansion of state environmental regulations has required increasing agency funding and the incorporation of expert personnel with higher levels of professional training and technical skills (Andonova & Mitchell, 2010).

The Development of Expert Environmental Agencies: An Example

The forty-year evolution of the national environmental agency in Argentina (Secretary of the Environment and Sustainable Development,

[5] Neumayer asserts: "As regards most international environmental problems, the affected countries are confronted with a basic Prisoner's Dilemma. The following situation is illustrative: all countries have an interest in reducing harmful emissions, and all countries are better off with international environmental cooperation, but each of them also has an incentive to free-ride on the others' efforts and to enjoy the benefits of abatement without incurring any of the costs of emission reduction" (Neumayer, 2001: 124).

[6] This cooperation has often been groomed by international organizations, intergovernmental treaty secretariats, and international donors, as I discuss further. See Bauer (2006), Hicks, Parks, Roberts, & Tierney (2008), and Biermann & Siebenhüner (2009).

or SAyDS in Spanish) illustrates how environmental bureaucrats' incentives to acquire skills and access funding have changed over time. Similar to environmental agencies in other developing countries, the SAyDS evolved from an institution with few well-defined functions and a small staff into a large agency with broad responsibilities that demand higher levels of technical expertise from its staff (Hochstetler, 2002; Gutierrez & Isuani, 2013). Created as a national secretariat for natural resources in 1973 by President Juan D. Perón, its institutional and budgetary status changed dramatically over the years (Hochstetler, 2002; Gutierrez & Isuani, 2013).[7]

For most of its history, the SAyDS lingered as an under-secretariat financed with discretionary resources from the national executive, and it was only in 2002 that the Argentine National Congress enacted legislation to guarantee the agency an earmarked budget, with the mission to protect and regulate the natural resources of the country (Gutiérrez & Isuani, 2014).[8] Despite recurrent institutional crises and endemic financial instability, the Argentine environmental sector steadily expanded both its jurisdictional claims to new policy areas as well as the numbers of its scientific personnel. More recently, a few persistent and nationally salient crises (like the worsening pollution of the Matanza River and the corruption scandals surrounding its failed cleanup attempts) raised the profile of the Argentine agency and gave a renewed urgency to increasing its existing resources (Alcañiz & Gutiérrez, 2009; Auyero & Swistun, 2009).[9]

When the Secretariat was created in the early 1970s, most of its activities concentrated on greening industrial production, which included

7 See www.pagina12.com.ar/diario/dialogos/21-227579-2013-08-26.html.

8 See www.greenpeace.org/argentina/es/informes/ley-de-presupuestos-m-nimos-de.

9 The Matanza River, also known as the Riachuelo, separates the capital city from the largest national steel belt in the Province of Buenos Aires. It is one of the most polluted rivers in the country (and in the world, see www.blacksmithinstitute.org/new-report-cites-the-world-s-worst-polluted-places.html). During the administration of President Menem in the 1990s, funds were appropriated for a cleanup in record time. But the projected multi-million-dollar cleanup did not occur and instead, the head of the environmental agency was charged with corruption and misappropriation of public funds. The mishandling of millions of dollars slated for remediation of the Matanza River brought into sharp relief the plight of the people living on its shores and the need for greater professionalization of the SAyDS. Another crisis that brought national attention to the SAyDS and an increased awareness of the need for greater resources (professional and monetary) was the conflict stemming from the construction of two pulp mills by Uruguay on the eastern shore of the shared Uruguay River, whereupon the agency was given additional resources, and a leader of the protests against the paper factories (an environmental lawyer), was appointed the new head of the agency (Alcañiz & Gutiérrez, 2009).

non-environmental quality controls of industrial imports and monitoring working conditions for labor.[10] At present, the SAyDS looks very different. It has over thirty administrative divisions that regulate critical environmental policy areas, such as climate change, biodiversity, desertification, water, and the environmental rights of indigenous peoples to mention a few.[11] With over sixty active programs and projects, including the National Administrative Center of Forests and the National Office for Water, the need for up-to-date skills is critical.[12]

To help supplement the scarce resources available at their home agencies, environmental bureaucrats seek cooperation opportunities abroad. Most green state agencies in the Global South, like the Argentine SAyDS, have "an office of projects of international financing" to help find opportunities for cooperation and external funding "like the ones with GEF."[13] A senior Model Forest officer of the Argentine Environmental Secretariat explained how she and her colleagues look for training opportunities outside the state. For example, they remain active in the Ibero-American Model Forest Network. But as this network does not always offer the "technical level that you would expect," these state experts also seek to participate at low cost in the prestigious Tropical Agricultural Research and Higher Education Center (CATIE) of Costa Rica and in programs sponsored by Japan and Germany.[14]

As discussed at length in previous chapters, expert bureaucrats have incentives to increase their operational budgets in order to fulfill their assigned responsibilities and, most important, to invest in their professional skills. Networking abroad and accessing foreign skills in turn increases their career prospects and market value. Training adds value to the professional portfolio of the state expert, and it can help advance her career within or outside the bureaucracy. A liaison for West Africa with the GEF and the United Nations Environment Programme observed: "Once you train someone, they become highly marketable."[15]

[10] See http://ambientalabp.blogspot.com/2013/08/entrevista-la-primer-secretaria-de.html and http://www.pagina12.com.ar/diario/dialogos/21-227579-2013-08-26.html.

[11] See www.ambiente.gov.ar/?idseccion=195.

[12] See www.ambiente.gov.ar/?aplicacion=proypro.

[13] Senior Director of the Secretariat for the Environment and Sustainable Development (SAyDS). Interview with the author in Buenos Aires, Argentina, April 2013.

[14] Senior bureaucrat from the Directorate of Forestry at the SAyDS. Interview with the author in Buenos Aires, Argentina, January 2014.

[15] Senior Programme Officer, Climate Change at the United Nations Environmental Programme. Interview with the author in Nairobi, Kenya, March 2013.

Inter-Agency Networks in Environment: The Role of the Global Environment Facility

There are many institutional settings that facilitate cooperation between domestic environmental bureaucrats and their foreign peers.[16] Here I focus on the collaborative network sponsored by the Global Environment Facility (GEF). GEF partially funded cooperation constitutes the largest global network of environmental state agencies.

The GEF was created by the World Bank and donor governments from the Organisation for Economic Co-operation and Development (OECD) in 1991 with an endowment of one billion dollars (Young, 2002; Hicks, Parks, Roberts, & Tierney, 2008; Andler, 2009). The purpose of the organization was to help fund environmental protection and remediation policies in developing countries as well as to serve as a financial mechanism for the implementation in the Global South of several UN treaties. Compliance with these agreements, the Convention on Biological Diversity (CBD); United Nations Framework Convention on Climate Change (UNFCCC); Stockholm Convention on Persistent Organic Pollutants (POPs); the UN Convention to Combat Desertification (UNCCD); and the Minamata Convention on Mercury, was expected to be onerous.[17] Thus, "some sort of fund was needed to persuade Southern governments to agree to the conservation and constraints on their national development implied in the Conventions" (Young, 2002: 6).

The GEF is the largest public fund in the world for environmental grants to developing and emerging economies in the areas of Biodiversity, Mitigation and Adaption to Climate Change, Chemicals, International Waters, Land Degradation, Sustainable Forest Management, and Ozone Layer Depletion. It has assisted in the funding of 5,435 environmental projects at the country, region, and global level since its creation in 1991.[18] The number of countries in collaborative projects ranges from two to sixty, with close to two-thirds of collaborative projects, including regional partners (346 grants), and the other third, including global partners (seventy-seven grants). GEF grants cover partial project

[16] Examples of institutions that foster such cooperation are the global Intergovernmental Panel on Climate Change (IPCC) and the South American Mercosur Environmental Information System (SIAM). In the last two decades, the number of coordinating institutions has been steadily increasing. See Biermann and Siebenhüner (2009) for an analysis of these organizations.

[17] Also, the GEF assists in the implementation of the Montreal Protocol on Substances That Deplete the Ozone Layer in the countries of Eastern Europe. See www.thegef.org.

[18] See www.thegef.org.

costs, leaving national environmental agencies to procure their share (i.e., co-financing) of the funding. Since its creation, GEF has disbursed directly $13.5 billion in individual, regional, and global grants to about 155 states, which include all developing countries as well as the former Soviet republics. GEF funds the "incremental cost" of "transforming a project with national benefits into one with global environmental benefits" (Hicks, Parks, Roberts, & Tierney, 2008: 206). In turn, these countries have provided co-financing for almost $65 billion. The organization awards full-size (over $2 million) and medium-size grants (up to $2 million) to individual countries, a group of countries within its designated regions (Africa, Asia, Latin America, Oceania, and most recently, Eastern Europe), or a group of countries across one or more regions. In this book I focus on GEF regional and global projects.

What kind of projects does GEF help finance? The two main focal areas of GEF grants are biodiversity and climate change. As Table 6.1 shows, when disaggregated by region and project type, all three regions of interest have a majority of projects in these two areas. Latin America has the greatest concentration in projects that attempt to stop the

TABLE 6.1. *Projects by Policy Area and Region*

	Eastern Europe	Latin America	Africa	Asia	Oceania	Total
Biodiversity	206	436	628	330	78	1,678
(%)	22.91	39.14	31.86	29	24.92	30.87
Climate change	200	288	496	352	110	1,446
(%)	22.25	25.85	25.16	30.93	35.14	26.61
International waters	220	98	224	162	52	756
(%)	24.47	8.8	11.36	14.24	16.61	13.91
Land degradation	53	28	188	34	3	306
(%)	5.9	2.51	9.54	2.99	0.96	5.63
Multi-focal area	97	196	236	170	43	742
(%)	10.79	17.59	11.97	14.94	13.74	13.65
Ozone depleting subst	59	0	0	0	0	59
(%)	6.56	0	0	0	0	1.09
POPs	64	68	199	90	27	448
(%)	7.12	6.1	10.1	7.91	8.63	8.24
Total	899	1,114	1,971	1,138	313	5,435
(%)	100	100	100	100	100	100

Source: Global Environmental Fund. Focal areas described in this table report on country, regional, and global projects.

deterioration of diverse ecosystems with 40 percent of its grants in Biodiversity, followed by Africa, with 32 percent, and Asia, with 29 percent. Given that the vast majority of participating countries across the three regions have important agricultural sectors, which need to balance economic development and environmental sustainability, this concentration is not surprising. The second largest concentration is in Climate Change. Here, Asian environmental bureaucrats come in first, with 31 percent of their projects in Climate Change adaptation and remediation, followed by Latin America (26 percent) and Africa (25 percent). It should be noted that Oceania, another region that is eligible for GEF grants, has the highest overall concentration in this area, with 35 percent of all its projects focused on Climate Change. This is consistent with the fact that island states are more vulnerable to global warming and changing weather patterns than continental states, and consequently have a greater incentive to invest in remediation skills and policy. In addition, these two areas receive greater attention by GEF because it is the financial mechanism of Biodiversity and Climate change conventions. GEF also helps fund large projects that focus on multiple environmental issues (known as "multifocal areas").

For example, one of the largest regional projects in Latin America – with a budget of US$ 10,730,000 in GEF funding and US$ 50,562,000 in co-financing – includes components on International Waters, Land Degradation, Climate Change, and Biodiversity.[19] This project, involving the five countries of the La Plata River basin (Argentina, Bolivia, Brazil, Paraguay, and Uruguay), advances an integrated water management approach in the riparian zones of the basin and adopts capacity-building measures aimed at climate change prediction.[20] Like the multifocal project of the La Plata Basin, most projects are technology-intensive and cover a wide range of themes, such as coral reef rehabilitation, investment in renewable energy, and creating wildlife and biological corridors. GEF grants typically include explicit goals for the adoption of common practices across borders and for policy convergence (Young, 2002; Hicks, Parks, Roberts, & Tierney, 2008).

[19] See project number 2095 "Sustainable Management of the Water Resources of the la Plata Basin with Respect to the Effects of Climate Variability and Change" at www.thegef.org.

[20] See project number 2095 "Sustainable Management of the Water Resources of the la Plata Basin with Respect to the Effects of Climate Variability and Change" at www.thegef.org.

Over 36 percent of the projects target Africa, followed by 20.9 percent in Asia and 20.4 percent in Latin America. Different from the NEST collaborative network, the regional distribution of project suggests strategic policy goals that appear more salient in the protection of the environment than in advancing nuclear development. Consequently, environmental bureaucrats in the Global South need to juggle the policy demands from political principals as well as their own professional goals. This will be more extensively discussed in Chapter 7, as I measure the cooperation decisions of bureaucrats as it is informed by both the demand for skills and the availability of resources in strategic areas targeted by donor agencies.

Adoption and Implementation of Projects in the Protection of the Global Environment

Similar to the NEST projects described in Chapters 5 and 6, GEF projects also pivot around national bureaucrats in charge of environmental policy. While non-state actors, like national universities or NGOs, may participate in GEF grants, expert bureaucrats are the ones that decide design, adoption, and implementation of tasks. Bureaucrats in environmental agencies are the liaisons with peers within and across regions, as well as with officials from the participating international organizations.

Larger cohorts of expert personnel, resulting from the expansion of environmental bureaus, also provide fertile grounds for inter-agency collaboration, as many of these bureaucrats share common professional backgrounds, scientific interests, and often common education networks (Biermann & Siebenhüner, 2009).[21] A consultant on a GEF International Waters project explained these common ties as:

> either formal or informal relationships between governments on environment projects . . . [for example] some of the Atlantic Ocean small islands, the Ministries of Environment all know each other very well, so all know each other by first name. This is true [because of] conferences they attend.[22]

Domestic bureaucrats vary in their participation from project to project as well. As discussed earlier, the number of environmental bureaucrats, and their agencies, has expanded greatly over the past two decades. As in Argentina, most countries have more than one state institution that

[21] International environmental bureaucracies also help forge common professional and normative ties among state experts across the world (Biermann & Siebenhüner, 2009).

[22] Interview with UNEP-GEF project consultant in Nairobi, Kenya, March 2014.

deals with the protection and remediation of the natural environment. The participation of different administrative units and their staff is contingent on the content and application of the project. For example, in the multi-focal project for the La Plata basin discussed earlier, environmental bureaus participate together with other state agencies. The executing agencies include the Argentine Sub-secretariat of Water Resources, the Bolivian General Direction of Land and Basins, and the Paraguayan General Direction for the Protection and Conservation of Water Resources.[23]

The decision to put forward a project may come from national environmental agencies or the GEF itself, with technical support offered throughout the project cycle by international implementing agencies, such as the UNEP or the United Nations Development Programme (UNDP) (Young, 2002). Often, GEF will recommend that countries focus on a particular environmental challenge and will allocate resources to that end. Still, environmental bureaus must commit large amounts of co-financing and, therefore, ultimately it is their decision how to target those funds. A GEF/UNEP program manager describes how the project cycle might initiate:

> The countries themselves come and approach you and say: "Look, we have a problem of this nature, it's happening in this critical ecosystem, can you be of help in accessing resources to solve the problem? We as a government, we're ready to put so much in." And then you can dialogue with the individual countries and their capacities, you can see all the partners who are interested to come and help. So you put the partnership together with a little bit of resources from GEF, because all GEF resources have to be co-financed. So the GEF resource sometimes is just the catalytic and that's what it's meant to be. The bigger part is usually the countries themselves, what they put in, and the partners, what they bring on board without the GEF manager.[24]

Without a doubt, international organizations like UNEP have the advantage of a bird's-eye view when it comes to national investment preferences for the natural environment. This greatly facilitates the coordination needed, especially at the initial stages of the project cycle. A

[23] See project number 2095 "Sustainable Management of the Water Resources of the la Plata Basin with Respect to the Effects of Climate Variability and Change" at www.thegef.org.

[24] Regional Coordinator for Africa in Biodiversity, Division of GEF Coordination, United Nations Environment Programme. Interview with the author in Nairobi, Kenya, March 2013.

senior official at UNEP Latin America describes the role played by the IO in helping countries come together for a GEF grant:

> We have regional mechanisms that allow us to see priorities. We have the Forum for Ministers of the Environment of Latin America and the Caribbean, whereby we are the Secretariat where the ministers meet every two years and they discuss their priorities.... So that forum allows us to see with them the priorities because when we are talking specific themes, Argentina comes and says "for us, this is fundamental," so then we are clear, that is how we do the matching. When the opportunity arrives, I can say "I have so much to finance this work area" and we already know that these three or four [countries] are interested.[25]

Similar to the evolution of projects in NEST, environmental bureaucrats network with peers in international meetings, like the Forum for Ministers or global meetings sponsored by UNEP.[26] Pre-existing ties between state experts also greatly facilitate the process of grant application and implementation. For example, Argentine and Uruguayan state water experts used the experience of past collaboration and existing regional institutions as leverage to secure sustained financing from GEF for a project in the Plata River.[27] The South American countries received two GEF grants to implement two large projects. The first grant, from 1999 to 2008, addressed the problem of pollution and habitat restoration of the Plate

[25] Senior official of UNEP for Latin America. Interview with the Author in Panama City, Panama June 2013.

[26] Interview with senior bureaucrat at the Secretary of the Environment and Sustainable Development (SAyDS) in the area of International Cooperation in Buenos Aires, Argentina, April 2013.

[27] In 1973, Argentina and Uruguay signed a comprehensive treaty (The Treaty between Uruguay and Argentina concerning the Rio de la Plata and the Corresponding Maritime Boundary) establishing a legal framework for co-management. Specifically, the Treaty (1) determined exclusive jurisdiction areas on each side of the River, (2) ended all claims to border disputes, (3) established a dispute settlement mechanism, and (4) regulated fishing and navigation in the Plata River. This treaty also called for the creation of two bilateral institutions to facilitate joint administration of this major natural resource. Both the Joint Technical Commission of the Maritime Front (CTMFM) and the Administrative Commission of the River Plate (CARP) have research mandates, but chronically underfunded, experts have had to seek international donations to carry them out. In 1990, for example, CTMFM and CARP obtained support from the United Nations Educational, Scientific, and Cultural Organization (UNESCO) and Shell Uruguay to assess pollution in the River. This in turn triggered a series of scientific meetings held between the technical personnel of the two agencies between 1991 and 1993. See www.un.org/Depts/los/LEGISLATIONANDTREATIES/PDFFILES/TREATIES/URY-ARG1973MB.PDF and GEF-Proposal for PDF Block B Grant, 1996.

River.[28] It funded a series of activities to remediate the waterway, culminating with the design of a Transboundary Diagnostic Analysis (TDA), a "procedure intended to provide a means of identifying the proximal, intermediate and fundamental causes of environmental problems and threats in shared (multilateral) water bodies" (Pernetta & Bewers, 2012: 1). The second grant, approved in 2009 and still under implementation, is geared toward the remediation of land-based pollution and the implementation of the "FrePlata Strategic Action Programme" that establishes action guidelines for a number of stakeholders using the River, such as local governments, the Navy and Coast Guard, and the private sector.[29]

Two points are worth highlighting here. First, the fact that Argentina and Uruguay had cooperated in the past on co-managing the Plata River was duly noted in the GEF grant applications.[30] In fact, the expectation is that past collaboration would make the project more effective and fruitful: "Based on the extensive political and technical bi-national and intra-national networks that have been established, cross-sectoral responses that bring together public and private partners will be developed."[31] Second, precisely because of their extensive history of cooperation, a significant percentage of Argentine and Uruguayan "co-financing" (the funds GEF requires countries to obtain on their own in order to approve their grant applications) does not involve a direct monetary transaction. For example, in the 1999–2002 budget, out of a grand total of US$ 8.874.036, the two South American states delivered US$ 1.568.000 in in-kind contributions. This type of joint funding is a major facilitator of regional cooperation between impoverished environmental bureaucrats.

Another facilitator of inter-agency cooperation in the protection of the global environment is the breaking up of large, complex projects into smaller, more manageable components. For example, in the Guarani Aquifer Project, described in Chapter 1, participants designed subprojects to divide the survey of the entire 1.200.000 km² of the Aquifer into areas ranging between 500 and 1,000 km².[32] This distribution allowed project partners to form working groups in Argentina and Uruguay, in Brazil and Uruguay, and in Paraguay and Brazil. In addition,

28 See www.thegef.org/gef/project_detail?projID=613.

29 See www.thegef.org/gef/project_detail?projID=3519.

30 One such document listed all past instances of international funding of Argentine-Uruguayan waterway projects. See www.thegef.org/gef/project_detail?projID=3519.

31 Approval/Endorsement by GEF Operational Focal Point and GEF Agency, p. 2.

32 Interview with senior state water expert, coordinator of GEF project for Argentina in Paraná, Argentina, July 2013.

they functioned as "pilot plans" to be used in future research on the Guarani Aquifer, or other GEF project involving groundwater measurements.[33]

How are these projects initiated? Often, participating countries make explicit requests on UNEP/GEF. A senior official at the UNEP Regional Office for Latin America and the Caribbean explains: "Sometimes they send us a very clear letter saying that they would like for us to organize a course in strategic evaluation, for example."[34] Other times, when technological innovation is a central part of the training and the skill disparity of participants is significant, coordination costs go up and UNEP takes on a larger role. Discussing a UNEP/GEF project to extend the use of geothermal energy in East Africa, involving Kenya, Ethiopia, Djibouti, Tanzania, Uganda, and Eritrea, a senior climate change official of UNEP/GEF explains:

> We deal with a whole range of different people, starting from government staff responsible for the policy making all the way down to the people who drill the holes when doing the surface surveys. There's no question that one of the fundamental points in a project like this is to transfer those capabilities. So the way that we're trying to do that in this particular project is to build up a project management unit in each and every one of those countries who become responsible, empowered, and feel a sense of ownership of this project. They will be following the teams, working together with the teams that do the work. In some cases, there is minimal expertise in the country, there are some parts missing. [As a survey technology, the capability for] geo-physical is quite new and probably there aren't many except in Kenya. Geo-physical capability, we're mainly procuring and bringing into these countries so the idea is to work with them to bring in technical expertise when needed, even buying the equipment as well when it's also needed and that will stay there.[35]

Even with increased assistance by UNEP/GEF, smaller environmental bureaus that are characterized by low skill levels face great challenges in project participation. Notwithstanding skill level, there are some practical obstacles that bureaucrats in these agencies face. To begin with, extra bodies are needed to travel to training sessions and meetings with project partners, and then to work in projects, so short-staffed agencies already are at a disadvantage. Furthermore, even before an evaluation of

33 Interview with senior state water expert, coordinator of GEF project for Argentina in Paraná, Argentina, July 2013.

34 Senior official of UNEP for Latin America. Interview with the Author, Panama City, Panama, June 2013.

35 Senior official in Climate Change, UNEP/GEF. Interview with the author, Nairobi, Kenya, March 2013.

her technological literacy, a participating bureaucrat must speak the same language as her partners. The official language of international cooperation is English, and not all state experts are sufficiently proficient to carry out a project with poor language skills. This challenges state institutions when they have to decide whom to send for training. As a senior environmental bureaucrat from Argentina puts it: "The real limitation these programs have is that they are in English. So we do not have that many people who are proficient in English at the level needed to take a course; it's not that easy. And those are very good opportunities."[36]

The GEF and International Implementing Organizations

As stated above, the GEF is an international organization that provides a financial mechanism for environmental cooperation in the developing world and transitioning countries. To channel its funding into the protection of the global environment, GEF works together with international agencies that help participating countries adopt and implement national and international projects. Because GEF is primarily a financial institution, it lacks many of the resources that policy-specific IOs have. Thus, GEF partners with implementing agencies that have know-how and capabilities on the ground in order to assist countries throughout the project cycle. Internally, GEF relies on the expertise of an independent Scientific and Technical Advisory Panel (STAP) made up of seven renowned environmental scientists to help shape its policy principles and objectives.[37] Also, the Council, the GEF governing board of directors, represents the constituencies of developing and transitioning countries of the organization. In addition, every four years members gather in the Assembly to discuss GEF goals and give input to the Council. To date, the Assembly has met five times: in 1998, 2002, 2006, 2010, and 2014. Finally, the Secretariat, based in Washington DC, is in charge of operations and management of all GEF programs and projects. Basically, its function is "to develop operational policies that lay down the foundation for the GEF's efforts in the six focal areas" (Andler, 2009: 207).

Without doubt, much of the coordination costs involved in GEF-sponsored cooperation fall on implementing agencies. The most active implementing agencies are the United Nations Environmental Program

[36] Senior official at the Directorate of Forestry of SAyDS. Interview with the author in Buenos Aires, Argentina, January 2014.

[37] See www.stapgef.org/.

(UNEP), the United Nations Development Programme (UNDP), and the World Bank (Young, 2002; Andler, 2009). Of the three, UNEP, created in 1972 within the United Nations system to promote conservation, is the only one fully specialized in environmental protection and remediation. The World Bank has extraordinary economic resources and UNDP has a worldwide institutional reach. On the other hand, UNEP has expertise and skills in environmental policy, but lacks significant monetary and institutional resources. Despite that, it is the agency that is most involved in green cooperation. To date, UNEP has coordinated 250 regional and global projects, followed closely by the UNDP, with 218, and the World Bank, with 130.[38] A UNEP/GEF official explains the differences in project coordination between UNEP and UNDP:

> I'll use UNDP and UNEP as a contrast. UNDP is a resident agency, which means it has an office in every single country in the world. UNEP is not. It has an office here [Nairobi, Kenya], and 4 or 5 regional offices. So we don't have the ability to go country by country. We don't have the contacts to go country by country. So we are very much more reliant on countries coming to us. But, we tend to do regional and global projects. So there's a bit of a tension there. If you waited forever for countries to come to you and suggest a regional and global project, you might be waiting forever. So you have to be a bit more proactive and pick up on the ideas that are emerging. I think if you're a non-resident agency you have to be more sensitive to country driven projects than if you were a resident.[39]

GEF Funding and Country Co-funding

As discussed earlier, GEF funding covers only a marginal part of projects, regardless of whether they are country-specific, regional, or global. Table 6.2 offers a breakdown of mean percentages of GEF funding and countries co-financing. On average, GEF funding does not exceed 30 percent of project costs. The difference in country and region-wide mean in this region is of seventeen points. This is explained by the great disparity in wealth across Asia (as discussed in Chapter 4), a region that includes giants, like China and India, and some of the poorest, like Bangladesh and Sri Lanka. Correspondingly, Asia is the region with the highest mean of co-financing, reaching almost 87 percent on average in what countries invest in these projects. For a better view of regional differences, the next

[38] See www.thegef.org/gef/gef_projects_funding.

[39] Senior official in Climate Change, UNEP/GEF. Interview with the author, Nairobi, Kenya, March 2013.

TABLE 6.2. *Percentages of GEF Financing and Countries' Co-financing by Region*

	Eastern Europe	Latin America	Africa	Asia	Oceania
Percent of GEF financing (Mean by country)	20.89%	24.75%	24.88%	29.55%	26.28%
Percent of GEF financing (Mean by region)	16.56%	23.73%	20.98%	13.37%	26.85%
Percent of co-financing (Mean by region)	83.44%	76.27%	79.02%	86.63%	73.15%
GEF financing (mean by country in US$)	86,329,435	218,960,149	175,410,169?	243,110,746	118,477,777
Co-financing (mean by country in US$)	434,956,030	703,657,445	660,654,956	1,574,621,911	322,859,837
Total financing (mean by country in US$)	521,285,464	922,617,591	836,065,117	1,817,732,649	441,337,612

Source: Global Environmental Fund.

section offers a visualization of the networks that make up international inter-agency cooperation in the global environment.

Visualizing Networks in the Environment

Finally, I present an affiliation matrix as a first step in visualizing the network of collaboration for all regions. As in Chapter 4, where I described instances of collaboration among state agencies, I created an affiliation matrix of GEF projects, where the diagonal elements describe the total number of environmental projects by country and the off-diagonal elements describe the number of times that each pair of countries collaborates. Table 6.3 presents a sample of Latin American countries that shows,

TABLE 6.3. *Affiliation Matrix of Collaboration in GEF Projects, Selected Latin American Countries*

	Argentina	Bolivia	Brazil	Chile	Colombia	Ecuador	Mexico	Paraguay	Peru	Uruguay	Venezuela
Argentina	**51**										
Bolivia	7	**33**									
Brazil	9	7	**88**								
Chile	6	3	9	**45**							
Colombia	3	6	9	3	**61**						
Ecuador	8	11	9	8	11	**58**					
Mexico	6	3	18	9	6	7	**79**				
Paraguay	4	6	4	2	4	4	3	**19**			
Peru	8	12	14	11	13	20	10	5	**72**		
Uruguay	5	1	5	3	2	2	3	3	3	**30**	
Venezuela	2	5	6	3	7	7	5	1	9	1	**25**

Note: Affiliation matrix of collaborative ties. Diagonal counts describe the total number of projects by country. Off-diagonal counts describe the number of collaborative projects by each pair of countries *i* and *j*.
Source: Global Environment Facility Projects.

for example, that Argentina and Brazil worked together in nine projects (out of the fifty-one and eighty-eight projects each country carried out, respectively).[40]

A full affiliation matrix, which uses all GEF project data (at the country, regional, and global level) to create a valued network of 152 rows and 152 columns, reveals the prominence of African countries in environmental cooperation.[41] Sub-Saharan states are particularly active at the regional level, with Kenya topping the list with participation in forty-three regional projects, followed by Tanzania (thirty-six), Mali (thirty-two), South Africa (thirty), and Senegal (thirty). The only African country to have participated in just one regional project is Somalia. When it comes to GEF global or inter-regional grants, it seems size does matter as only the larger countries of the developing world are frequent collaborators. At the top we find Brazil, with participation in twenty-one global projects, followed by Indonesia (eighteen), Kenya (eighteen), and China (sixteen). Correspondingly, at the other end of the spectrum, there is El Salvador, Gabon, and Uruguay with participation in only one global project.

From the full affiliation matrix we can produce descriptive graphs that visualize collaboration within and across regions. Figure 6.1 presents the network of high collaborators, which only counts those dyads in which a pair of countries collaborated at least four times. Figure 6.1 uses a force-directed algorithm to map the proximity of countries by their level of collaboration in GEF projects. In this thinned down network of high collaborators,[42] we observe significant regional differences in the structure of collaborative networks. Descriptive statistics show that almost all countries of Oceania are at least two degrees removed from other regions of the world, only connected through Papua and Timor. Furthermore, Asia is a continent with very different subgroups of collaborators, with a few countries such as China that are consistently collaborating

40 While Argentina and Brazil share significant interests in NEST, they have less in common in environmental policy. Undeniably, they find common ground in transboundary waters and the shared Guaraní Aquifer. But as the largest stakeholder of the Amazon rain forest and the country with the greatest biodiversity of flora and fauna in the world, Brazil has distinct preferences and favors a host of green partners, such as the other Amazon states or regional giants, like Mexico, China, and India.

41 The three less frequent participants were dropped from the affiliation matrix and analysis.

42 I define high collaborators as those that participated in more than +7 projects. In the next chapter I provide extensive analyses of collaboration that consider the full affiliation matrix as well as thinned versions with higher collaboration thresholds as in Cranmer & Desmarais (2011).

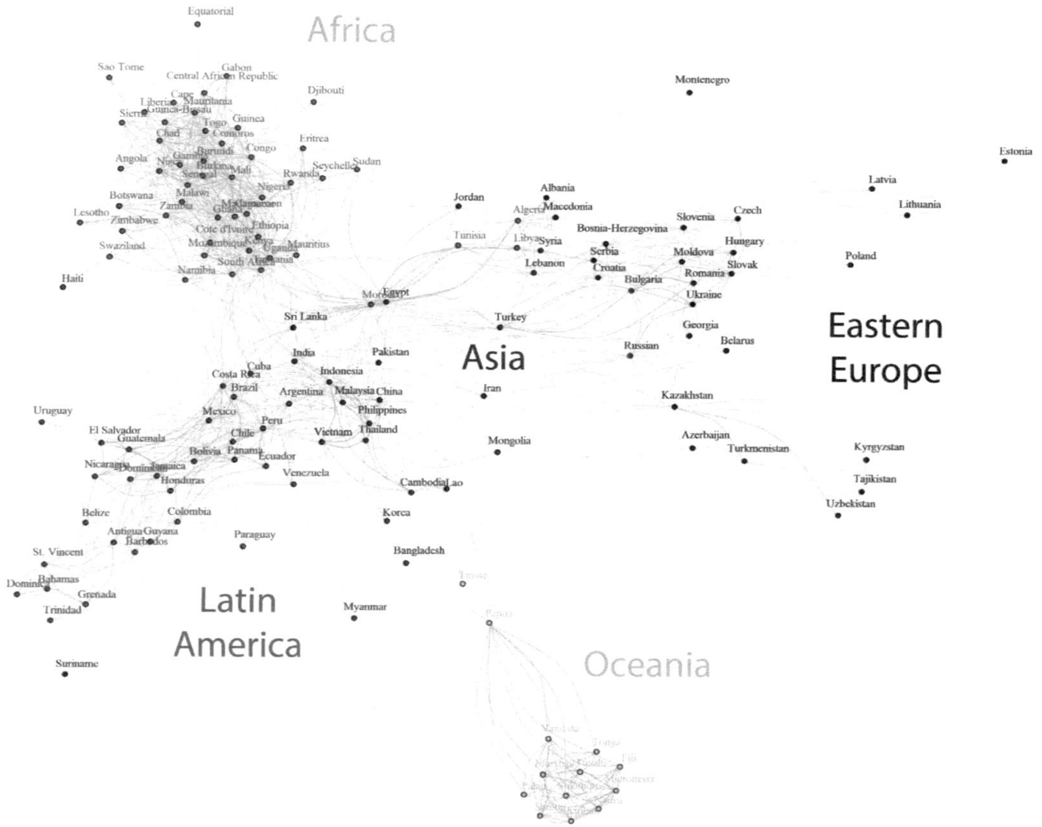

FIGURE 6.1. Collaboration network, thinned by high (frequent) collaborators.
Note: Network of collaboration of GEF projects. Fruchterman-Reingold layout on a thinned affiliation matrix with threshold $\frac{n-ties}{7}$. Size of the node describes level of dependency on GEF funding to implement the environmental proposal.

with Latin America while other countries such as Turkey that are more actively cooperating with Europe. In the next chapter I use Exponential Random Graph Models (ERGM) to provide more precise estimates of these regional differences.

Conclusion

This chapter describes the world's largest network of cooperating state agencies in the protection of the global environment. Since the early 1990s, expert bureaucrats from developing and emerging countries have worked together on large, technical projects with peers. These projects have been a source of skills for environmental experts in areas ranging from biodiversity, climate change, and transboundary water. Descriptive data analyzed in this chapter offers a first look at how agencies with low levels of human capital participate in less than skilled ones in cross-national projects. This is despite the fact that the Global Environment Facility helps partially fund these projects and its partner IOs, like the United Nations Environmental Program and the United Nations Development Programme, assist with their technical expertise.

Furthermore, the preliminary evidence in this chapter suggests that not all international inter-agency networks are the same. Indeed, a summary comparison of the descriptive evidence for cooperation in NEST and the protection of the environment reveals that environmental networks are not as dense as the nuclear ones. In the next chapter I test my theory of the expert bureaucrat against project participation data from the GEF. I use Exponential Random Graph Models (ERGM) in order to determine the drivers of international inter-agency cooperation and partner selection in NEST networks.

Appendix 6.A

TABLE A.6.1. *Participating Countries in GEF Grants and Number of Projects*

	Countries	Countries	Countries	Countries	Countries
	Afghanistan	Albania	Algeria	Angola	Antigua
Total no. of projects	14	32	37	22	28
	Argentina	Armenia	Azerbaijan	Bahamas	Bahrain
Total no. of projects	51	27	23	21	3
	Bangladesh	Barbados	Belarus	Belize	Benin
Total no. of projects	24	23	28	38	20

TABLE A.6.1. (continued)

	Countries	Countries	Countries	Countries	Countries
	Bhutan	Bolivia	Bosnia-Herzegovina	Botswana	Brazil
Total no. of projects	21	33	26	31	88
	Bulgaria	Burkina	Burundi	Cambodia	Cameroon
Total no. of projects	42	62	38	42	46
	Cape Verde	Central African Republic	Chad	Chile	China
Total no. of projects	27	27	35	45	153
	Colombia	Comoros	Congo	Cook	Costa Rica
Total no. of projects	61	26	41	23	56
	Côte d'Ivoire	Croatia	Cuba	Czech	Djibouti
Total no. of projects	44	32	37	26	20
	Dominica	Dominican	Ecuador	Egypt	El Salvador
Total no. of projects	19	24	58	66	30
	Equatorial	Eritrea	Estonia	Ethiopia	Fiji
Total no. of projects	13	24	14	51	32
	Gabon	Gambia	Georgia	Ghana	Grenada
Total no. of projects	24	35	33	62	24
	Guatemala	Guinea	Guinea-Bissau	Guyana	Haiti
Total no. of projects	41	41	28	24	21
	Honduras	Hungary	India	Indonesia	Iran
Total no. of projects	43	34	83	90	35
	Iraq	Jamaica	Jordan	Kazakhstan	Kenya
Total no. of projects	3	30	47	46	92
	Kiribati	Korea	Kyrgyzstan	Lao	Latvia
Total no. of projects	26	15	30	34	18
	Latvia	Lebanon	Lesotho	Liberia	Libya
Total no. of projects	18	31	26	29	13
	Lithuania	Macedonia	Madagascar	Malawi	Malaysia
Total no. of projects	17	25	42	38	42
	Maldives	Mali	Malta	Marshall	Mauritania
Total no. of projects	15	60	2	21	38
	Mauritius	Mexico	Micronesia	Moldova	Mongolia
Total no. of projects	35	79	20	29	41

(*continued*)

TABLE A.6.1. (continued)

	Countries	Countries	Countries	Countries	Countries
	Montenegro	Morocco	Mozambique	Myanmar	Namibia
Total no. of projects	14	65	46	8	47
	Nauru	Nepal	Nicaragua	Niger	Nigeria
Total no. of projects	19	26	40	47	49
	Niue	Oman	Pakistan	Palau	Panama
Total no. of projects	24	4	35	21	40
	Papua	Paraguay	Peru	Philippines	Poland
Total no. of projects	32	19	72	80	27
	Romania	Russian	Rwanda	Samoa	São Tomé
Total no. of projects	38	80	32	30	17
	Senegal	Serbia	Seychelles	Sierra	Slovak
Total no. of projects	60	26	30	27	31
	Slovenia	Solomon	Somalia	South Africa	Sri Lanka
Total no. of projects	17	25	4	73	32
	St. Vincent	Sudan	Suriname	Swaziland	Syria
Total no. of projects	20	35	15	25	26
	Tajikistan	Tanzania	Thailand	Timor	Togo
Total no. of projects	35	79	49	14	32
	Tonga	Trinidad	Tunisia	Turkey	Turkmenistan
Total no. of projects	19	19	46	42	25
	Tuvalu	Uganda	Ukraine	Uruguay	Uzbekistan
Total no. of projects	21	64	48	30	34
	Vanuatu	Venezuela	Vietnam	Zambia	Zimbabwe
Total no. of projects	33	25	77	38	28

7

Explaining International Inter-Agency Cooperation in the Protection of the Environment

What are the determinants of international inter-agency cooperation in the protection of the environment? The present chapter explains inter-agency cooperation and partner selection under the Global Environment Facility (GEF), the largest public fund in the world for inter-state environmental projects in the Global South. As described in the previous chapters at length, the GEF offers significant funding to its members (i.e., national environmental agencies) to meet the expenses of cross-national technical projects in environmental remediation and adaptation. To get at the causal mechanism driving states' decision to collaborate with others in IO sponsored projects, I examine the effect of these two resources – funds and skills – on international environmental cooperation. I will show that, while member states respond to the monetary incentives to collaborate (that is, IO donations should be a predictor of project participation), a key driver of cooperation in environmental policy is the need to acquire and update skills. I expect results in this chapter to reinforce the findings of previous chapters on the determinants of inter-agency collaboration in the nuclear sector and, more importantly, explain in detail how domestic and international sources of funding affect the cooperative behavior of expert bureaucrats.

As described in previous chapters, the central argument of this book centers on the career incentives of the expert bureaucrat, who seeks to invest in her skills if and when her employer, the state, does not. Through IO-sponsored projects, state experts not only pool resources and share research costs, but also and perhaps more critically, keep their professional portfolio current. Indeed, a wealth of qualitative evidence and expert interviews points to the centrality of professional development and training strategies which expert bureaucrats consider when making decisions to cooperate. These decisions are then incorporated into the strategic planning of environmental agencies through program development, grant application, and the design and execution of environmental projects.

Choosing partners for a project is not done lightly and carries important implications for expert bureaucrats and their agencies. Skilled partners bring their know-how, existing networks, and financial resources, assuring donors and political principals that ambitious project goals can be met. At the same time, bureaucrats know that unskilled and poorly funded partners may syphon time and money away from the agency. Thus, I argue that skills and resources are key causal mechanisms behind inter-agency cooperation. In analyzing partner selection in GEF projects, this chapter will reveal the strong homophily effect predicted by my theory of inter-agency cooperation while controlling for differences in the access to financial resources.[1]

Access to Domestic Resources vs. Access to Skills

In analyzing the incentives for inter-agency cooperation in the Global South, prior chapters argued that exogenous shocks that reduce agency funding signaled bureaucrats that they needed to take skill investment and upgrading in their own hands. Government shocks that reduce the funds held by agencies, however, are not the only type of economic shock that may trigger cooperation. For example, exogenous increases in the demand for skills as a result of new technologies will also require investment and updating, triggering demands for more resources or, alternatively, for more cooperation. Similarly, international donor agencies that provide seed money may also incentivize cooperation. If cooperation allows bureaucrats to invest in their skills when state funding withdraws, we should expect the availability of program funds from international agencies to increase cooperation as well.

A unique contribution of this chapter is that it analyzes the effect of money, disbursed both by the IO and by each of the environmental agencies, on international environmental cooperation. This gives us a measure

[1] As previously discussed, the meaning of homophily is captured in the phrase "birds of a feather flock together," whereby actors who share traits are more likely to come together than those who do not (McPherson, Smith-Lovin, & Cook, 2001; Maoz, 2012; Kinne, 2013; Videras, 2013). If bureaucrats' priority is to advance their skills, they will seek out partners who have either superior or equal training.

of the willingness of states to invest in coordinated environmental protection (and the effectiveness of the IO strategy to "buy" cooperation). As discussed in the previous chapter, the GEF has disbursed $13.5 billion directly in individual, regional, and global grants to Global South countries and former Soviet republics over twenty years.[2] GEF funds a part of project costs; the rest is co-financed by each participating environmental state agency. Since 1991, countries co-financing approximates $65 billion.[3]

To analyze the drivers of international inter-agency cooperation in the protection of the global environment, I constructed a database with information on GEF funding, co-financing by individual countries, various measures of skill levels of countries and bureaucràcies, as well as other international, country, and agency-specific data. Data come from GEF, the International Debt Statistics of the World Bank, and the Quality of Government Project. To explain the determinants of partner selection in GEF projects, I take advantage of new advances in the measurement of social networks. I run Exponential Random Graph Models (ERGM), which estimate the probability of observing a collaborative tie between each pair of country agencies. ERGMs allow us to include homophily terms, which measure the effect of shared traits on environmental collaboration, and consequently, the determinants of partner selection in the GEF green network.

Models show that two environmental bureaus are more likely to cooperate in GEF projects when they (1) have similar levels of bureaucratic competence, (2) invest similar *overall* amounts of co-financing,[4] (3) receive similar *overall* amounts of GEF funding, and (4) have similar country levels of scientific productivity. I interpret these findings as confirming my argument: in order to increase their access to resources needed to solve common problems and advance their professional careers, expert bureaucrats are willing to bear the costs of international collaboration with foreign peers under IO technical cooperation programs.

The chapter makes two important contributions. First, it offers empirical analyses of the effects of IO funding on environmental cooperation. If, as practitioners and advocates maintain, international collaboration is necessary in order to solve dire environmental problems, then

[2] See www.thegef.org/gef/home.
[3] See www.thegef.org/gef/home.
[4] By *overall* I mean the totality of GEF funding (as well as country co-financing) for all projects in which each country has participated.

understanding the determinants of inter-state cooperation and the role that multilateral organizations play is essential. Further, this second empirical test of my theory of the expert bureaucrat deepens our understanding of homophily in international cooperation (Maoz, 2012; Kinne, 2013). Often observed in social networks, its precise causal mechanism remains under-theorized in the study of international cooperation (McPherson, Smith-Lovin, & Cook, 2001; Videras, 2013). My theory of expert bureaucrats, who pursue collaboration with foreign peers as part of a skill-investment strategy, explains the incentives to collaborate in IO technical programs among state agencies with similar levels of development and funding.

The fact that domestic agencies with similar levels of development have a higher propensity to collaborate under technical cooperation programs has neither been noted in the extant literature, nor has it been explained. This finding should be of special interest to managers of these programs in IOs, who strive to distribute scarce resources in the most efficient and effective way. It creates a dilemma for the international manager as well. On the one hand, more equal country pairings are more likely to work, thus effectively advancing cooperation in the protection of the global environment. On the other, when unequal pairings "stick," they can be a great source of needed training and expertise for the lesser developed partner.

Differences in Environmental and NEST Data and Analyses

In contrast to the NEST data analyzed in Chapter 5, the GEF data studied in the present chapter discriminate by type of funding, whether domestic or foreign. Consequently, I will be able to assess if cooperation increases when there are more resources available abroad and declines when there are larger shares of resources domestically. In particular, this allows me to distinguish the effect of asymmetries on the level of resources that partners can commit as well as when there are larger gains to be made from donor agencies that contribute to the cooperative effort. Because substituting local resources for cooperation will only be beneficial if programs are at comparable levels of development, the flow of resources among peer programs can be analyzed as a function of differences in the share of resources that these programs are willing to commit. Different from the prior analysis of NEST data, in this chapter I can distinguish homophily effects that result from the share of resources that domestic environmental programs are willing to invest and from the type of endowments (scientific and technical) that are at the disposal of expert bureaucrats. Another difference in the analysis of the two policy sectors is that the global nature of the environmental network allows me to estimate a set of models that includes all countries of the Global South (and emerging economies) simultaneously.

Results that follow provide support for the main hypotheses of the book: first, when the domestic share of resources increases (decreases), then domestic environmental agencies step up (scale down) international cooperation. Similarly, when the share of resources available abroad increases (decreases), then domestic environmental agencies increase (decrease) cooperation. Second, the projects that are favored by local bureaucrats are those that provide the highest returns to skills. As it was also the case in the analyses of nuclear collaborative networks, I interpret these findings as evidence that bureaucrats favor cooperation in order to update their professional skills. Finally, collaboration is more likely to emerge among peer programs that are at relatively similar levels of development (homophily). This last result is consistent with the qualitative evidence in previous chapters and in interviews with expert bureaucrats. In all, it shows that cooperation in environmental programs is not merely a strategy to transfer knowledge from skilled to unskilled bureaucrats, but also a strategy to pool common resources in order to update and upgrade skills.

Hypotheses and the Data

Briefly, I reiterate the main hypotheses to be tested in this chapter. The partner selection or homophily hypotheses are:

Hypothesis HomophilyA: The smaller the difference in countries' dependence on GEF funding, the more likely two environmental bureaus will collaborate (Homophily Effect in Funding).

Hypothesis HomophilyB: The smaller the difference in technical expertise between countries, the more likely two environmental bureaus will collaborate (Homophily Effect in Technical Expertise Levels).

Hypothesis HomophilyC: The smaller the difference in bureaucratic competence between countries, the more likely two environmental bureaus will collaborate (Homophily Effect in Bureaucratic Competence).

The book's central hypothesis on the expected effect of skills on international inter-agency cooperation is:

Hypothesis Bureaucratic Competence: The more competent the national bureaucracy, the more likely its environmental bureau will collaborate with foreign peer institutions in GEF projects.

Hypotheses testing the effect of availability and origin of funding for cross-national projects in the protection of the environment are:

Hypothesis Funding: The less funding available to an environmental bureau at home, the more likely it will cooperate with foreign peer institutions.

Hypothesis IO Funding: The more funding available from the IO, the more likely a national agency will cooperate in a GEF grant.

Finally, an alternative explanation testing the effect of domestic regulation follows.

Hypothesis Domestic Regulations: The more regulations on business in a country, the less likely its environmental bureau will collaborate with foreign peer institutions in GEF projects.

The Dependent Variable

The network of collaboration in GEF projects, described by the affiliation matrix in Table 6.3 and visualized in Figure 6.1 in Chapter 6, considers each member country as a node and collaboration between each pair of countries as an edge. Consistent with the hypotheses described in previous chapters, I seek to explain the determinants of peer selection in GEF projects. In other words, the objective is to calculate the probability of observing a collaborative tie between pairs of environmental agencies in two different countries.

As in Chapter 5, to estimate the determinants of inter-agency cooperation I take advantage of new modeling strategies in social network analysis that use ERGM. These models allow me to assess the probability of observing a network tie (here, cooperation in the GEF network) both as a function of covariates and network structure. Given that the GEF network is valued, with higher counts describing more active collaboration, I follow Cranmer and Desmarais' strategy and estimate different ERGM models on progressively thinned networks, with higher thresholds to form less dense networks that describe ties between more active partners (Cranmer & Desmarais, 2011).[5]

[5] As I clarified in Chapters 2 and 5, bureaucrats' previous level of skills (i.e., the independent variable) creates incentives to cooperate with foreign peers (i.e., the dependent variable).

The Covariates

To explain international inter-agency cooperation in the protection of the global environment, I consider a number of independent variables similar to the ones used in the analysis of NEST networks. I distinguish among three different groups of variables that test for the hypotheses of the book. The first group of variables measures the effect of both GEF and domestic financing on the probability of collaboration. The first variable describes the total financing provided by GEF *to* each country *i* (each node) in US$ dollars (LN), **GEF (US$)**. I expect that higher levels of financing by GEF will make collaboration in its projects more attractive. The second variable, **Co-financing US$**, measures the total financing provided *by* each country *i* in US$ dollars (LN). Consistent with the proposed theory, higher (lower) levels of domestic financing will reduce (increase) the probability of country collaboration in the GEF network.

A second group of variables test for the overall effect of program development on collaboration. These variables are expected to be positive, with higher development (i.e., higher skill level) increasing the incentives to collaborate in order to maximize already existing skills in the bureau. I include the average number of **Scientific Publications (LN)** over ten years for each country *i* as a proxy for the relative skills of experts in each country. I expect higher overall scientific skills in a country to correlate positively with GEF cooperation. From the Quality of Government Dataset, I include the variable **Bureaucratic Competence** that measures on a four-point scale the capacity of the bureaucracy, based on how professionalized and autonomous it is.

A third group of covariates tests for homophily/heterophily effects in network collaboration. Here, I consider the extent to which differences in resources (money), skills (program development), and capacities (bureaucratic competence) reduce the probability of any pairs of countries selecting one another. A measure of **Inter-Country Differences in GEF Financing** is expected to reduce partner selection the greater the difference in GEF funding allocation among pairs of countries. A measure of **Inter-Country Differences in Co-financing** is expected to reduce collaboration the greater the difference in overall domestic investment. This is so because greater differences in domestic co-financing would represent a net transfer of resources from countries that invest more to countries that invest less, which would reduce the incentives of the former to cooperate. Another variable, **Inter-Country Differences in Scientific**

But the decision to collaborate has no direct effect on bureaucratic expertise, thus it does not create an endogeneity problem.

Publications, measures differences in technical skills, using the number of scientific publications for each country in the network. I expect the variable to be negative, indicating that programs with expert bureaucrats that have significantly different skills will be less likely to collaborate in GEF projects. Finally, I include a variable that measures differences in bureaucratic competence. I expect the variable **Inter-Country Differences in Bureaucratic Competence** to be negative as well, with larger differences in bureaucratic competence decreasing the probability of collaboration.

I also consider other controls, measuring the **Number of Technical Cooperation Grants** (US$) a country has received as an alternative of transfers of technology and skills to recipient countries.[6] **Multilateral Financing** (US$) combines all publicly guaranteed multilateral loans and credit from international and regional development banks.[7] Also, **GDP** per capita and level of trade exposure (**Openness**), as a measure of country wealth and of exposure to globalization, respectively. Finally, **CPIA Environmental Regulation** rates the environmental regulatory agencies and policies of a country from one (low) to six (high).[8] All control variables (except **Bureaucratic Competence** and covariates generated from GEF data) come from the International Debt Statistics of the World Bank. Finally, using the GEF grant data, I create regional and subregional controls: **Region**, that captures any regional effect; dummy variables for **Latin America, Africa, Asia,** and **Oceania**; and **Constituency,** which controls for the thirty-two GEF-defined sub-regional constituencies clusters.

Models and Results

In an Exponential Random Graph Model a collaborative tie between two country agencies is assumed to be a random variable with each i and j as distinct members of a set of actors. The dependent variable of the estimated model takes the value of one if there is a network tie from actor

[6] The World Bank, International Debt Statistics describes this variable as follows: "Technical cooperation grants include free-standing technical cooperation grants, which are intended to finance the transfer of technical and managerial skills or of technology for the purpose of building up general national capacity without reference to any specific investment projects; and investment-related technical cooperation grants, which are provided to strengthen the capacity to execute specific investment projects." Data are in current U.S. dollars. See http://data.worldbank.org/indicator/BX.GRT.TECH.CD.WD.

[7] See http://data.worldbank.org/indicator/DT.AMT.MLAT.CD.

[8] See http://data.worldbank.org/indicator/IQ.CPA.ENVR.XQ.

i to actor j, and zero otherwise. The probability of observing a set of network ties is:

$$P(Y_{ij} = 1) = exp[\theta T g(y, X)]/k(\theta)$$

where Y_{ij} describes a tie between environmental agencies in countries i and j, X is a matrix of country attributes associated with the agencies in the network, $g(y, X)$ is a vector of network statistics, θ is a vector of coefficients, and $k(\theta)$ is a normalizing constant.

Model results are presented in Tables 7.1 and 7.2, with coefficients for the most important variables plotted in Figure 7.1 to facilitate interpretation. Coefficients report log-odds-ratio describing the effect that a one-unit change in the independent variable has on the probability of observing a tie between agencies from two countries. Given that I have not included structural network variables in the model, coefficients can be interpreted as logistic results, without requiring simulated networks to assess the magnitude of change.

To explain the determinants of collaboration I use standard ERGM terms to measure the effects of domestic funding; regional membership (homophily within region); constituency membership (homophily within cluster); and differences in GEF funding (heterophily) on the probability of cooperation. I also compare homophily across regions in order to measure inter-regional differences on the probability that two countries will collaborate with each other.

Table 7.1 presents restricted results that include regional and constituency cluster variables. The variable ***edge*** represents the probability of observing a tie when all other covariates are equal to zero, similar to the *constant* in the standard generalized linear models. The models in Table 7.1 present estimates of the region homophily, describing the effect that membership in the same region has on inter-agency collaboration. Readers will note that there is no baseline, as parameters of each region describe the extent to which co-membership in a region increases cooperation. Model results yield positive coefficients for all countries, which indicate that being in the same region increases the probability of cooperation. The increase in the probability of cooperation that results from being in the same region is rather dramatic. When considering the full network (Model 1A), results show that a country in Latin America is forty times more likely to collaborate with another country of Latin America than with a country from another region – i.e., $exp(3.7) \approx 40$. The effect is also large for Africa, where the likelihood that the partner

TABLE 7.1. *Explaining the Determinants of Collaboration in GEF Projects, Regional Model*

		Model 2.A	Model 2.B	Model 2.C	Model 2.D	Model 2.E	Model 2.F	Model 2.G
		Low Collaborators		=========================			High Collaborators	
Homphily Terms	Edge	-0.55^{***}	-1.8^{***}	-1.8^{***}	-2.82^{***}	-2.82^{***}	-3.65^{***}	-3.65^{***}
		(0.022)	(0.030)	(0.030)	(0.046)	(0.046)	(0.067)	(0.067)
	Others	0.58^{***}	1.11^{***}	1.11^{***}	1.59^{***}	1.59^{***}	2.03^{***}	2.03^{***}
		(0.101)	(0.106)	(0.106)	(0.119)	(0.119)	(0.137)	(0.137)
	Latin America	3.7^{***}	3.18^{***}	3.18^{***}	3.15^{***}	3.15^{***}	3.01^{***}	3.01^{***}
		(0.274)	(0.137)	(0.137)	(0.117)	(0.117)	(0.126)	(0.126)
	Africa	2.52^{***}	2.61^{***}	2.61^{***}	2.81^{***}	2.81^{***}	3.04^{***}	3.04^{***}
		(0.096)	(0.072)	(0.072)	(0.075)	(0.075)	(0.091)	(0.091)
	Asia	0.8^{***}	1.12^{***}	1.12^{***}	1.52^{***}	1.52^{***}	1.73^{***}	1.73^{***}
		(0.111)	(0.115)	(0.115)	(0.131)	(0.131)	(0.158)	(0.158)
	Oceania	14.2	3.96^{***}	3.96^{***}	3.61^{***}	3.61^{***}	3.71^{***}	3.71^{***}
		(128.354)	(0.727)	(0.727)	(0.442)	(0.442)	(0.361)	(0.361)
	GEF constituency	1.42^{***}	1.47^{***}	1.47^{***}	1.69^{***}	1.69^{***}	1.86^{***}	1.86^{***}
		(0.157)	(0.124)	(0.124)	(0.115)	(0.115)	(0.110)	(0.110)
	AIC	30821.9	26958.2	26958.2	23643.5	23643.5	21675.8	21675.8
	BIC	30873.6	27009.9	27009.9	23695.2	23695.2	21727.5	21727.5
	LogLik	−7131.3	−5199.4	−5199.4	−3542.1	−3542.1	−2558.2	−2558.2

Note: Dependent variable is the network of collaboration in GEF projects. Threshold for collaboration increases from $\frac{n-ties}{1}$ tie in Model 1.A to $\frac{n-ties}{k}$ for thinned networks of higher collaboration, where k takes values of two in Model B, three in Model C, all the way to seven in Model G.

TABLE 7.2. *Explaining the Determinants of Collaboration on GEF Projects, Full Model*

		Model A	Model B	Model C	Model D	Model E	Model F	Model G
		Low Collaborators		=======	=======	=======	High Collaborators	
Financing Terms	Edge (constant)	−40.97***	−53.42***	−53.42***	−52.4***	−52.4***	−47.64***	−47.64***
		(1.416)	(1.907)	(1.907)	(2.291)	(2.291)	(2.563)	(2.563)
	GEF (US$)	1.43***	1.92***	1.92***	1.64***	1.64***	1.13***	1.13***
		(0.050)	(0.068)	(0.068)	(0.081)	(0.081)	(0.089)	(0.089)
	Co-financing (US$)	−0.31***	−0.47***	−0.47***	−0.27***	−0.27***	0.13*	0.13*
		(0.032)	(0.044)	(0.044)	(0.059)	(0.059)	(0.069)	(0.069)
Homophily Terms	Same region	2.37***	3.06***	3.06***	3.38***	3.38***	3.49***	3.49***
		(0.069)	(0.071)	(0.071)	(0.082)	(0.082)	(0.097)	(0.097)
	Inter-country differences in GEF financing	−0.3***	−0.67***	−0.67***	−0.59***	−0.59***	−0.44***	−0.44***
		(0.054)	(0.077)	(0.077)	(0.099)	(0.099)	(0.116)	(0.116)
	Inter-country differences in domestic cofinancing	0.04	0.091*	0.091*	0.01	0.01	−0.16*	−0.16*
		(0.033)	(0.047)	(0.047)	(0.068)	(0.068)	(0.080)	(0.080)
	Inter-country differences in scientific publications	−0.26***	−0.3***	−0.3***	−0.3***	−0.3***	−0.28***	−0.28***
		(0.013)	(0.018)	(0.018)	(0.022)	(0.022)	(0.026)	(0.026)
	Inter-country difference in bureaucratic competence	0.08*	0.01	0.01	−0.24***	−0.24***	−0.26***	−0.26***
		(0.046)	(0.062)	(0.062)	(0.078)	(0.078)	(0.091)	(0.091)
	Inter-country difference in GDP per capita	−0.2***	−0.33***	−0.33***	−0.33***	−0.33***	−0.35***	−0.35***
		(0.029)	(0.038)	(0.038)	(0.047)	(0.047)	(0.056)	(0.056)
	Inter-country difference in polity	0.013	−0.002	−0.002	−0.043**	−0.043**	−0.074***	−0.074***
		(0.011)	(0.014)	(0.014)	(0.017)	(0.017)	(0.020)	(0.020)
	Inter-country difference in openness	0.16**	−0.37***	−0.37***	−0.37***	−0.37***	−0.44***	−0.44***
		(0.074)	(0.098)	(0.098)	(0.120)	(0.120)	(0.140)	(0.140)

(*continued*)

TABLE 7.2. *(continued)*

		Model A	Model B	Model C	Model D	Model E	Model F	Model G
		Low collaborators		=====	=====	=====	High collaborators	
Program Development Variables	Scientific publications (LN)	0.01	0.06***	0.06***	0.02	0.02	0.02	0.02
		(0.011)	(0.014)	(0.014)	(0.017)	(0.017)	(0.019)	(0.019)
	Number of technical cooperation agreements	0.01	0	0	0.065**	0.065**	0.04	0.04
		(0.019)	(0.026)	(0.026)	(0.032)	(0.032)	(0.036)	(0.036)
	Multilateral financing	0.01	−0.02	−0.02	−0.05***	−0.05***	−0.11***	−0.11***
		(0.012)	(0.015)	(0.015)	(0.018)	(0.018)	(0.020)	(0.020)
	CPIA environmental regulation	−0.01	−0.02	−0.02	−0.15***	−0.15***	−0.19***	−0.19***
		(0.035)	(0.043)	(0.043)	(0.052)	(0.052)	(0.061)	(0.061)
	Bureaucratic competence	−0.13***	−0.06	−0.06	0.19***	0.19***	0.08	0.08
		(0.044)	(0.057)	(0.057)	(0.070)	(0.070)	(0.080)	(0.080)
	GDP per capita (LN)	−0.03	−0.01	−0.01	0.03	0.03	0.07**	0.07**
		(0.024)	(0.029)	(0.029)	(0.034)	(0.034)	(0.037)	(0.037)
	Polity	0.01	0.02*	0.02*	0.02*	0.02*	0.04***	0.04***
		(0.008)	(0.010)	(0.010)	(0.012)	(0.012)	(0.013)	(0.013)
	Openness	−0.01	−0.048	−0.048	−0.053	−0.053	0.042	0.042
		(0.055)	(0.073)	(0.073)	(0.089)	(0.089)	(0.102)	(0.102)
	Countries	152	152	152	152	152	152	152
	N	23104	23104	23104	23104	23104	23104	23104
	AIC	11364.05	7647.50	7647.50	5505.06	5505.06	4297.99	4297.99
	BIC	11503.66	7787.11	7787.11	5644.67	5644.67	4437.60	4437.60
	LogLik	−5663.03	−3804.75	−3804.75	−2733.53	−2733.53	−2129.99	−2129.99

Note: Dependent variable is the network of collaboration in GEF projects. Threshold for collaboration increases from $\frac{n-ties}{1}$ tie in Model 3.A to $\frac{n-ties}{k}$ for thinned networks of higher collaboration, where k takes values of two in Model B, three in Model C, all the way to seven in Model G.

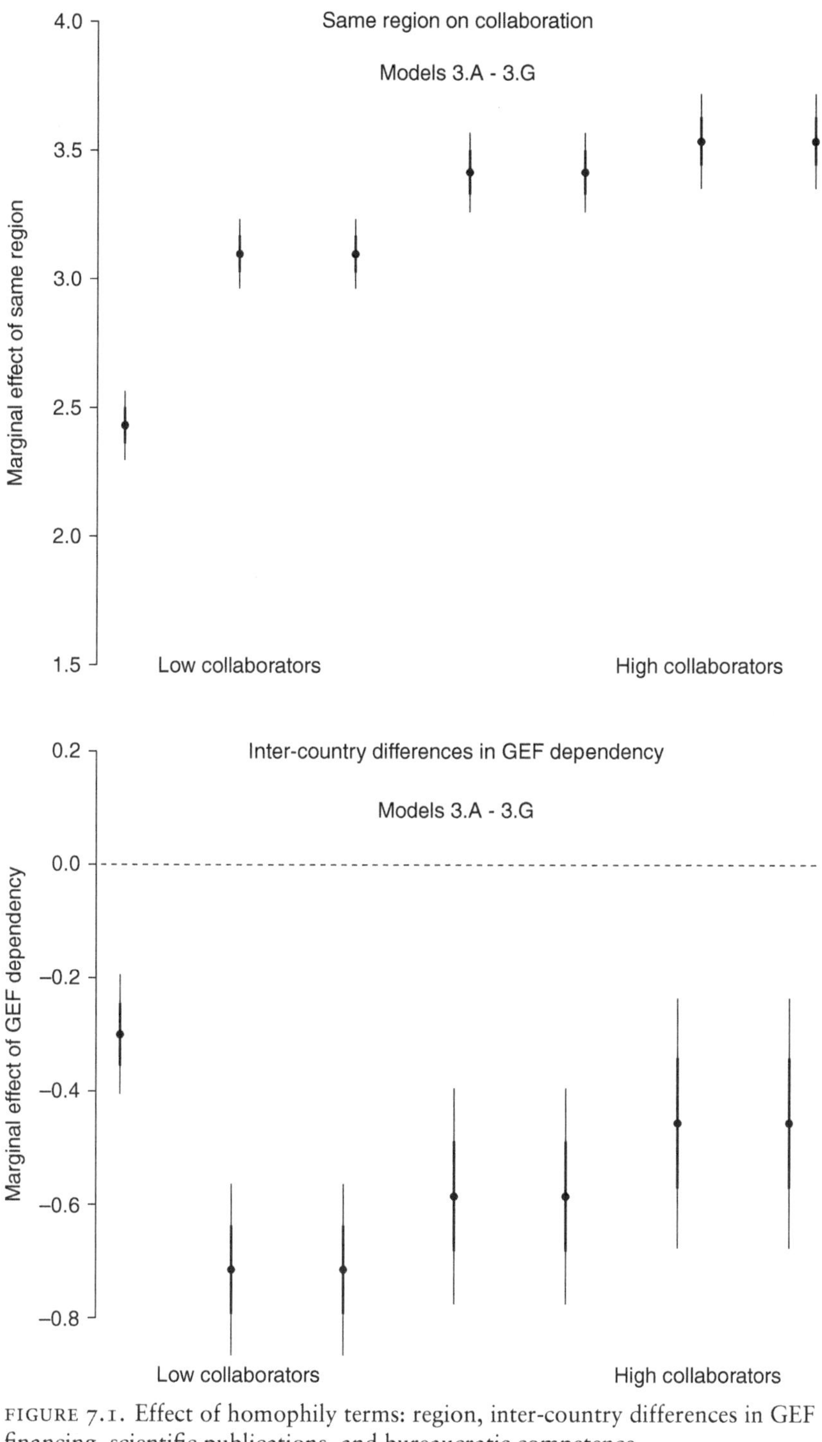

FIGURE 7.1. Effect of homophily terms: region, inter-country differences in GEF financing, scientific publications, and bureaucratic competence.
Note: Marginal effect of coefficient estimates on collaboration. Exponential Random Graph Model Estimates, with 95 percent confidence intervals.

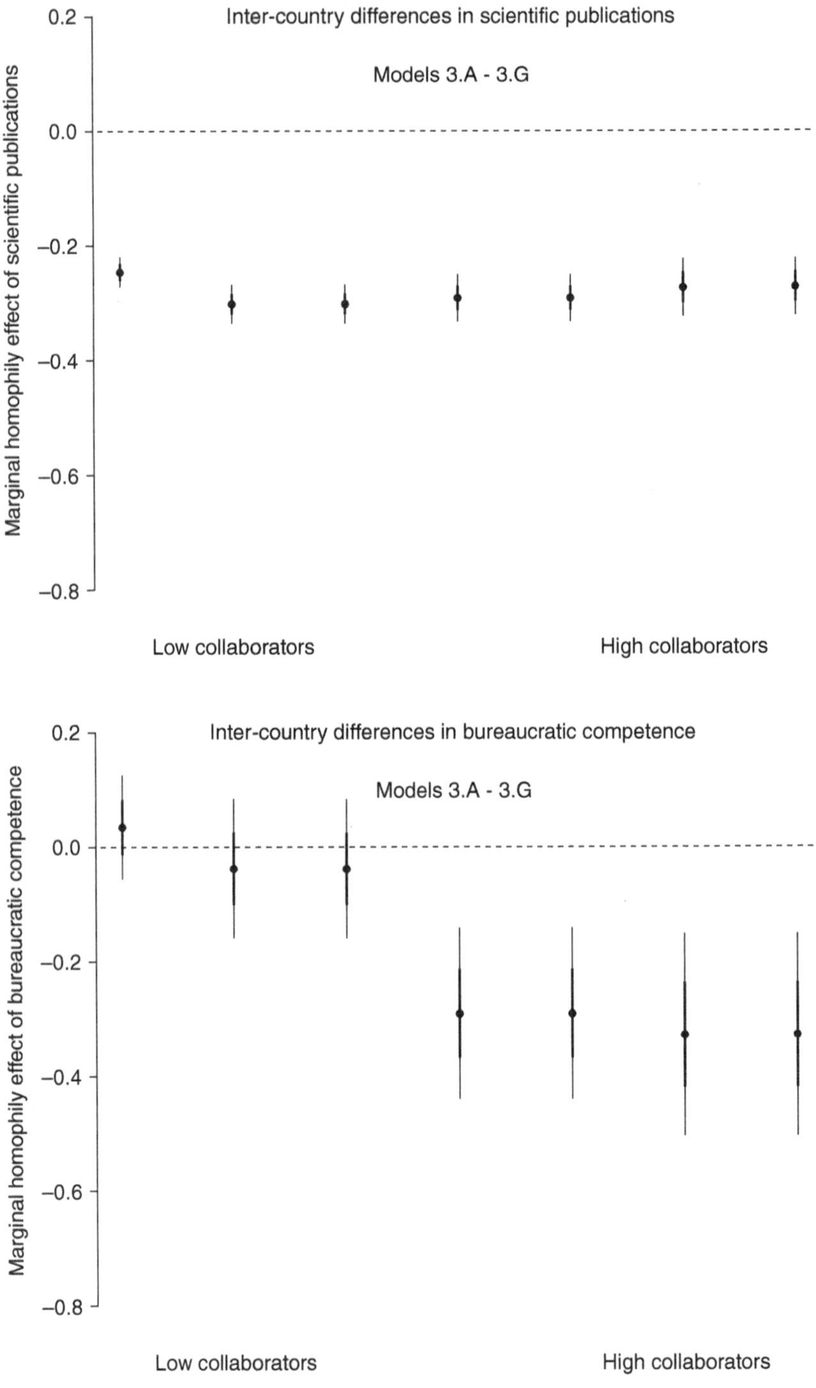

FIGURE 7.1. (*continued*)

will be from the same continent being almost twelve times larger than if the partner was from a different continent.

Model results in Table 7.1 are estimated for different collaboration thresholds,[9] from very occasional collaborators (one instance of collaboration is already enough to define a tie), to very high collaborators (collaboration in at least seven projects is required to consider that a tie exists). The effect of co-membership in the same continent is slightly less dramatic among high collaborators from Latin American, which are twenty times more likely to collaborate with another country of the region. In contrast to Latin America, being in the same region has a very small effect among countries in Asia, which are twice as likely to collaborate with countries from their same region. Meanwhile, regional homophily effects are highest among countries in Oceania, well above those of all other regions. Overall, results show that for both high and low-level collaborators, the most connected continent is Oceania, followed closely by Africa and Latin America.

Table 7.2 incorporates all covariates, including measures of GEF and domestic financing, all homophily terms, and the indicators of program development. Results show that the greater the overall financing by GEF, the more countries collaborate in the network with peers. The effect of GEF financing is positive and statistically significant for all thinned networks, from low-level collaborators to high-level collaborators. Among low-level collaborators, GEF financing results in a fourfold increase in the probability of observing a tie, $exp(1.4) \approx 4$. Among high-level collaborators, GEF financing makes it three times more likely that two countries will collaborate. This confirms a central hypothesis of the present study: more GEF funding increases agency participation in environmental cooperation. By contrast, the greater the amount of co-financing of a country, the less the environmental agencies will participate in GEF projects. The effect remains negative and statistically significant for occasional or intermediate collaborators, reducing collaboration by 25 percent, $exp(-.3) \approx .74$. Among high collaborators the increase in co-financing is associated with a small but statistically significant 10 percent increase in collaboration. Indeed, among high collaborators, pooling resources – whether international or domestic – facilitates cooperation.

The interpretation is straightforward and intuitive: the more funding provided by IOs, the greater the level of collaboration. The greater the

9 This is defined as "thinning" a network, by establishing different thresholds at which we consider whether there is a collaborative tie.

amount of money provided by the domestic agency, the less significant the level of collaboration. Results show the expected substitution effect, whereby countries that have more resources are less likely to engage in cooperative projects that risk spreading those resources on poorer partners.

The effect of shared funding provides a strong test for the arguments of this book: increased differences in co-financing by the countries reduce the likelihood of cooperation significantly. That is, significant asymmetries in domestic funding between state agencies deter cooperation. Consequently, both the availability of significant domestic financing, which would be shared with other agencies when cooperating, as well as large differences in the money to be contributed by different programs, will result in declines in inter-agency cooperation.

Other homophily terms also work in the expected direction. Increased differences in GEF financing, scientific publications, and bureaucratic competence all result in large and significant declines in GEF project cooperation. Indeed, model results provide extensive evidence that, when explaining environmental collaboration, *birds of a feather flock together*. This is verified when considering the allocation of resources, the level of development of the expert bureaucrats' community, and the level of administrative competence of bureaucracies in each country. Membership in the same region significantly increases partner selection, as reported in Table 7.2.

Figure 7.1 provides a more intuitive view of model results. First, the evidence in the upper-right plot of Figure 7.1 supports the hypothesis that countries that receive similar levels of GEF financing are more likely to select each other to collaborate on a project. The lower left plot of Figure 7.1 also shows that larger inter-country differences in the number of annual scientific publications – as a proxy for the level of development of the community of experts – decreases the level of collaboration. Here, homophily effects are roughly similar among low- and high-level collaborators. Finally, the lower right plot in Figure 7.1 shows that inter-country differences in bureaucratic competence reduce collaboration. The effect is not statistically significant among low-level collaborators, but it is very large and significant among high-level collaborators. In fact, homophily in bureaucratic quality has the second largest effect on cooperation among high-level collaborators, after the very large regional effects.

As stated, both the average number of scientific publications in a country and level of bureaucratic competence increase collaboration. These two findings provide strong evidence for the argument presented here and based on past studies in the political economy of skills: the more skills bureaucrats have, the more cooperation they seek. The positive effect of bureaucratic competence, particularly notable among high collaborators, also supports Bach and Newman's theory (i.e., a more independent and professionalized regulatory body increases transgovernmental cooperation) for the field of environmental protection (Bach & Newman, 2014). Similarly, environmental regulation is statistically significant, and as expected, has a negative effect on green cooperation, especially among high collaborators. This finding is also consistent with Bach and Newman's work.

On the other hand, model results do not support standard explanations of cooperation that focus on the role of international actors. While statistically significant, the variable multilateral financing carries a negative sign which means that larger pools of multilateral credit actually reduce cooperation. I interpret this result as showing that having more resources diminishes the incentive to cooperate with peers to substitute skills, given that the available financing comes free of any transgovernmental commitments. This relationship brings into question any possible effect of lenders' conditionality clauses on cooperation, as multilateral agreements do not increase the propensity to collaborate in cross-national environmental projects. Also, the number of technical cooperation agreements a country has signed shows no effect on cooperation and is not statistically significant, except for low-level collaborators. Overall, there seems to be very little spillover from technical agreements on the level of cooperation in GEF projects. Finally, and somewhat surprisingly, there is no globalization effect on international inter-agency cooperation in the protection of the global environment.

Thus, consistent with the theory, study findings show that larger amounts of GEF financing, greater overall levels of program development, and greater homophily among countries in program development increase collaboration. Taken together, results provide strong support of a skill-driven strategy as a driver of cross-national project cooperation in the protection of the global environment.[10]

Conclusion

The study of environmental networks sponsored by the Global Environment Fund is revealing. Results in this chapter provide empirical support

[10] Data and alternative specifications can be requested from the author.

for the hypotheses that inter-agency cooperation among expert bureaucrats is enhanced by the availability of foreign resources, by the level of program development, and by the similarity among environmental programs (homophily). As was also the case when analyzing the NEST sector, results show that reductions in the pool of domestically available resources increase cooperation. Different from the nuclear sector, however, data provided by GEF allows for better discrimination between the pool of domestic and foreign available resources, adding further support for the resource hypotheses proposed in this book.

There are also a number of other interesting findings that emerge from the study of environmental networks and expand results from previous chapters. Different from the nuclear collaborative network, the existence of global projects under GEF sponsorship also allows closer examination of cross-regional patterns. Results show that homophily effects hold at the regional and global scale, with collaboration being more likely to be observed across strata of countries at similar levels of development in different regions of the world.

The environmental data, as well as the model estimates in this chapter, provide interesting information about occasional and frequent environmental cooperation. Results show that the proposed hypotheses hold across the board for occasional versus frequent collaborators. However, they also show that shared funding, skills, and bureaucratic capacity become more important determinant of program behavior as the frequency of collaboration increases. In all, the model of skill updating conditional on funding shocks is well supported by the predictors of collaborative behavior in environmental networks. Further, this model of inter-agency cooperation provides a clear rational for collaborative behavior and, more importantly, show how the effect of shared agency traits becomes stronger among those that collaborate the most.

8

After Austerity

The theory of the expert bureaucrat posits an inverse relation between the skill levels in a country and its participation in international technical cooperation. For most of the book, I focus on the effect of varying skill levels on cooperation when government spending declines. That is, I have explained the two top quadrants of Table 1.1, where bureaucrats endowed with either high or low skills face incentives to cooperate because they are operating under austerity conditions. As predicted by my theory, empirical analyses show that when government spending decreases, nuclear and environmental bureaucrats cooperate more with their foreign peers on cross-national projects. I take this consistent and robust finding as evidence that when governments cut spending, bureaucrats in technical agencies are motivated to seek alternative resources such as funding and skills through international cooperation. This finding is also corroborated by the state experts interviewed for this book.

Far-reaching fiscal crises have been common in the developing world. Because of this regularity it is particularly relevant to study the effect of austerity on bureaucracies in the Global South. Over the years and across countries, government spending cuts have been enacted repeatedly on already inadequate public budgets. Indeed, there is a rich tradition in the social sciences of examining the political consequences of poverty and austerity on the state (Goldsmith, 1999; Schneider & Heredia, 2003; Wibbels, 2006; Murillo, 2009; Falleti, 2011; Kaplan, 2013). After the widespread implementation of neoliberal reforms across the developing world in the 1990s, social scientists in general, and political scientists in particular, became very interested in studying the effects of austerity and state withdrawal (Rauch & Evans, 2000; Alcañiz, 2005a; Murillo, 2009). But in the first decade of the twenty-first century, the state in the Global South has experienced several years of bonanza due to a record-breaking commodities supercycle. Do cooperative networks continue after austerity? The theory of the expert bureaucrat would predict a decrease in international cooperation when government spending increases. That is, under surplus conditions at their home institutions, bureaucrats in technical agencies have less incentive to seek participation in cross-national projects with foreign peers. Yet, given what we know about self-enforcing networks, where pre-existing ties provide an inertia-like effect on actors' interactions, will cooperation drop at the same rate it increases when state resources increase than when they decline?

This chapter examines what happens to international inter-agency cooperation when government spending increases after bureaucrats have forged stable ties with their peers across borders and collaboration networks have been established. This is an important question to ask at this time as a great number of developing countries still benefit from sustained high export prices, which consequently have increased – quite dramatically – the coffers of the state.[1] That is, after years of retreat, in the first decade of the new millennium, the state has gained. The famed commodity boom of the 2000s, greatly driven by the industrial transformation of countries like Brazil, Russia, India, and China (i.e., the BRICs), have helped advance in turn the economies of a majority of primary product producers in the Global South. This, coupled with a leftist and populist turn in many countries outside the industrial North, entailed renewed investments by the state in social, science, and energy policies in the first decade of the 2000s (Morrison, 2009; Rudra & Jensen, 2011; Huber & Stephens, 2012; Weyland, Madrid, & Hunter, 2010).

In short, this chapter fills in the bottom row of Table 1.1 from Chapter 1; the two quadrants in which skill levels may be high or low, but austerity as a motivator to cooperate is absent. In the next pages, I explore the effect of "bringing the state back in" after extensive international cooperation has occurred (Evans, Rueschemeyer, & Skocpol, 1985). I

[1] There is evidence that the overheated world economy, driven by the extraordinary growth rates of China and other emerging markets, started to cool down early in the second decade of the twenty-first century. In particular, China's slowdown will have negative effects in both the industrial North and the Global South. Still, some non-oil commodity prices remain high, especially food goods, which continues to benefit many agricultural producers in the developing world.

use data from the Global Environment Facility (GEF) on cross-national environmental projects for 155 countries. In Chapters 6 and 7, I used GEF data to model the probability of cooperation given a number of covariates, such as the amount of funds for all projects dispersed by the GEF and participating countries. Here, I utilize the same data to model cooperation over time and reflect changing funding policies of the GEF in the 2000s, when it increased the co-financing share of participating countries. In this chapter, I explain the impact of previous cooperation on new partnerships; the impact of recent trends in the Global South (e.g., the sustained rise of commodity prices); and GEF reforms. Given the theory of the expert bureaucrat, the central expectation is that international inter-agency cooperation will decrease when government spending increases. Nonetheless, given the effect of previous existing ties and the self-enforcing nature of networks, I expect the decline of cooperation to be less marked than its rise under austerity.

The Theory of the Expert Bureaucrat under High Government Spending

The theory of the expert bureaucrat is predicated on the fluctuation of government spending and states' endowment of skills. The argument put forth is simple: when government spending goes down, ensuing austerity creates incentives to cooperate and the availability of skills enables bureaucrats to do so. As shown in the empirical chapters of this book, low government spending and a higher level of skills greatly explain international inter-agency cooperation in environmental protection and nuclear energy, science, and technology (NEST). Expert bureaucrats seek out partnerships with peers abroad as a means to access resources that are being cut at home. When government spending declines, research programs are interrupted, budgets are cut, and vital training disappears. Bureaucrats in technical agencies, who depend on updating their skills for career advancement, go outside their state institutions and work on international projects as a compensatory strategy. As previous chapters revealed, bureaucrats with expertise in NEST and environmental protection often forge lasting ties with project partners in other countries. Furthermore, state professionals endeavor to associate with foreign colleagues in true peer institutions with similar levels of skills and resources (i.e., homophily). Consequently, once those equal partnerships form, they will be more likely to persist over time. For example, over the years,

Argentina and Peru have chosen often to collaborate in NEST projects, as Kenya and Tanzania have in environmental ones.[2]

What are the effects of high government spending on cooperation when collaborative networks have been forged already? Put differently, if foreign bureaucrats have cooperated before (regardless of whether with one another or third party partners), will they continue to seek participation in cross-national projects in good economic times? The theory of the expert bureaucrat would tell us to expect a significant drop in international inter-agency cooperation under conditions of economic surplus. This is so, not only because austerity acts as a motivator, but also because more resources at home mean more projects and programs in operation, which in turn demand the inward-focus of agency professionals. International technical cooperation requires many man-hours that cannot be applied to domestically generated projects. Even the larger agencies, like the National Commission of Nuclear Energy in Argentina, experience a trade-off between additional funding available at home and participation in foreign technical projects.[3]

Yet, after agencies have partnered up with foreign institutions and established ongoing projects, do they fully abandon the collaborative networks to which they belong when domestic budgets go up again? I posit that cooperation should drop, as predicted by the theory of the expert bureaucrat, but *over time* we should expect some cooperation to continue, albeit much less intensely, even when austerity as a motivator is absent. The intuition that transgovernmental collaboration does not end abruptly when countries experience surplus government spending is based on several factors. First, with each passing year, the costs of international technical cooperation continue to decrease. Continuous revolutionary advances in information technology (IT) greatly facilitate the coordination of cross-national teams of government scientists working together. Many project tasks can be coordinated remotely through common use of simulators or other IT programs. I expect the positive effect of the digital revolution on international inter-agency cooperation to be most observable in the last decade, given that in the last ten years we have seen the greatest advances and sophistication in the relevant technology. Relatedly, sometimes new cross-national projects build on

[2] See Figures 4.4 in Chapter 4 and 6.1 in Chapter 6, which show how reiterated participation in cross-national projects develops stable networks in NEST and environmental protection across the Global South.

[3] Former Director of International Relations of CNEA, Capitan Roberto Ornstein. Interview with the author in Buenos Aires, Argentina, July 2006.

old ones, either as an expansion or a new version of an original pilot. This also requires a smaller investment of time and resources to get them off the ground and contributes to the decrease of cooperation costs over time.[4]

Second, there is a definite learning curve associated with navigating the administrative bureaucracy of international donor organizations, which often is steep in the beginning but should diminish over time (Young, 2002). Many if not most IOs have rigid regulations and bureaucratic cultures. In their influential book, *Rules for the World: International Organizations in Global Politics*, Barnett and Finnemore point out that:

> IOs often generate their own mistakes, perversities, even disasters. In fact, it is often the very features that make bureaucracies authoritative and effective that can encourage bureaucratic dysfunction... Division of labor and specialization can create tunnel vision among staff. Standardized rules of action can make it difficult to respond to unique situations. Expert knowledge may solve some problems but inevitably carries biases and limitations that can create new problems. Bureaucracies can thus become obsessed with their own rules and captives of parochial outlooks and internal culture.
>
> (Barnett & Finnemore, 2004: 8)

This can be especially true of international financial institutions involved in economic assistance to its membership, where administrative rigidities mix with shareholder and domestic politics (Copelovitch, 2010; Caraway, Rickard, & Anner, 2012).

Grants disbursement at GEF has been shaped by bureaucratic red tape and donor-recipient politics as well, and in its twenty-year history it has undergone numerous policy reforms responding to demands from shareholders and changing international circumstances. As the GEF is set up solely as a financial mechanism, it requires partnerships with other IOs that have more institutionally rich bureaucracies (e.g., with multiple and diverse institutional capacities, not just financial), such as the United Nations Environmental Program (UNEP) and the United Nations Development Program (UNDP). This in turn complicates the grant process for country applicants. Consequently, the often cumbersome and changing intricacies involved in applying for grants from IOs like the GEF are better managed when applicants have previous experience with the donor organization. Additionally, program officers will note explicitly past success-rates of applicants, like in the GEF grant awarded to

[4] See Project and Funding at www.thegef.org.

Argentina and Uruguay to clean up the shared Rio de la Plata discussed in Chapter 6.

Third, past ties forged with project partners should make future collaboration easier as bureaucrats will seek out peers they already know. The literature on networks also offers strong evidence that iterated social interactions tend to be self-sustaining or to put it differently, networks help sustain cooperation through "social inertia" (Marsden, 1983).

> Generally, preexisting network structures can be expected to create a sort of "social inertia" or "commitment" (Cook and Emerson 1978) analogous to "brand loyalty" in which a focal actor considers only certain other actors as possible exchange or coalition partners.
>
> (Marsden, 1983: 690–691)

This relates to what we know of networks and how they shape the cooperative behavior of actors by facilitating collaboration (Hochstetler & Keck, 2007; Scholz, Berardo, & Kile, 2008; Berardo, Alcañiz, Hadden, & Jasny, 2016). This assumption also stems from the widely held understanding that institutions tend to be "sticky," whereby once a political arrangement arises it is hard to dismantle it and a certain "path dependence" of behavior is observable (Pierson, 2000, 2001; Thelen, 2009). Paul Pierson describes how institutional stickiness leads to path dependency:

> Certain courses of political development are hard to reverse. It is not just that institutional veto points make a reversal of course difficult. Individual and organizational adaptations to previous arrangements may also make reversal unattractive.... [this] can become self-reinforcing over time.
>
> (Pierson, 2001: 414)

Given all this, in the case at hand, we should expect the existing networks in NEST and environmental protection to have continued effects on expert bureaucrats even when they are not motivated by austerity.

Finally, incentives to cooperate in the global environment have never been higher. In the past decade or so, a number of global initiatives and inter-governmental organizations have risen to prominence. These endeavors clearly result from loud societal demands for states to coordinate policy response to the numerous and increasingly severe crises of the natural world (Hadden, 2015). Moreover, international environmental law has never been more developed. In fact, the GEF is a financial mechanism of several major international treaties, including the Convention on Biological Diversity (CBD) and the United Nations Framework Convention on Climate Change (UNFCCC) (Biermann & Siebenhüner, 2009). These treaties have well over 150 signatories, and a clear majority of those countries are in the developing world. Therefore, some incentives and pressures to cooperate on the protection of the global environment should remain for developing and emerging powers, even when the bureaucrats' motivation of accessing external resources diminishes.

Emerging Powers and the Commodity Boom: New Funding for the State and Transgovernmentalism in the Global South

The data analyzed in previous chapters cover over twenty years from the late 1980s through the 2000s. These were years of state retreat. As discussed at length earlier, the 1980s were especially challenging for primary product producers, and became known as the Lost Decade precisely because of the foreign debt crisis and negative growth rates caused by a dramatic reversal in the terms of trade against commodities (Frieden, 1991; Murillo, 2000). The 1990s saw similarly low prices on primary exports as well as a major retraction of state investment given the widespread adoption of neoliberal reforms in the developing world (Helbling, Mercer-Blackman, & Cheng, 2008). But the 2000 began auspiciously for many developing countries. Rising prices of food and energy exports and a Chinese economy that was beginning to heat up helped create the conditions that resulted in a record number of "emerging economies" over the past fifteen years. While clearly not the only cause of the commodity boom, dramatic growth rates in China and the resulting demand for food products and energy acted as the proverbial *rising tide that lifts all boats*, helping fuel price increases for primary products across the globe.

China has been an exceptional contributor to record commodity prices worldwide and the country – once with little economic and political presence in Latin America and Africa – has now developed an active role in all regions of the developing world. As a major consumer of oil, natural gas, and soy products, China has had a direct hand in the economic bonanza experienced by agricultural and energy producers in Argentina, Brazil, and Angola. As recently as 2010–2012 and even with evidence of the beginning of an economic slowdown, China consumed over half of world production of metals, close to 30 percent of soybeans, and 15 percent of oil.[5] Soybean, soybean oil, and meal are other major imports to China. Argentina and Brazil, together with the United States, are its

[5] See the World Bank Group Commodities Market Outlook, October 2014, accessed at http://econ.worldbank.org.

main suppliers of soybean and related products. Chinese demand helped increase Argentine exports of soybean, soybean oil, and meal by 300 percent in just ten years, and by 2012 the South American country was selling over 18 billion dollars of that commodity (Murillo & Mangonnet, 2013). Between 2009 and 2013, China consumed a total of 20 percent of Latin American iron ore and 24 percent of copper and copper ore concentrates from the region.[6]

Sub-Sahara African economies have also benefited from Chinese consumption. In 2012 alone, China accounted for the total oil exports of Angola, Congo, and Sudan.[7] Also in that year, over half of the copper exports of the Democratic Republic of Congo and virtually all Zambian copper exports went to China.[8] By 2013, the United Nations Conference on Trade and Development found that China had become "the largest developing country foreign investor in Africa."[9] China has been so central to the growth rates of so many countries, especially developing economies, that it has been said that "when China sneezes, the world gets a cold."[10] From 2003 to 2008, the country maintained double-digit growth rates, peaking at 14.2 percent in 2007; since then Chinese economic growth has slowed to a pace slightly in excess of 7 percent from 2012 to 2014.[11] Other emerging powers have had high growth rates as well, although few as spectacular as the Asian giant. India comes close, hovering around 9–10 percent growth between 2005 and 2011.[12] Many Latin American economies had record growth years, but nothing comparable to the stable trend of China. Furthermore, some were coming off either negative or low growth rates, partly triggered by the Argentine financial collapse in 2001. Many had much catching up to do. Figure 8.1 shows the growth rates for the regions of the developing world over the past decades.

[6] China-Latin America Economic Bulletin, 2015 Edition. Discussion Paper 2015, #9.

[7] See "Mapping and comparing China's imports from Africa" accessed at http://ecdpm.org/great-insights/emerging-economies-and-africa/mapping-comparing-chinas-imports-africa.

[8] See "Mapping and comparing China's imports from Africa" accessed at http://ecdpm.org/great-insights/emerging-economies-and-africa/mapping-comparing-chinas-imports-africa.

[9] See Linkages between China and Sub-Saharan Africa, Global Economic Prospects by the World Bank accessed at www.worldbank.org/en/publication/global-economic-prospects.

[10] See "Low Oil Prices And China Pull The Rug From Under Latin America" accessed at http://oilprice.com/Energy/Energy-General/Low-Oil-Prices-And-China-Pull-The-Rug-From-Under-Latin-America.html.

[11] See World Bank Data Indicators accessed at http://databank.worldbank.org/data/home.aspx.

[12] See World Bank Data Indicators accessed at http://databank.worldbank.org/data/home.aspx.

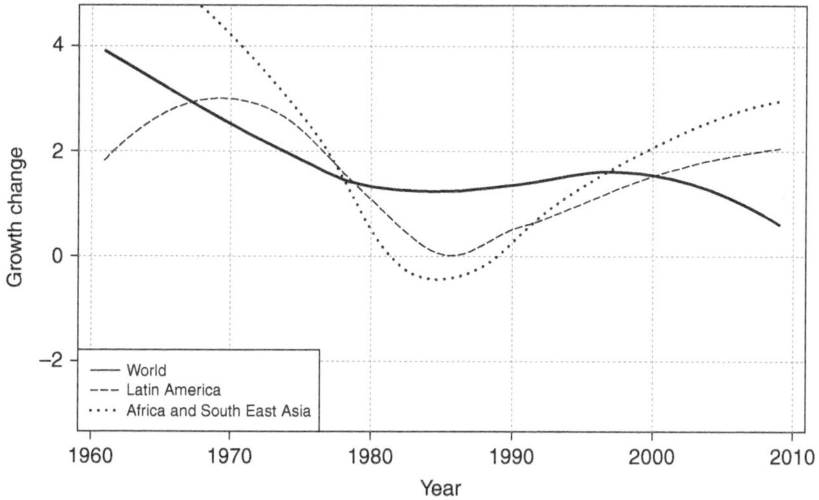

FIGURE 8.1. Growth rates for the world and the regions of the Global South, 1961–2009.
Note: LOESS estimates from the World Development Indicators (WDI), World Bank.

The commodity boom of the twenty-first century has had widespread effects across the entire Global South. The boom has been exceptional, primarily for two reasons. First, it has avoided a bust for record time, with prices remaining high in a sustained way. Second, it involved a wide range of commodities (from energy to food to metals), which means that it affected an inordinate number of developing countries (Conceição & Marone, 2008; Erten & Ocampo, 2013). Indeed, countries producing and exporting a diverse assortment of primary products, like natural gas, oil, soy beans, wheat, and tin, have benefited from exceedingly favorable terms of trade. The commodity boom has raised living wages and improved development indicators in many countries. Given its global impact and length, it is not surprising that the commodity supercycle has rearranged the existing world order in significant ways. Analysts describe this commodities supercycle:

> The current boom has also been more broad based and longer lasting than is usual, and it contrasts noticeably with the 1980s and 1990s, when most commodity prices were on a downward trend.
>
> (Helbling, Mercer-Blackman, & Cheng, 2008: 11)

For the larger states in the Global South, the price bonanza and the trading power that comes with it have translated into economic and political influence in international affairs. In the past few years, the emerging powers have produced a number of initiatives that seek to coordinate and institutionalize their growing clout relative to the United States and Europe. Many ambitious transgovernmental initiatives, both intra- and inter-regional, are being funded by the trade surplus of the last decade. These initiatives tackle shared political, economic, and trade goals of the emerging and regional powers. One pressing concern, for countries in the Global South, has been the problem of accessing international credit. Historically, developing countries have struggled to get credit at competitive rates from private international financial institutions, and while multilateral banks offer lower interest rates, they attach onerous reform conditions (the so-called conditionality clauses) to their loans (Vreeland, 2003; Kaplan, 2013).

Thus, not surprisingly, a number of emerging markets riding the commodity wave used their trade surpluses to fund the creation of new regional and cross-regional multilateral banks. In contrast to the International Monetary Fund (IMF), the World Bank, and the Inter-American Development Bank (IADB), multilateral financial institutions stemming from the post-War order and managed by non-borrowers from industrial economies, the new development banks of the twenty-first century will not use conditionality clauses. Once again, China is poised to become a major regional and global financial player. Its brand new Asian Infrastructure Investment Bank (AIIB) is set to rival the World Bank in infrastructure loans to developing and OECD countries alike.[13]

China is helping redefine policy coordination in the developing world, especially in finance and development aid, and has forged strong ties with other leading regional powers – namely, Brazil, Russia, India, and South Africa – in this area. Collectively known as the BRICS, these countries are making significant investments in deepening South to South cooperation. In 2014, for example, the five countries signed the founding treaty of the BRICS New Development Bank.[14] This financial institution explicitly seeks to challenge the dominance of OECD countries in multilateral lending and signal the rise of a new order, dominated by emerging markets. Other examples of transgovernmental initiatives in the Global South financed by the commodities boom include the Bank of the South

[13] See http://blogs.wsj.com/chinarealtime/2015/04/15/chinas-infrastructure-bank-attracts-57-founding-members-prospectively/.

[14] See www.washingtonpost.com/blogs/monkey-cage/wp/2014/07/17/what-the-new-bank-of-brics-is-all-about/.

(BancoSur) and the IBSA trilateral. BancoSur was founded by the center-left governments of Argentina, Bolivia, Brazil, Ecuador, Paraguay, Uruguay, and Venezuela in 2009. Like the BRICS New Development Bank, it will have a similar mission to the World Bank – to serve as a lender for social and infrastructure programs – but without conditionality clauses requiring market reforms.[15] In 2003, India, Brazil, and South Africa created the IBSA Dialogue Forum to promote South-South cooperation and policy coordination in such key areas as pharmaceuticals and patent disputes as well as science and technology.[16] The IBSA trilateral is a transgovernmental initiative that remains loosely institutionalized yet has become increasingly relevant in South-South cooperation.

The commodity boom is a critical backdrop to test the theory of the expert bureaucrat in times of increased government spending. The surge in export prices started a solid decade after the rise of transgovernmental cooperation in environmental protection. As the next section shows, GEF funding policies beginning around 2005 seemed to respond to the overall trend of economic growth in the Global South. At that time, the environmental IO increased significantly the amount of country co-financing (i.e., the money that each participant contributes to a project), consequently decreasing the size of the grant it disbursed.

"Pick Up the Tab": From GEF Financing to Self-Sustained Cooperation

The empirical analyses of Chapter 7 revealed that inter-agency cooperation in the protection of the global environment is driven by declines in government spending that place domestic environmental programs under stress, demands for new sources of training and skills by bureaucrats at greater levels of expertise, and selective monetary incentives provided by the Global Environmental Fund. In the early 1990s, GEF resources gave environmental bureaucrats an initial push to cooperate by reducing the cost burden of coordinating policies and programs with peers across the

[15] See www.unasursg.org/es. The Bank of the South comes out of UNASUR, the Union of South American Nations. UNASUR, in turn, was created in 2008. It brings together the countries of the Common Market of the South or the Mercosur (Argentina, Brazil, Paraguay, Uruguay, and Venezuela), the countries under the customs union of the Andean Community of Nations (Bolivia, Colombia, Ecuador, and Peru) and Chile, Guyana, and Suriname. Its main objective is to expand regional integration to all of South America.

[16] See www.ibsa-trilateral.org/.

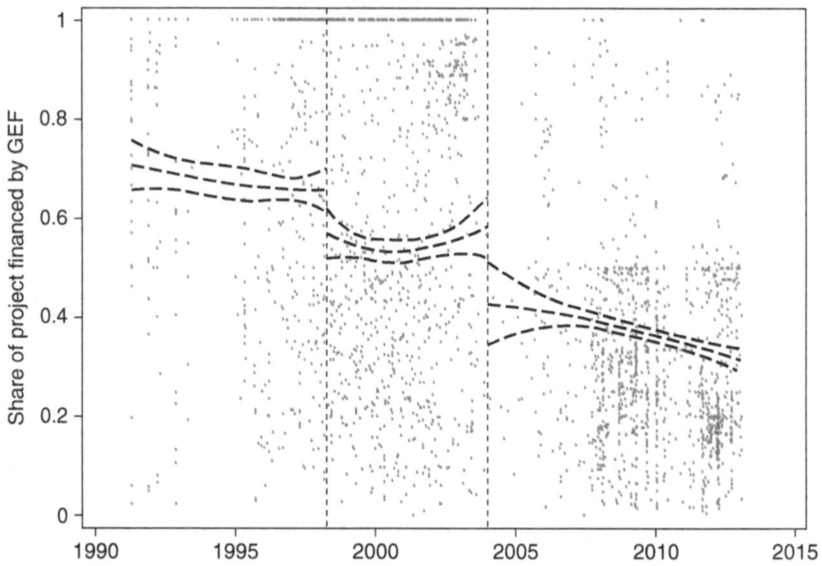

FIGURE 8.2. Share of the total project cost financed by GEF, 1991–2011.
Note: Mean financing provided by GEF in three separate periods: 1991–1997, 1998–2003, 2004–2011.

border. Chapter 7 also showed that the more money GEF was willing to disburse in a country grant, the more likely the recipient would be able to participate in a cross-national project. In contrast, when national agencies had to put up a greater share of the cost of the project (i.e., increase their co-financing), the less likely they would cooperate, holding all other variables constant.

The importance of self-sustained and self-financed cooperation, however, is thrown into sharp relief as soon as we observe the changing trend of the 2000s, when GEF financing declines dramatically and member countries were required to finance at least 50 percent of the investment for a project. Figure 8.2 illustrates this change in share. We can see that while in the early 1990s GEF financed approximately 70 percent of the total cost of projects, the IO funding declined to less than half that amount by 2012.

The data show that between 1991 and 2012 GEF financing changed in different ways. First, in the late 1990s, GEF increased its total participation in the financing of projects that involved small, low-income states. On the other hand, the larger economies of the Global South, like Brazil, India, and China, were expected to commit more resources to cross-national projects. We can see this clearly in Figure 8.2 for the years 1999 to 2003, in which a small group of countries had projects fully funded by GEF (upper middle quadrant) and a much larger cluster of countries participated in projects that received very little financing from the IO (lower middle quadrant).

GEF policy of considerably subsidizing low-income countries while expecting the larger economies to contribute more co-financing would change mid-decade. Beginning in 2004, we can observe how on average country financing reached 50 percent for all projects, reducing the disparity in collaboration costs between large and small countries. Consequently, the field was leveled again but with state agencies being required to shoulder most expenses in the collaborative effort. After 2005, when more project co-financing was left in the hands of member countries, cooperation among peers from programs at comparable levels of development strengthened. In short, when state co-financing increases, homophily in the network strengthens. As I will show in the next sections, the wave of economic growth in the Global South in the mid-2000s (after environmental transgovernmentalism was well-established), enhanced partnerships between similarly skilled national programs to the detriment of cooperation with the relatively poorer states, which previously had been financed more heavily by GEF. To explore this dynamic in further detail, the next sections estimate different Exponential Random Graph Models (ERGM) for each of the three periods described in Figure 8.2.

The Data

The Dependent Variable

As in the previous chapter, the dependent variable of the Exponential Random Graph Models considers each member country as a node and collaboration between each pair of countries as an edge. Consistent with the description from the previous section, I explain the determinants of peer selection in GEF projects, estimating the probability of observing a collaborative tie between pairs of environmental agencies in each pair of countries.

Given that the GEF network is valued, with higher counts describing more active collaboration, I follow Cranmer and Desmarais' strategy and estimate the probability of low-level collaboration and high-level collaboration, thinning the affiliation matrix of each period network. I estimate six different models, with low- and high-level collaboration for each of the three periods.

The Covariates

To explain international inter-agency cooperation in the protection of the global environment for each of the three periods, I consider the same variables used in the analysis of Chapter 7. I distinguish three different groups of variables that explain the effect of financing, peer program similarity, and country-level traits.

The first group of variables measures the effect of both GEF and domestic financing on the probability of collaboration. The first variable describes the total funding provided by GEF *to* each country *i* (each node) in US$ dollars (LN), **GEF (US$)**. I expect that higher levels of financing by GEF will make collaboration in cross-national projects more attractive to country participants. The second variable, **Co-financing (US$)**, measures the total financing provided *by* each country *i* in US$ dollars (LN). Consistent with the proposed theory, higher (lower) levels of domestic financing will reduce (increase) the probability of country collaboration in the GEF-sponsored network.

A second group of variables tests for the overall effect of program development on collaboration. These variables are expected to be positive, with higher development (i.e., higher skill level) increasing the incentives to collaborate in order to maximize already existing (yet depreciating) skills in the bureau. I include the average number of **Scientific Publications (LN)** over ten years for each country *i* as a proxy for the relative skills of experts in each country. As in the previous chapter, I expect higher overall scientific skills in a country to correlate positively with cooperation. I also consider the overall change in **government spending** and **GDP per capita.**

As in Chapter 7, a third group of covariates tests for homophily effects in network collaboration. I consider the extent to which differences in resources (money) and skills (program development) reduce collaboration. A measure of **Inter-Country Differences in GEF Financing** is expected to decrease partner selection, the greater the difference in GEF funding allocation between pairs of countries. A measure of **Inter-Country Differences in Co-financing** is expected to reduce collaboration the greater the difference in overall domestic investment between partners. **Inter-Country Differences in Scientific Publications** measures differences in technical skills, using the number of scientific publications for each country in the network. I expect this estimate to be negative, indicating that programs with expert bureaucrats that have significantly different skills will be less likely to collaborate in GEF projects. The models also include **Inter-Country Differences in GDP per capita** and level of trade exposure (**Inter-Country Differences in Openness**), as a measure of country wealth and of exposure to globalization, respectively. The variable **Inter-Country Difference in Polity** seeks to capture the effect of differences in political regime types, along the ten-point scale of Polity IV. All control variables (except the covariates generated from GEF data) come from the International Debt Statistics of the World Bank. Finally, using the GEF grant data, I created the control **Region**, which captures any regional effect.

Models and Results

As I anticipated above, I estimated six different models that capture differences by period as well as differences between high- and low-level environmental collaborators. Model results are presented in Table 8.1. Coefficients report log-odds-ratios describing the effect that a one-unit change in the independent variable has on the probability of observing a tie between national environmental agencies from two countries. Given that I have not included structural network variables in the model, coefficients can be interpreted as logistic results, without requiring simulated networks to assess the magnitude of change.

The edge, which should be interpreted as a constant in standard OLS models, shows that collaboration increased significantly over time. This is more noticeable when comparing Models A and E in Table 8.1, which have roughly similar parameter estimates but a much larger estimate for the edge parameter after 2004.

Consistent with the evolution of GEF financing described in Figure 8.2, results show that more financing from GEF-increased collaboration in the early 1990s. In the first period, GEF financing was critical to the expansion of environmental cooperation among country agencies. As in Chapter 7, collaboration in this early period is associated with larger GEF financing and lower levels of co-financing by participating state agencies. Further, cooperation is more likely among programs that share relatively similar skills and invest comparable resources. Finally, as the theory of the expert bureaucrat predicted: the higher the government spending, the lower the level of cooperation between national state agencies.

For the second period (1998–2003), Table 8.1 shows that cooperation is driven by the investment made by domestic programs rather than GEF, with the environmental IO disproportionally allocating its resources into smaller, poorly funded state agencies.

TABLE 8.1. *Determinants of Inter-Agency Cooperation in GEF Projects*

		Model A 1991–1997 Low Collaborators	Model B 1991–1997 High Collaborators	Model C 1998–2003 Low Collaborators	Model D 1998–2003 High Collaborators	Model E 2004–2011 Low Collaborators	Model F 2004–2011 High Collaborators
Financing Terms	Edge (constant)	−16.76***	−15.61***	−6.98***	−0.86	−4.44***	1.83*
		(1.488)	(2.682)	(1.186)	(1.726)	(0.809)	(1.041)
	GEF (US$)	0.48***	0.52***	0.1***	−0.31***	0.47***	0.48***
		(0.046)	(0.084)	(0.036)	(0.050)	(0.027)	(0.033)
	Co-financing (US$)	−0.03***	−0.05**	0.12***	0.22***	−0.31***	−0.58***
		(0.011)	(0.020)	(0.016)	(0.024)	(0.022)	(0.028)
Homophily Terms	Same region	2.24***	3.11***	2.5***	3.57***	1.57***	1.89***
		(0.070)	(0.146)	(0.068)	(0.139)	(0.054)	(0.060)
	Inter-country differences in GEF financing	−0.52***	−0.58***	−0.37***	−0.56***	−0.12***	−0.17***
		(0.069)	(0.132)	(0.058)	(0.088)	(0.034)	(0.045)
	Inter-country differences in domestic co-financing	−0.09***	−0.22***	−0.11***	−0.18***	−0.03	−0.24***
		(0.016)	(0.033)	(0.021)	(0.035)	(0.026)	(0.033)
	Inter-country differences in scientific publications	−0.04***	−0.13***	−0.08***	−0.03	−0.14***	−0.2***
		(0.017)	(0.033)	(0.017)	(0.027)	(0.011)	(0.015)
	Inter-country difference in GDP per capita.	−0.1**	−0.11	0.03	−0.07	−0.02	−0.01
		(0.048)	(0.087)	(0.044)	(0.067)	(0.027)	(0.035)
	Inter-country difference in polity	−0.01***	−0.01**	0.000	−0.01	0.01**	0.000
		(0.003)	(0.005)	(0.003)	(0.004)	(0.003)	(0.004)

	Inter-country difference in openness	0.16	−0.11	−0.09	−0.01	0.16***	0.13*
Program Development Variables	Inter-country difference in openness	0.16	−0.11	−0.09	−0.01	0.16***	0.13*
		(0.113)	(0.201)	(0.111)	(0.167)	(0.058)	(0.077)
	Scientific publications (LN)	0.06***	0.06***	0.05***	−0.03*	0.05***	0.11***
		(0.010)	(0.017)	(0.012)	(0.018)	(0.007)	(0.009)
	GDP per capita	0.08	−0.16	−0.04	0.04	−0.04	−0.03
		(0.056)	(0.104)	(0.050)	(0.072)	(0.032)	(0.041)
	Polity	−0.01**	−0.01*	0.000	0.000	0.000	0.000
		(0.002)	(0.003)	(0.002)	(0.003)	(0.003)	(0.003)
	Openness	−0.03	0.18	−0.08	0.14	0.11***	−0.21***
		(0.080)	(0.136)	(0.080)	(0.118)	(0.042)	(0.057)
	Government spending	−3.71**	−13.64***	0.3	2.24	0.9	1.1
		(1.875)	(3.662)	(1.470)	(2.083)	(1.130)	(1.412)
	Countries	142	142	146	146	142	142
	N	20022	20022	21170	21170	20022	20022
	AIC	12214.00	12449.00	12318.00	12916.00	13189.00	12016.00
	BIC	12330.00	12565.00	12433.00	13031.00	13306.00	12132.00

Note: Exponential Random Graph Models for the three different periods (1991–1997, 1998–2003, and 2004–2011), for low and high collaborators.

Changes in the GEF financing strategy, however, did not alter the patterns of partner selection by cooperating national agencies. Homophily effects remain very similar, with inter-country differences in both GEF financing and in domestic co-financing reducing the log-odds of cooperation.

Two important variations on the determinants of cooperation directly speak to the larger debate of what happens when the state comes back. In the first place, the effect of declining government spending on international inter-agency cooperation is large and statistically significant for the first period. However, in the second and third periods, government spending no longer has any significant effect. That is, once the transgovernmental network of cross-national projects on the protection of the global environment was forged, cooperation among country participants did not decline with sustained economic growth. In other words, a spending shock (i.e., a decline) on the part of the government generates incentives to cooperate with peers abroad, but once the network is established, national agencies tend to maintain that cooperation. Consequently, while there is a strong association between state retrenchment and international inter-agency cooperation, we do not observe a decline in that cooperation when the state comes back in.

Second, while in the early years cooperation was encouraged by GEF financing, allowing both small and large programs to cooperate more actively, in the later periods, program homophily becomes more affected by country co-financing. That is, state programs that received similar levels of GEF funding were more likely to work together in the early 1990s; whereas in the later periods, domestic agencies that are willing to contribute similar number of resources are more likely to collaborate with each other. Consequently, while in the early 1990s GEF financing helped facilitate cooperation between more and less skilled environmental state agencies; cooperation today is more likely to emerge among environmental bureaus at similar levels of funding.

Conclusion

This chapter set out to test an extension of the theory of the expert bureaucrat: What happens to environmental international inter-agency cooperation when government spending increases? To a great extent, the question is motivated by the commodity boom of the twenty-first century, which helped replenish the depleted coffers of many developing states between 2001 and 2011. The theory of the expert bureaucrat predicts a decline in cooperation when government spending increases, but I qualify this prediction with findings from network theory and historical institutionalism, as I also expect ties between participating national agencies to be "sticky" and endure when the state comes back. Furthermore, the cost of remote collaboration on large international technical projects continues to go down, which should also facilitate the continuation of collaboration under surplus economic conditions at home.

Model results confirmed the expectation that there is an institutional inertia at work, whereby once environmental networks of cooperation have been established in the Global South, they tend to remain active even when the factors that led to its origin are reversed. The empirical section of the chapter took into account the different patterns of funding by the Global Environment Facility over time. Overall, the results of this chapter mirror model coefficients from Chapter 7. GEF financing makes cooperation more likely, country co-financing less likely, and homophily effects remain strong.

The analysis presented here should encourage practitioners and advocates of the conservation and protection of the global commons. Even when done "on the cheap," cooperative networks have proved to be resilient to significant changes in the home economy. Once forged, bureaucratic networks in the Global South are hard to dismantle. What is less encouraging is the findings of this chapter, and consistent with the results from Chapters 5 and 7, that disparity in skills and funding among potential project partners matters. The propensity of a participating state agency to seek partnerships with foreign peers at similar levels of development and economic resources endures over time, whether the economy is on a downward or upward trend.

9

Conclusion

The Hidden Costs of Low Skills

> There is little doubt that experts and expertise will be highly in demand as long as modern societies keep evolving towards higher complexity, as they have done in recent centuries.
>
> Evetts, Mieg, & Felt, 2006: 120 in *Expertise and Expert Performance*

A recent piece on public radio asked: "What do you do when you are a scientist and you have no money for your research?"[1] The report featured a molecular biologist in the United States who studied the effects of addiction on the brain: "He's interested in doing something about mental illness and addiction, but he needs a lot more basic information about the brain before he can invent a new drug or treatment. Now, most of the time the federal government funds the basic biomedical research in this country. But it's getting harder and harder to snag one of those government research grants." So, the story continues, the scientist took matters into his own hands by crowdsourcing: he organized a campaign using different types of social media to ask the public to fund his research project. His goal was to raise the equivalent to a small seed grant, which he did. Like this professional, other American scientists are networking in new and resourceful ways to cope with widespread government spending cuts, which tend to affect disproportionately Research and Development (R&D) budgets.[2] Crowdsourcing has enabled the implementation

[1] See www.npr.org/2013/02/14/171975368/scientist-gets-research-donations-from-crowdfunding

[2] For example, the grants program at the National Institutes of Health (NIH) has cut funding by almost 2 percent on a yearly basis since 2003. See http://yaledailynews.com/blog/2013/10/18/amidst-budget-cuts-science-appeals-to-public/.

of projects that tend to be low on costs but high on innovation.[3] Thus, soliciting "ideas, skills, or participation" from a wide network is one strategy scientists follow in the face of declining state sponsorship.[4] More critically, as monies raised through this networking method are typically supplemental to the level that is needed to support a science research program, the most significant contribution of crowdsourcing is the access it provides to innovation and expertise.

In the developing world, where R&D budgets turn on a dime, state scientists have been "crowdsourcing" for decades. Accustomed to regular cuts in government spending, which can quickly derail research programs, expert bureaucrats network with peers outside their agencies to pool scarce resources, access new technology, and keep up with professional best practices. In non-OECD countries a majority of technology-intensive scientists work in government agencies, as employment alternatives for them in the private sector or university are few and infrequent. For this kind of expert, networking to access new resources in response to the withdrawal of state support often entails going beyond national borders. While overlooked by the existing literature, cooperation in technology-intensive sectors is on the rise among skilled bureaucrats and their national agencies in the developing world.

As discussed throughout the book, if the incentive to invest in skills drives the international behavior of the bureaucrat, three empirical observations should follow. First, higher-skilled bureaucrats should be more active in NEST and environmental collaborative networks. The reason for this is that bureaucrats and agencies with greater levels of human capital have the most to lose when governments fail to invest in them and the most to gain by updating and upgrading skills. As a result, the theory of the expert bureaucrat predicts that skilled professionals will be more likely to cooperate with foreign peers. Second, declines in government spending will correlate with increased participation of bureaucrats in international inter-agency cooperation. This expectation stemmed from the understanding that government cuts signal lean times ahead and cue state experts to seek alternatives to state funding. Working together on cross-national projects allows bureaucrats to pool existing resources and better the chances of accessing donor funds. Third, if skill

[3] See http://yaledailynews.com/blog/2013/10/18/amidst-budget-cuts-science-appeals-to-public/ and http://dailycrowdsource.com/training/crowdsourcing/what-is-crowdsourcing.

[4] See http://dailycrowdsource.com/training/crowdsourcing/what-is-crowdsourcing.

upgrading is the primary causal mechanism behind inter-agency cooperation in expert agencies, cooperation should be characterized by homophily effects. If bureaucrats' priority is to update and upgrade their skills, they will want to seek out partners who have superior training. The rationale for this is straightforward; most professionals will prefer to collaborate with peers in advanced programs. Bureaucrats at higher skill levels, however, will also favor working with colleagues from more advanced or equal agencies. The resulting coordination game should facilitate cooperation among programs at comparative levels of development, as agencies at greater levels of expertise will reject partners that are further down the skill chain.

To be sure, support for the theory of the expert bureaucrat is strong. All three expectations are observed and the predicted relationships proved. As model results in Chapters 5, 7, and 8 show, there is significant and robust evidence to uphold the main hypotheses of the book. Furthermore, the wealth of qualitative data collected through archival research and numerous interviews with expert bureaucrats in two continents, also supports the study's hypotheses. Thus, in the following sections, I discuss some of the policy implications and possible extensions of my argument.

No Skills, No Cooperation: International Collaboration as a Public Good

The key finding of this book is that higher levels of human capital and greater parity in program development matter enormously for international cooperation. It shows how state experts with poor skills cannot forge collaborative ties with peer programs and, consequently, cannot benefit from the technology transfer entailed in it. "No skills, no cooperation" is the opening line of the book because regardless of how closely international development agencies work with low-skilled state experts, or how democratic or open their countries are, low-skill agencies are unable to access the benefits of inter-agency collaboration in the Global South. This book makes an original contribution, with important implications that have been overlooked by the existing literature. While the scholarship on skills has overwhelmingly focused on the link between domestic skills and international competition, my book reveals crucial links between domestic skills *and* international cooperation.

Thus, the book tackled an important question that should be of interest to students of international cooperation: How do differing bureaucratic skill levels and the scientific reservoir of a country affect its participation in collaborative transgovernmental networks? My theory provides a general answer and shows that there are barriers to access international cooperation that lie outside the political will of domestic actors. Not only must countries be willing to join in coordinated international endeavors, they must be able also. Especially in the information age, with all policy sectors increasing their technical complexity, bureaucratic skills remain critical to working with peers at the international level.

Over the past decades, many long-established barriers to international collaboration have been lowered or removed. Inexpensive communication channels, which have multiplied in the information age, make it easier to coordinate remote work. As discussed at length in this book, the main mission of IOs is to advance inter-state cooperation, for which they bring to bear numerous resources (e.g., annual membership assemblies, training workshops, funding). One exclusive tool available to them is the collection of programs and projects they manage and through which members – especially developing countries – can work together on common problems. Because of scarce resources and pressure to deliver results and remain accountable to country donors, IOs aim to enlarge the number of participants (Kahler, 1992; Young, 2002; Biermann and Siebenhüner, 2009). In contrast to individual country assistance, multilateral partnerships "spreads the wealth" of state agency resources more efficiently and effectively (Schiff & Winters, 2002). Just as critically, these partnerships multiply the effects of cooperation and create networks of knowledge, as project participants (i.e., national bureaucrats) forge lasting ties, share knowledge and practices, and address common problems (Carmen, Nesshöver, Saarikoski, Vandewalle, Watt, Wittmer, & Young, 2015).

Globalization, the process through which domestic economic markets and actors progressively integrate and internationalize, has also increased state-to-state cooperation. As countries become more open and exposed to the global economy, they face greater incentives to coordinate policy and find common solutions to shared problems. Finally, the wave of democratization that transformed so many authoritarian regimes in the Global South has lowered security concerns among states and facilitated greater cooperation. Indeed, there is a wealth of research that shows that democracies are much more likely to collaborate with foreign peers than dictatorships (Fredriksson & Gaston, 2000; Mansfield, Milner, & Rosendorff, 2000; Simmons & Hopkins, 2005; Goodliffe & Hawkins, 2006; Alcañiz, 2012). All of these processes have pulled domestic actors – state experts, government officials, and NGOs – into the global sphere.

To the extent that inter-state collaboration results in benefits that are shared by all and withheld from none (such as the reduction in size of the ozone hole or fewer atomic weapons), we can characterize international cooperation as a public good. Yet, even this type of good may have hidden costs that restrict the right to use it (Alesina, Baqir, & Easterly, 1997; Cremer & Laffont, 2003; Raleigh, 2010). In particular, "access to the good may be costly. In other words, some private good or service must be consumed along with the public good" (Cremer & Laffont, 2003: 2). Despite its relevance, the problem of costly access to public goods has not been examined much in political science. Rather, we tend to assume all consumers have equal access to public goods – even global ones like "the environmental commons and global knowledge for development."[5] But as this book has shown, lack of skills can be costly in the information age and hinder actors from reaping the benefits of international collaboration.

This is a question of particular importance to countries in the Global South. When domestic budgets falter, international donors and IOs can help supplement the funds needed for participation in cross-national projects. But skills, which take a medium to long-term investment in human capital, cannot be easily covered by outsiders (Amirault & Branson, 2006). When skills are severely lacking, countries miss out on significant opportunities to advance domestic programs through international technical cooperation. In other words, countries fail to benefit from accessing new knowledge, know-how, best practices, and innovative techniques. Further, it exacerbates the gap between the developing South and the industrial North, as the prospect of accessing international sources of learning and training is contingent on existing levels of skills, an area in which the latter has significant advantages over the former.

Policy Implications for Transparency, Good Governance, and Nonproliferation

In 2005, Anne-Marie Slaughter published her seminal book *A New World Order* where she brings to our attention the extraordinary number of bureaucrats and state regulators who are forging transgovernmental ties with their foreign peers in order to exchange critical information and coordinate policy across borders. Slaughter hails transgovernmentalism as an effective and efficient strategy for global governance.

[5] The World Bank provides other examples of global public goods that include the treatment of "communicable diseases (including HIV/AIDS, tuberculosis, malaria, and avian influenza), international trade, international financial architecture." See http://web.worldbank.org.

The more decentralized and specialized the state is, the better equipped it is to deal with the many challenges it faces: international terrorism, organized crime, global finance, and the environment, to mention just a few. Many of those who oppose the state, she points out, are already organized through global networks. Thus, governments are best served by decentralizing and coordinating their response. In other words, global governance can be achieved if state experts, rather than politicians, partner up with their peers across borders. In her book, Slaughter makes the argument that transgovernmentalism is more democratic and inclusive, and produces better governance than direct negotiations carried out by national governments.

Consequently, a valid question to ask is whether the bureaucratic networks in NEST and the protection of the global environment also help create good global governance. Does international inter-agency cooperation further policy coordination among countries? To begin with, the case studies of Argentina and Brazil are good examples of how a "partner or perish" mandate increases transparency. The two countries made the heaviest investment in nuclear expertise and capacity during military rule (1966–1973 and 1976–1983 in Argentina, and 1964–1985 in Brazil). Not surprisingly, the *Juntas* in both countries empowered the more recalcitrant factions of the national state agencies (namely, the Argentine National Atomic Energy Commission, or CNEA and the Brazilian National Nuclear Energy Commission, or CNEN), which in turn pushed for exploring some of the strategic uses of nuclear energy. During the 1970s, the two countries refused to sign the Non-Proliferation Treaty, which was interpreted by some in the international community as evidence of a potential nuclear arms race brewing in South America. Argentina and Brazil were deemed "countries to be monitored" for their nuclear activities and were often compared to India and Pakistan as potential nuclear enemies. In the 1970s, a small group of Argentine nuclear scientists, under the protection of an undercover program, developed native technology to enrich uranium. At the same time, Brazilians developed the Parallel or Autonomous Program (placed completely outside IAEA safeguards) that sought to control the full cycle of nuclear energy, including the enrichment phase as well as reprocessing spent fuel. Furthermore, the scientists of this program were also working on building a nuclear submarine.

As described in Chapter 3, the severe economic crisis of the early 1980s and the lack of investment in nuclear expertise in the two countries left state experts with few options. Partnering would entail opening up both programs to each other in order to pool existing resources and share in some of the costs of R&D. The loss of autonomy (and secrecy) would be offset by the gain in skills and other resources. Staying the course (i.e., preserving a closed-off program) without state funding, on the other hand, was a problematic alternative. Nuclear bureaucrats would have retained some autonomy, but at the same time, they would have had very few investment options. Staying within the confines of an impoverished state makes it very difficult for bureaucrats to avoid the depreciation of their skills.

More importantly, cooperation across borders forces disclosure. In the case of Argentina and Brazil, working together on technical projects resulted in an unprecedented reversal of their respective nuclear foreign policies. After years of refusing to endorse the NPT and to place their programs under full IAEA safeguards, the two countries began regular cross-national inspections, whereby Argentine inspectors were given access to Brazilian facilities and vice versa. A few years later, the South American countries signed an agreement that committed the two to periodic inspections, allowing IAEA oversight in the accounting and control of all nuclear material within Argentina and Brazil. Thus, what began as informal collaboration between state experts across the border, culminated with an institutionalized commitment to transparency and accountability that continues to this day. International inter-agency cooperation increases transparency even beyond the densely knit ties of two neighboring countries at similar levels of development. Region-wide, project-based cooperation in NEST and in the protection of the environment also forces disclosure and opening up. By working together, expert bureaucrats not only develop personal ties with their foreign peers (which facilitate more and deeper cooperation), but also enhance the state of their institutions; that is, their skill level, financial resources, existing technology, and infrastructure. The sustained exchanges of state agencies help build trust across participating actors and lower future transaction costs.

Even where security concerns are lower (for the time being), like in the protection of the environment, the increase of transparency and accountability brought about by international inter-agency cooperation is critical for political action. Transparency builds trust, and trust reduces commitment problems. Given that environmental treaties are based on voluntary compliance because of the weak enforcement mechanisms of the international community in this policy area, trust among bureaucrats – who will implement the terms of the agreement – is invaluable. Similarly, international cooperation among state experts in HIV/AIDS (i.e.,

Human Immunodeficiency Virus and Acquired Immune Deficiency Syndrome) helped increase the transparency and accountability of national anti-AIDS and pandemic policies in the field of public health. Moreover, the transnational network forged by state experts, scientists, policymakers, specialized IOs (such as UNAIDS), and NGOs – all working together to find solutions to the AIDS crisis – allowed activists to pursue accountability politics and often bypass politicians and directly target government scientists for information and influence in policy implementation.

In short, as Slaughter posited in 2005, international networks of state experts have the potential to deepen global governance by offering a more transparent and democratic alternative to the high politics of government-to-government negotiations. In the next sections, I discuss some other extensions of the theory of the expert bureaucrat, beginning with how I expect the theory to perform regarding the international behavior of state experts in the industrial North.

Policy Extensions of *How Skills Shape Cooperation*

A common assumption in the field of bureaucratic politics is that state agencies in OECD countries have a surplus of highly skilled workers, whereas bureaucracies in the Global South do not. While this account of state expertise is often accurate, it masks two key facts. First, even expertise-rich bureaucracies in developed countries need to make sustained investments in personnel training in order to avoid skill depreciation. Second, within developing states we find institutions with niche expertise, where bureaucrats are better trained and specialized than their national colleagues in other agencies. These two facts have been discussed at length throughout the book, but below I elaborate on how the study of bureaucratic politics should incorporate them into the prevailing views of the discipline.

Chapters 1 and 2 of this book surveyed the extant literature and found that when scholars examine skill formation within the state, the focus tends to be on whether politicians (often in partnership with business) have made necessary *initial* investments to ensure expertise. While this is a critical question, less attention has been paid to the ongoing challenge of skill upgrading. But in the information age, know-how, technology, and skills are susceptible to rapid depreciation, thus requiring constant investments in updating and upgrading. In other words, an initial investment in institutional and financial resources will not be sufficient to maintain sharp and current skills among state experts. Existing expertise needs to be deepened and tailored to the new discoveries and technical innovations of the field. Skill upgrading is a costly and ongoing process, one which all technical bureaucracies (including state agencies in the industrial North) must engage in order to keep abreast of swift technological change. This problem is likewise shared by the workforce in the private sector. This topic has been extensively debated in the United States and Europe in recent years as politicians and businesses are concerned with loss of innovation and a diminishing competitive edge (in particular against the better trained workforces of some emerging markets).

In the United States, labor experts continue to debate whether the country has a *skill gap* problem.[6] That is, while there is an abundance of unskilled labor, American employers increasingly struggle to fill positions that require greater skill levels. Consistent with the argument presented in this book, deficits in the general education and technical training of the workforce are exacerbated once the economy declines. While not all labor scholars are in agreement that there is in fact a gap,[7] there is nevertheless a growing and significant concern with how well the United States can keep its workforce competitive in the global market. Data continue to show that skill formation in many emerging markets, such as China, India, and South Korea, is becoming more technical and adaptable and is exceeding some OECD countries in the production of flexible workforces that can respond quickly to dizzying changes in technology and know-how.

Similarly, the skill debate also takes place in American public bureaucracies. The case of U.S. scientists who crowdsource research monies discussed at the beginning of this chapter reveals how cuts in government spending greatly hurt investment in R&D activities and limit access to innovative techniques. In lean economic times, government grants are fewer and dispersed using more stringent and conservative criteria. This means that projects based on safe rather than untested (yet potentially innovative) technologies are rewarded.

The United States also exemplifies how partisan battles function as exogenous shocks to government spending, which may yield outcomes that are similar to the ones resulting from economic crises. Partisanship affects government spending. For example, the U.S. Environmental

6 See www.nytimes.com/2013/10/09/business/economy/stubborn-skills-gap-in-americas-work-force.html?pagewanted=all&_r=0 Also, http://skills.oecd.org/skillsoutlook.html.

7 Some argue that rather than the so-called gap resulting from a supply deficit (i.e., the United States no longer produces highly skilled workers because its education system is broken), it is a problem of rewards, whereby employers are not willing to pay better-trained workers more.

Protection Agency (EPA) has benefited more from the financial and institutional resources granted by Democratic governments, whereas it has received little support from Republican administrations. But partisan conflict and polarization also have an effect on the state's ability to update and upgrade skills (Huber & Shipan, 2002). Witness the brutal partisan fighting over the U.S. budget and national deficit in recent times that resulted in the decision to sequester massive funding across the American bureaucracy and later to shut down the government for sixteen days in the fall of 2013.

These events have led some to question the future of expertise in the American state. Others are finding early evidence of a brain drain of technical personnel in the U.S. bureaucracy, whereby workers with (tech) skills in high demand do not stay in the state.[8] This trend has been particularly sharp among younger skilled workers, who in contrast to many of the experts featured in this book, have viable employment opportunities in the private sector.[9] Recently, the first survey of Millennials employed in the U.S. federal government was conducted. It found that young skilled professionals hired at the beginning of the 2008 Obama Administration are now leaving the bureaucracy at alarming rates, in part because of dissatisfaction with innovation and creativity in their jobs, in part because of the insecurity resulting from partisan fighting over government spending. One report of the survey highlighted a young professional with a graduate degree who after only a few years of being employed at the country's top research agency in public health, the National Institutes of Health (NIH), and despite holding a managerial position, left the NIH for a job in the private sector shortly after the 2013 sequestration spending cuts:

> I was starting to feel like I was ready for the next challenge [just as agencies imposed hiring freezes] I had fantastic mentors and teachers in government. But there was a big question mark about what opportunities would be available for me.[10]

Cooperation with peer agencies is also a strategy for bureaucrats in OECD states who face dwindling resources at their home institutions. Yet there is one crucial difference between countries in the industrial North and

[8] See http://blogs.wgbh.org/innovation-hub/2014/10/30/governments-tech-brain-drain.

[9] See www.nbcnews.com/news/us-news/60-percent-millennial-government-workers-job-n221601.

[10] See www.washingtonpost.com/politics/millennials-exit-the-federal-workforce-as-government-jobs-lose-their-allure/2014/12/15/ea3d4418-7fd4-11e4-9f38-95a187e4c1f7_story.html.

those in the Global South. Typically, the private sector in the former offers many more employment alternatives than in the latter, especially for professionals with technical skills in NEST and the environment. Expert bureaucrats in the United States and other developed economies have a better chance of finding a similar paying job outside of the state. Like the Millennials in the U.S. government survey, they are better able to leave and seek employment in the private sector. For example, government contractors in the industrial North offer employment opportunities to many professionals seeking to quit their state jobs. In the United States alone, the government spends billions of dollars each year via contract.

Leaving the state is more difficult in countries of the Global South. Similar to the industrial North, employment in developing bureaucracies offers stability and benefits that might be hard to find in the private sector. Different from OECD countries, the state is often the only viable employer for a professional with training in NEST or the environment. In most of the developing world, the state has a virtual monopoly on nuclear activities. The *green* private sector is rather incipient – often completely absent – in the Global South, although there is a growing nonprofit sector in environmental conservation. But, similar to practices in many OECD countries, the salary and employment benefits offered by NGOs and foundations in developing countries cannot compete with state jobs.

How do fewer employment opportunities in the private sector shape the incentives of expert bureaucrats to cooperate with peers outside their agency in search of updated and upgraded skills? First, as career opportunities in the private and semi-private markets are fewer and less frequent, they tend to be quite competitive. Thus, staying marketable with sharp technical skills is key, especially when the government is not making appropriate investments in training and R&D. Second, there are clear internal incentives to gain international experience. If the career prospects of a professional lie squarely in the state, then and as discussed at length in the earlier chapters of this book, training abroad can help advance a bureaucrat's career at home. Participation in international technical projects, workshops, and symposia not only increases the professional reputation of the state expert, it also increases her instrumental network of professional and political connections. Third, and related to this last point, inter-agency cooperation should help expand the autonomy of the skilled bureaucrat. In his 2001 seminal book, *The Forging of Bureaucratic Autonomy*, Carpenter asserts that bureaucratic autonomy "was not captured, but earned" (Carpenter, 2001: 6). According to Carpenter, state experts gain autonomy when they offer politicians unique solutions that distinguished them from bureaucrats in other domestic agencies, with whom they compete for scarce financial, political, and institutional resources. Similarly, I argue that by seeking inexpensive sources of additional training and R&D, expert bureaucrats establish themselves as problem-solvers to their political principals. Going international raises the profile of their agency, as it embeds it in global policy debates and connects it to a vital network of states and international organizations, from which it can draw additional resources. As Carpenter posits, the more an agency solves problems on its own, the more it increases the room to maneuver outside of the terms of political delegation.

Bureaucratic autonomy has been found to correlate closely with expertise and reputation. While some of the poorest, most corrupt, and unskilled bureaucracies in the world are in developing economies, we find also countless state agencies with niche expertise outside of the industrial North. In earlier chapters, I highlighted some examples of distinct specialization, such as the expertise of Costa Rica in tropical forestry, Kenya in geothermal energy, and Cuba in nuclear medicine. The case studies featured in Chapter 3 of the Argentine CNEA and the Brazilian CNEN brought attention to the goal of reputation and how it is more likely to matter to bureaucrats who are highly skilled and want to maintain their authoritative claim to knowledge in their policy sector. This poses an interesting question for future research: How exactly do reputational concerns for expertise shape the behavior of governments and bureaucrats?

Bring Back the Comparative Study of the State

In 1985, Evans, Rueschemeyer, and Skocpol made an appeal to comparative social scientists to bring the state back in (Evans, Rueschemeyer, & Skocpol, 1985). This call, based on the understanding that state institutions matter to politics everywhere, inspired a renewed interest in the capacity and autonomy of bureaucracies across the world. In the following decade, a rich literature emerged that examined how the competence of the state bureaucracy shaped policy outcomes (Hall, 1986; Sikkink, 1991; Thelen, Longstreth, & Steinmo, 1992; Evans, 1995; Maxfield & Schneider, 1997). After the wave of privatization and deregulation reforms of the 1990s transformed bureaucracies across the world, the state lost its primacy in the field of Comparative Politics. Yet, it remains front and center in defining and shaping politics in the twenty-first century. This book makes a call to revisit the state under globalization and the information age as a critical actor and arena of contemporary politics.

Furthermore, this book also makes a call to examine extensively the preferences and strategies of bureaucrats to update and upgrade skills when international and domestic politico-economic conditions change. Here, I have focused on the *broad* causal patterns of international inter-agency cooperation of 150 countries. While Chapter 3 offers two detailed case studies that help flesh out the mechanisms driving the behavior of expert bureaucrats in two agencies with advanced skills in NEST, more in-depth research is needed. There is a basic trade-off between depth and breadth, with the former necessarily requiring fewer cases. Future in-depth research should analyze the precise effects that different skill thresholds have on inter-agency cooperation as well as on the type of state institutions in charge of skill formation in the Global South. Research addressing these questions would expand and enrich an exciting recent body of work that is revisiting the role of the state in skill acquisition. Since, with few exceptions, most of this literature focuses on states in the industrial North and on private labor, there is great potential for contribution.

A final yet crucial question that my research leaves unanswered concerns whether there is a gender effect in accessing skills. In this book, I have assumed that *all* bureaucrats, whether women or men, are affected by the same incentives and constraints to invest in their expertise to keep it current. The book shows that previous levels of skills may deter (or facilitate) inter-agency cooperation. Does gender shape international cooperation in a similar way? How do female career bureaucrats develop professional networks to access skills? These are fundamental questions. This book has shown how important it is for career civil servants in technology-driven sectors to acquire and maintain appropriate skills by forging critical ties with like experts inside and out of the home agency. At the same time, there is also evidence that professional networks differ in size and in career value by gender, with women's networks being smaller and less effective for career enhancement (Campion & Shrum, 2004).

Research on gender inequality has focused mostly on women in legislative representation or as cabinet members (Taylor-Robinson & Heath, 2003; Krook, 2009; Arriola & Johnson, 2014; Escobar-Lemmon & Taylor-Robinson, 2014; Barnes, 2016). In contrast, despite its relevance, the study of women as career bureaucrats remains underdeveloped. This is a troubling lapse because, in addition to implementing policy, state institutions are frequently the locus for policy problem-solving, innovation, and the establishment of new norms of behavior and best practices. The shortage of research on gender and state experts is particularly striking in the Global South, as so much of R&D activities and scientific production occurs within the state. This lapse persists despite the fact that the number of women in research careers and employed by the state has been rising steadily in recent years (Schiebinger, 1999; Campion & Shrum, 2004).

Thus, more research is needed on female expert bureaucrats and the type of professional networks they develop inside and outside the state. International networks, like the ones analyzed in this book, would give them access not only to additional resources (critically, new skills) but also to professional distinction (and consequently better possibilities for career advancement) at home. Additionally, there is growing recognition of the need for more *gendered* policies as many state experts find that public interventions often fail because of a lack of understanding of gender inequalities on the ground. For example, environmental experts know that women tend to be affected differently by, and are more vulnerable to, crises arising from the mismanagement of natural resources and the effects of climate change (Dankelman, 2010). This knowledge is mirrored in public health, agriculture, and science, to name just a few policy sectors. The United Nations and a small number of national governments have adopted recent mandates to *mainstream gender* (i.e., evaluate the particular effects on women of a policy intervention before its adoption) into their programs and sponsored projects in order to improve the efficiency and effectiveness of implementation. In this context, the question of how women in the bureaucracy acquire the technical and political tools to implement policy becomes even more relevant. In short, does the involvement of expert women make a difference in the gendered component of the policies that are adopted? There is evidence that when women hold central positions in a bureaucracy, institutional policies reflect this and decrease gender inequality (Keiser, Wilkins, Meier, & Holland, 2002). If expertise is gendered as it seems to be, a skill-focused approach would reveal one possible mechanism through which gender inequality becomes reinforced in the state and in policy.

Bibliography

Abers, R. N., & Keck, M. E. (2013). *Practical authority: Agency and institutional change in Brazilian water politics*. New York: Oxford University Press.

Adler, E. (1987). *The power of ideology: The quest for technological autonomy in Argentina and Brazil*. Oakland: University of California Press.

(1992). The emergence of cooperation: National epistemic communities and the international evolution of the idea of nuclear arms control. *International Organization*, 46(01), 101–145.

(2008). The spread of security communities: Communities of practice, self-restraint, and NATO's post-Cold War transformation. *European Journal of International Relations*, 14(2), 195–230.

Agranoff, R. (2006). Inside collaborative networks: Ten lessons for public managers. *Public Administration Review*, 66(1), 56–65.

Agrawal, A. (2005). *Environmentality: Technologies of government and the making of subjects*. Durham: Duke University Press.

(2014). Studying the commons, governing common-pool resource outcomes: Some concluding thoughts. *Environmental Science & Policy*, 36, 86–91.

Alcañiz, I. (2000). Slipping into something more comfortable: Argentine-Brazilian nuclear integration and the origins of the MERCOSUR. In G. M. Derluguian & S. L. Greer (Eds.), *Questioning geopolitics: Political projects in a changing world-system* (pp. 155–168). Westport: Greenwood Press.

(2005a). Defeating welfare retrenchment: Privatization and conflict in the Argentine nuclear energy sector. *New Political Science*, 27(3), 331–344.

(2005b). La política nuclear Argentina y el Instituto Balseiro: Cincuenta años de historia (Argentine nuclear policy and the Balseiro Institute: Fifty years of history). *Ciencia Hoy*, 88, 20–25.

(2010). Bureaucratic networks and government spending: A network analysis of nuclear cooperation in Latin America. *Latin American Research Review*, 45(1), 148–172.

(2012). Democratization and multilateral security. *World Politics*, 64(02), 306–340.

Alcañiz, I., & Gutiérrez, R. A. (2009). From local protest to the International Court of Justice. In P. G. Harris (Ed.), *Environmental change and foreign policy: Theory and practice* (pp. 109–120). New York: Routledge.

Alcañiz, I., & Hellwig, T. (2011). Who's to blame? The distribution of responsibility in developing democracies. *British Journal of Political Science*, 41(02), 389–411.

Alemán, E., & Calvo, E. (2013). Explaining policy ties in presidential congresses: A network analysis of bill initiation data. *Political Studies*, 61(2), 356–377.

Alesina, A., Baqir, R., & Easterly, W. (1997). *Public goods and ethnic divisions*. Cambridge: National Bureau of Economic Research.

Amengual, M. (2016). *Politicized enforcement in Argentina: Labor and environmental regulation*. New York: Cambridge University Press.

Amirault, R. J., & Branson, R. K. (2006). Educators and expertise: A brief history of theories and models. *The Cambridge handbook of expertise and expert performance* (pp. 69–86). New York: Cambridge University Press.

Andler, L. (2009). The secretariat of the global environment facility: From network to bureaucracy. In F. Biermann & B. Siebenhüner (Eds.), *Managers of global change: The influence of international environmental bureaucracies* (pp. 203–223). Cambridge: MIT Press.

Andonova, L. B. (2014). Boomerangs to partnerships? Explaining state participation in transnational partnerships for sustainability. *Comparative Political Studies*, 47(3), 481–515.

Andonova, L. B., & Mitchell, R. B. (2010). The rescaling of global environmental politics. *Annual Review of Environment and Resources*, 35(1), 255.

Arriola, L. R., & Johnson, M. C. (2014). Ethnic politics and women's empowerment in Africa: Ministerial appointments to executive cabinets. *American Journal of Political Science*, 58(2), 495–510.

Auyero, J., & Swistun, D. A. (2009). *Flammable: Environmental suffering in an Argentine shantytown*. New York: Oxford University Press.

Bach, D., & Newman, A. L. (2010). Transgovernmental networks and domestic policy convergence: Evidence from insider trading regulation. *International Organization*, 64(3).

(2014). Domestic drivers of transgovernmental regulatory cooperation. *Regulation & Governance*, 8(4), 395–417.

Bafumi, J., Gelman, A., Park, D. K., & Kaplan, N. (2005). Practical issues in implementing and understanding Bayesian ideal point estimation. *Political Analysis*, 13(2), 171–187.

Baker, A. (2009). *The market and the masses in Latin America: Policy reform and consumption in liberalizing economies*. New York: Cambridge University Press.

Barnes, T. D. (2016). *Gendering legislative behavior*. New York: Cambridge University Press.

Barnett, M., & Finnemore, M. (2004). *Rules for the world: International organizations in global politics*. Ithaca: Cornell University Press.

Bauer, S. (2006). Does bureaucracy really matter? The authority of intergovernmental treaty secretariats in global environmental politics. *Global Environmental Politics*, 6(1), 23–49.

Becker, G. S. (2009). *Human capital: A theoretical and empirical analysis, with special reference to education*. Chicago: University of Chicago Press.

Bendor, J., & Meirowitz, A. (2004). Spatial models of delegation. *American Political Science Review*, *98*(02), 293–310.

Berardo, R., & Scholz, J. T. (2010). Self-organizing policy networks: Risk, partner selection, and cooperation in estuaries. *American Journal of Political Science*, *54*(3), 632–649.

Berardo, R., Alcañiz, I., Hadden, J., & Jasny, L. (2016). Environmental politics and networks. In J. Nicoll, M. Lubell, & A. H. Montgomery (Eds.), *Oxford handbook of political networks*. New York: Oxford University Press.

Biermann, F., & Siebenhüner, B. (2009). *Managers of global change: The influence of international environmental bureaucracies*. Cambridge: MIT Press.

Blais, A., & Dion, S. (1990). Are bureaucrats budget maximizers? The Niskanen model & its critics. *Polity*, *22*(4), 655–674.

Booth, A. L., & Snower, D. J. (1996). *Acquiring skills: Market failures, their symptoms and policy responses*. New York: Cambridge University Press.

Bresnahan, T. F., Brynjolfsson, E., & Hitt, L. M. (1999). Information technology, workplace organization and the demand for skilled labor: Firm-level evidence. Cambridge: National Bureau of Economic Research.

Brown, P. (2005). Skill formation in the twenty-first century. In P. Brown, A. Green, & H. Lauder (Eds.), *High skills: Globalization, competitiveness, and skill formation* (pp. 1–55). New York: Oxford University Press.

Brown, P., Green, A., & Lauder, H. (2005). *High skills: Globalization, competitiveness, and skill formation*. New York: Oxford University Press.

Busemeyer, M. R., & Trampusch, C. (2012). *The political economy of collective skill formation*. New York: Oxford University Press.

Calvo, E., & Murillo, M. V. (2013). When parties meet voters: Assessing political linkages through partisan networks and distributive expectations in Argentina and Chile. *Comparative Politics Studies*, *46*(07), 851–882.

Campion, P., & Shrum, W. (2004). Gender and science in development: Women scientists in Ghana, Kenya, and India. *Science, Technology & Human Values*, *29*(04), 459–485.

Carasales, J. C. (1997). *De rivales a socios: El proceso de cooperación nuclear entre Argentina y Brasil*. Buenos Aires: Grupo Editor Latinoamericano.

Carasales, J. C., & Ornstein, R. (1998). *La Cooperación Internacional de la Argentina en el Campo Nuclear*. Buenos Aires: Editorial CARI.

Caraway, T. L., Rickard, S. J., & Anner, M. S. (2012). International negotiations and domestic politics: The case of IMF labor market conditionality. *International Organization*, *66*(01), 27–61.

Carmen, E., Nesshöver, C., Saarikoski, H., Vandewalle, M., Watt, A., Wittmer, H., & Young, J. (2015). Creating a biodiversity science community: Experiences from a European network of knowledge. *Environmental Science & Policy*, *54*(01), 497–504.

Carpenter, D. P. (2001). *The forging of bureaucratic autonomy: Reputations, networks, and policy innovation in executive agencies, 1862–1928*. Princeton: Princeton University Press.

Chwieroth, J. M. (2007). Testing and measuring the role of ideas: The case of neoliberalism in the International Monetary Fund. *International Studies Quarterly*, *51*(1), 5–30.

(2010). How do crises lead to change? Liberalizing capital controls in the early years of new order Indonesia. *World Politics*, 62(03), 496–527.

Coll, J. A., & Radicella, R. (1998). First nuclear technology transfers and the subsequent developments in the radioisotope field. In J. C. Carasales & R. Ornstein (Eds.), *La Cooperación internacional de la Argentina en el campo nuclear*. Buenos Aires: Editorial CARI.

Conca, K. (2005). Old states in new bottles? The hybridization of authority in global environmental governance. In J. Barry & R. Eckersley (Eds.), *The state and the global ecological crisis* (pp. 181–205). Cambridge: MIT Press.

(2006). *Governing water: Contentious transnational politics and global institution building*. Cambridge: MIT Press.

Conceição, P., & Marone, H. (2008). Characterizing the 21st century first commodity boom: Drivers and impact. Working Paper of the Office of Development Studies, United Nations Development Programme, New York.

Copelovitch, M. S. (2010). Master or servant? Common agency and the political economy of IMF lending. *International Studies Quarterly*, *54*(1), 49–77.

Cranmer, S. J., & Desmarais, B. A. (2011). Inferential network analysis with exponential random graph models. *Political Analysis*, *19*(1), 66–86.

Cremer, H., & Laffont, J.-J. (2003). Public goods with costly access. *Journal of Public Economics*, *87*(9), 1985–2012.

Crowe, J. (2007). The forging of judicial autonomy: Political entrepreneurship and the reforms of William Howard Taft. *Journal of Politics*, *69*(1), 73–87.

Dankelman, I. (2010). *Gender and climate change: An introduction*. Washington DC: Earthscan.

Danziger, J. N., & Andersen, K. V. (2002). The impacts of information technology on public administration: An analysis of empirical research from the "Golden Age" of transformation. *International Journal of Public Administration*, *25*(5), 591–627.

Darnton, C. (2014). *Rivalry and alliance politics in cold war Latin America*. Baltimore: Johns Hopkins University Press.

Da Rosa, J. E. (1983). Economics, politics, and hydroelectric power: The Paraná river basin. *Latin American Research Review*, *18*(3), 77–107.

de Andrade, A. M. R., & dos Santos, T. L. (2013). A dinâmica política da criação da Comissão Nacional de Energia Nuclear, 1956–1960 (Political dynamics of the creation of the Brazilian National Commission for Nuclear Energy, 1956–1960). *Boletim do Museu Paraense Emílio Goeldi. Ciências Humanas*, *8*(1), 113–128.

De Ferranti, D. M. (2003). *Closing the gap in education and technology*. Washington DC: World Bank Publications.

De Grip, A., & Van Loo, J. (2002). The economics of skills obsolescence: A review. *Research in Labor Economics*, *21*, 1–26.

Ericsson, K. A. (Ed.). (2006). *The influence of experience and deliberate practice on the development of superior expert performance*. New York: Cambridge University Press.

Erten, B., & Ocampo, J. A. (2013). Super cycles of commodity prices since the mid-nineteenth century. *World Development*, 44, 14–30.

Escobar-Lemmon, M. C., & Taylor-Robinson, M. M. (2014). *Representation: The case of women*. New York: Oxford University Press.

Estévez-Abe, M. (2012). Gendered consequences of vocational training. In M. R. Busemeyer & C. Trampusch (Eds.), *The political economy of collective skill formation* (pp. 259–283). New York: Oxford University Press.

Estevez-Abe, M., Iversen, T., & Soskice, D. (2001). Social protection and the formation of skills: A reinterpretation of the welfare state. In P. A. Hall & D. Soskice (Eds.), *Varieties of capitalism: The institutional foundations of comparative advantage* (pp. 145–183). New York: Oxford University Press.

Evangelista, M. (1993). Internal and external constraints on grand strategy: The Soviet case. In R. N. Rosecrance & A. A. Stein (Eds.), *The domestic bases of grand strategy* (pp. 154–178). Ithaca: Cornell University Press.

(2002). *Unarmed forces: The transnational movement to end the Cold War*. Ithaca: Cornell University Press.

Evans, P. B. (1995). *Embedded autonomy: States and industrial transformation*. New York: Cambridge University Press.

Evans, P. B., Rueschemeyer, D., & Skocpol, T. (1985). *Bringing the state back in*. New York: Cambridge University Press.

Evetts, J., Mieg, H. A., & Felt, U. (2006). Professionalization, scientific expertise, and elitism: A sociological perspective. In K. A. Ericsson, N. Charness, P. J. Feltovich, & R. R. Hoffman (Eds.), *The Cambridge handbook of expertise and expert performance* (pp. 105–123). New York: Cambridge University Press.

Falleti, T. G. (2011). Varieties of authoritarianism: The organization of the military state and its effects on federalism in Argentina and Brazil. *Studies in Comparative International Development*, 46(2), 137–162.

Fan, S., & Rao, N. (2003). Public spending in developing countries: Trends, determination and impact. International Food Policy Research Institute.

Fredriksson, P. G., & Gaston, N. (2000). Ratification of the 1992 climate change convention: What determines legislative delay? *Public Choice*, *104*(3–4), 345–368.

Frieden, J. A. (1991). *Debt, development, and democracy: Modern political economy and Latin America, 1965–1985*. Princeton: Princeton University Press.

Gailmard, S. (2002). Expertise, subversion, and bureaucratic discretion. *Journal of Law, Economics, and Organization*, *18*(2), 536–555.

Gailmard, S., & Patty, J. W. (2013). *Learning while governing: Expertise and accountability in the executive branch*. Chicago: University of Chicago.

Goldsmith, A. A. (1999). Africa's overgrown state reconsidered: Bureaucracy and economic growth. *World Politics*, *51*(04), 520–546.

Goodliffe, J., & Hawkins, D. G. (2006). Explaining commitment: States and the convention against torture. *Journal of Politics*, *68*(2), 358–371.

Green, A., & Sakamoto, A. (2005). Models of high skills in national competition strategies. In P. Brown, A. Green, & H. Lauder (Eds.), *High skills: Globalization, competitiveness and skill formation* (pp. 56–161). New York: Oxford University Press.

Guadalupe, M. (2007). Product market competition, returns to skill, and wage inequality. *Journal of Labor Economics*, 25(3), 439–474.

Gutiérrez, R. A., & Isuani, F. J. (2014). The emergence of state and social environmentalism in Argentina. *Revista de Administração Pública*, 48(2), 295–332.

Haas, P. M. (1989). Do regimes matter? Epistemic communities and Mediterranean pollution control. *International Organization*, 43(03), 377–403.

(1992a). Banning chlorofluorocarbons: Epistemic community efforts to protect stratospheric ozone. *International Organization*, 46(01), 187–224.

(1992b). Introductions: Epistemic communities and international policy coordination. *International Organization*, 46(1), 1–35.

Hadden, J. (2015). *Networks in contention: The divisive politics of climate change*. New York: Cambridge University Press.

Haggard, S., & Kaufman, R. (1995). *The political economy of democratic transitions*. Princeton: Princeton University Press.

Hall, P. A. (1986). *Governing the economy: The politics of state intervention in Britain and France*. New York: Oxford University Press.

(Ed.). (1989). *The political power of economic ideas: Keynesianism across nations*. Princeton: Princeton University Press.

Harvey, D. (2005). *A brief history of neoliberalism*. New York: Oxford University Press.

Heclo, H. (1978). Issue networks and the executive establishment. In A. King (Ed.), *The new American political system*. Washington DC: American Enterprise Institute.

Helbling, T., Mercer-Blackman, V., & Cheng, K. (2008). Riding a wave. *Finance and Development*, 45(1), 10–15.

Hellwig, T. (2014). *Globalization and mass politics: Retaining the room to maneuver*. New York: Cambridge University Press.

Herrera, Y. M. (2010). *Mirrors of the economy: National accounts and international norms in Russia and beyond*. Ithaca: Cornell University Press.

Hicks, R. L., Parks, B. C., Roberts, J. T., & Tierney, M. J. (2008). *Greening aid? Understanding the environmental impact of development assistance*. New York: Oxford University Press.

Hochstetler, K. (2002). After the boomerang: Environmental movements and politics in the La Plata River basin. *Global Environmental Politics*, 2(4), 35–57.

Hochstetler, K., & Keck, M. E. (2007). *Greening Brazil: Environmental activism in state and society*: Durham: Duke University Press.

Hoel, M. (1992). International environment conventions: The case of uniform reductions of emissions. *Environmental and Resource Economics*, 2(2), 141–159.

Hoffer, A. J. (2013). Bureaucratic behavior: Budget cuts, imperfect information, and the 2013 sequester. Social Science Research Network.

Huber, E., & Solt, F. (2004). Successes and failures of neoliberalism. *Latin American Research Review*, 39(3), 150–164.

Huber, E., & Stephens, J. D. (2012). *Democracy and the left: Social policy and inequality in Latin America.* Chicago: University of Chicago Press.

Huber, J. D., & Shipan, C. R. (2002). *Deliberate discretion? The institutional foundations of bureaucratic autonomy.* New York: Cambridge University Press.

(2006). Politics, delegation, and bureaucracy. In B. R. Weingast & D. A. Wittman (Eds.), *The Oxford handbook of political economy.* New York: Oxford University Press.

Jordana, J., Levi-Faur, D., & i Marín, X. F. (2011). The global diffusion of regulatory agencies: Channels of transfer and stages of diffusion. *Comparative Political Studies*, 44(10), 1343–1369.

Kahler, M. (1992). Multilateralism with small and large numbers. *International Organization*, 46(03), 681–708.

Kamelarczyk, K. B. F., & Smith-Hall, C. (2014). REDD herring: Epistemic community control of the production, circulation and application of deforestation knowledge in Zambia. *Forest Policy and Economics*, 46, 19–29.

Kaplan, S. B. (2013). *Globalization and austerity politics in Latin America.* New York: Cambridge University Press.

Kapstein, E. B. (1992). Between power and purpose: Central bankers and the politics of regulatory convergence. *International Organization*, 46(01), 265–287.

Kassenova, T. (2014). *Brazil's nuclear kaleidoscope: An evolving identity.* Washington DC: Carnegie Endowment for International Peace.

Kauffman-Zeh, A. (1998). Brazil forced to cut back science funding. *Nature*, 395(6705), 831–835.

Keck, M. E., & Sikkink, K. (1998). *Activists beyond borders: Advocacy networks in international politics.* Ithaca: Cornell University Press.

Keiser, L. R., Wilkins, V. M., Meier, K. J., & Holland, C. A. (2002). Lipstick and logarithms: Gender, institutional context, and representative bureaucracy. *American Political Science Review*, 96(03), 553–564.

Keohane, R. O., & Nye, J. S. (1974). Transgovernmental relations and international organizations. *World Politics*, 27(01), 39–62.

Kinne, B. J. (2013). Network dynamics and the evolution of international cooperation. *American Political Science Review*, 107(04), 766–785.

Krook, M. L. (2009). *Quotas for women in politics: Gender and candidate selection reform worldwide.* New York: Oxford University Press.

Kurtz, M. J. (2004). *Free market democracy and the Chilean and Mexican countryside.* New York: Cambridge University Press.

Machin, S. (1996). Changes in the relative demand for skills. In A. Booth & D. J. Snower (Eds.), *Acquiring skills: Market failures, their symptoms and policy responses* (pp. 127–146). New York: Cambridge University Press.

Madero, C. C., & Takacs, E. A. (1991). *Política nuclear argentina: Avance o retroceso?* Buenos Aires: Instituto de Publicaciones Navales.

Maggetti, M. (2014). Institutional change and the evolution of the regulatory state: Evidence from the Swiss case. *International Review of Administrative Sciences*, 80(02), 276–297.

Mansfield, E. D., Milner, H. V., & Rosendorff, B. P. (2000). Free to trade: Democracies, autocracies, and international trade. *American Political Science Review*, 94(02), 305–321.

Maoz, Z. (2012). Preferential attachment, homophily, and the structure of international networks, 1816–2003. *Conflict Management and Peace Science*, 29(3), 341–369.

Marsden, P. V. (1983). Restricted access in networks and models of power. *American Journal of Sociology*, 88(04), 686–717.

Martin, C. J. (2012). Political institutions and the origins of collective skill formation systems. In M. R. Busemeyer & C. Trampusch (Eds), *The political economy of collective skill formation* (pp. 41–67). New York: Oxford University Press.

Maxfield, S., & Schneider, B. R. (1997). *Business and the state in developing countries*. Ithaca: Cornell University Press.

Mayer, K. U., & Solga, H. (2008). *Skill formation: Interdisciplinary and cross-national perspectives*. New York: Cambridge University Press.

McCarty, N. (2014). Complexity, capacity, and capture. In D. Carpenter and D. A. Moss (Eds), *Preventing regulatory capture: Special interest influence and how to limit it* (pp. 99–123). New York: Cambridge University Press.

McPherson, M., Smith-Lovin, L., & Cook, J. M. (2001). Birds of a feather: Homophily in social networks. *Annual Review of Sociology*, 27(01), 415–444.

Morrison, K. M. (2009). Oil, nontax revenue, and the redistributional foundations of regime stability. *International Organization*, 63(01), 107–138.

Murillo, M. V. (2000). From populism to neoliberalism: Labor unions and market reforms in Latin America. *World Politics*, 52(02), 135–168.

(2009). *Political competition, partisanship, and policy making in Latin American public utilities*. New York: Cambridge University Press.

Murillo, M. V., & Mangonnet, J. (2013). La economía política de la Argentina exportadora en el nuevo milenio: Proponiendo una nueva agenda de investigación. *Desarrollo Económico*, 53(209–210), 223–240.

Neumayer, E. (2001). How regime theory and the economic theory of international environmental cooperation can learn from each other. *Global Environmental Politics*, 1(1), 122–147.

Niskanen, W. A. (2007). *Bureaucracy and representative government*. Chicago: Aldine Transaction Publishers.

O'Connell, P. J., & Jungblut, J.-M. (2008). What do we know about training at work? In K. U. Mayer & H. Solga (Eds), *Skill formation: Interdisciplinary and cross-national perspectives* (pp. 109–125). New York: Cambridge University Press.

O'Donnell, G. (1978). State and alliances in Argentina, 1956–1976. *The Journal of Development Studies*, 15(1), 3–33.

Ostrom, E. (2008). The challenge of common-pool resources. *Environment: Science and Policy for Sustainable Development*, 50(4), 8–21.

Pavnick, N. (2000). What explains skill upgrading in less developed countries? NBER Working Paper.

Pernetta, J. C., & Bewers, J. M. (2012). Transboundary diagnostic analysis in international waters interventions funded by the global environment facility. *Ocean & Coastal Management*, 55, 1–12.

Pielke, R. A. (2007). *The honest broker: Making sense of science in policy and politics*. New York: Cambridge University Press.

Pierson, P. (1993). When effect becomes cause: Policy feedback and political change. *World Politics*, 45(04), 595–628.

(2000). The limits of design: Explaining institutional origins and change. *Governance*, 13(4), 475–499.

(2001). *The new politics of the welfare state*. New York: Oxford University Press.

Poole, K. T. (2005). *Spatial models of parliamentary voting*. New York: Cambridge University Press.

Raleigh, C. (2010). Political marginalization, climate change, and conflict in African Sahel states. *International Studies Review*, 12(1), 69–86.

Rauch, J. E., & Evans, P. B. (2000). Bureaucratic structure and bureaucratic performance in less developed countries. *Journal of Public Economics*, 75(1), 49–71.

Raustiala, K. (2002). Architecture of international cooperation: Transgovernmental networks and the future of international law. *The Virginia Journal of International Law*, 43(1), 1–92.

Roett, R. (1983). Democracy and debt in South America: A continent's dilemma. *Foreign Affairs*, 62(03), 695–720.

Rohrschneider, R., & Dalton, R. J. (2002). A global network? Transnational cooperation among environmental groups. *The Journal of Politics*, 64(02), 510–533.

Rudra, N., & Jensen, N. M. (2011). Globalization and the politics of natural resources. *Comparative Political Studies*, 44(6), 639–661.

Sabatier, P. A., & Jenkins-Smith, H. C. (1999). The advocacy coalition framework: An assessment. In P. A. Sabatier (Ed.), *Theories of the policy process* (Vol. 118, p. 188). Boulder: Westview Press.

Sarkar, J. (2012). Big state, big science, big projects: The nuclear energy programme and state (un)-managerialism in India. Paper presented at the "Rising Powers and the Future of Global Governance" International Conference, University of Sussex.

Schiebinger, L. (1999). *Has feminism changed science?* Cambridge: Harvard University Press.

Schiff, M., & Winters, L. A. (2002). Regional cooperation, and the role of international organizations and regional integration. *World Bank Policy Research Working Paper* (2872).

Schneider, B. R. (1999). The Desarrollista State in Brazil and Mexico. In M. Woo-Cumings (Ed.), *The developmental state* (pp. 276–305). Ithaca: Cornell University Press.

(2013). *Hierarchical capitalism in Latin America*. New York: Cambridge University Press.

Schneider, B. R., & Heredia, B. (2003). *Reinventing Leviathan: The politics of administrative reform in developing countries*. Miami: North-South Center Press.

Scholz, J. T., Berardo, R., & Kile, B. (2008). Do networks solve collective action problems? Credibility, search, and collaboration. *The Journal of Politics*, 70(02), 393–406.

Schrank, A. (2009). Professionalization and probity in a patrimonial state: Labor inspectors in the Dominican Republic. *Latin American Politics and Society*, 51(2), 91–115.

(2014). The German roots of Latin American vocational training institution. Paper presented at the Red para el Estudio de la Economía Política de América Latina (REPAL), Santiago, Chile.

Schrank, A., & Whitford, J. (2011). The anatomy of network failure. *Sociological Theory*, 29(3), 151–177.

Schwartzman, S. (1994). Brazil scientists and the state-evolving models and the "Great leap forward." In E. Solingen (Ed.), *Scientists and the state: Domestic structures and the international context* (pp. 171–188). Ann Arbor: University of Michigan.

Scott, J. (2000). *Social network analysis: A handbook*. New York: Sage.

Sikkink, K. (1991). *Ideas and institutions: Developmentalism in Brazil and Argentina*. Ithaca: Cornell University Press.

Simmons, B. A., & Hopkins, D. J. (2005). The constraining power of international treaties: Theory and methods. *American Political Science Review*, 99(04), 623–631.

Slaughter, A.-M. (2004). *A new world order*. Princeton: Princeton University Press.

Slaughter, M. J. (2002). Skill upgrading in developing countries: Has inward foreign direct investment played a role? Working Paper 192. OECD Development Center, Washington DC.

Solingen, E. (1994). *Scientists and the state: Domestic structures and the international context*. Ann Arbor: University of Michigan Press.

(1996). *Industrial policy, technology, and international bargaining: Designing nuclear industries in Argentina and Brazil*. Palo Alto: Stanford University Press.

Stephenson, P. J., & Baharani, M. L. (2012). Evaluation techniques applied to large-scale regional projects. In P. De Lombaerde, R. Flores, L. Iapadre, & M. Schulz (Eds.), *The regional integration manual: Quantitative and qualitative methods* (pp. 270–296). New York: Routledge Press.

Streeck, W. (2012). Skills and politics: General and specific. In M. R. Busemeyer & C. Trampusch (Eds.), *The political economy of collective skill formation* (pp. 317–352). New York: Oxford University Press.

Tarrow, S. (2005). *The new transnational activism*. New York: Cambridge University Press.

Taylor-Robinson, M. M., & Heath, R. M. (2003). Do women legislators have different policy priorities than their male colleagues? A critical case test. *Women & Politics*, 24(4), 77–101.

Teodoro, M. P. (2011). *Bureaucratic ambition: Careers, motives, and the innovative administrator*. Baltimore: Johns Hopkins University Press.

Thelen, K. (2004). *How institutions evolve: The political economy of skills in Germany, Britain, the United States, and Japan*. New York: Cambridge University Press.

(2009). Institutional change in advanced political economies. *British Journal of Industrial Relations*, 47(3), 471–498.

(2014). *Varieties of liberalization and the new politics of social solidarity*. New York: Cambridge University Press.

Thelen, K., Longstreth, F., & Steinmo, S. (1992). *Structuring politics: Historical institutionalism in comparative analysis*. New York: Cambridge University Press.

Thurner, P. W., & Binder, M. (2009). European Union transgovernmental networks: The emergence of a new political space beyond the nation-state? *European Journal of Political Research*, 48(1), 80–106.

Treier, S., & Jackman, S. (2008). Democracy as a latent variable. *American Journal of Political Science*, 52(1), 201–217.

Ulph, D. (1996). Dynamic competition for market share and the failure of the market for skilled labour. In A. L. Booth & D. J. Snower (Eds.), *Acquiring skills: Market failures, their symptoms and policy responses* (pp. 81–108). New York: Cambridge University Press.

Velho, L. (2005). S&T institutions in Latin America and the Caribbean: An overview. *Science and Public Policy*, 32(2), 95–108.

Videras, J. (2013). Social networks and the environment. *Annual Review of Resource Economics*, 5(1), 211–226.

Von Bülow, M. (2010). *Building transnational networks: Civil society and the politics of trade in the Americas*. New York: Cambridge University Press.

Vreeland, J. R. (2003). *The IMF and economic development*. New York: Cambridge University Press.

Walton, M. (2004). Neoliberalism in Latin America: Good, bad, or incomplete? *Latin American Research Review*, 39(3), 165–183.

Wasmer, E. (2006). General versus specific skills in labor markets with search frictions and firing costs. *The American Economic Review*, 96(3), 811–831.

Weber, M. (1958). *From Max Weber: Essays in sociology*. New York: Oxford University Press.

Webster, F. (2006). The Information Society revisited. In L. A. Lievrouw & S. Livingstone (Eds.), *Handbook of new media: Social shaping and consequences of ICTs* (pp. 443–457). London: Sage Publications.

Weyland, K. G. (2002). *The politics of market reform in fragile democracies: Argentina, Brazil, Peru, and Venezuela*. Princeton: Princeton University Press.

Weyland, K. G., Madrid, R. L., & Hunter, W. (2010). *Leftist governments in Latin America: Successes and shortcoming*. New York: Cambridge University Press.

Wibbels, E. (2006). Dependency revisited: International markets, business cycles, and social spending in the developing world. *International Organization*, 60(02), 433–468.

World Bank (2012). *World Development Indicators 2012*. Washington DC: World Bank Publications.

Wrobel, P. S., & Redick, J. R. (1998). Nuclear cooperation in South America: The role of scientists in the Argentine-Brazilian rapprochement. *Annals of the New York Academy of Sciences*, 866(1), 165–181.

Young, Z. (2002). *A new green order? The World Bank and the politics of the Global Environment Facility*. London: Pluto Press.

Index

Adler, Emmanuel, 6
Affordable Care Act, 32
African Regional Cooperative Agreement for Research, Development and Training Related to Nuclear Science and Technology (AFRA), 76
Algeria, 50
Alvaro Alberto, Admiral, 58
Amazon, 134
Andean Group, 77
Angra I and II, 61, 62
Argentina, xi, xxi, 3, 7, 19, 21, 48, 54, 64, 66, 69, 74, 79, 82, 93, 119, 125, 163, 181
Argonaut Reactors, 50
Asian Infrastructure Investment Bank (AIIB), 166
Atoms for Peace, 50, 58, 60, 84
Atucha I, 51
Atucha II, 53, 54
Austerity, 9, 13, 28, 37, 66, 67, 68, 157, 158, 160, 162

Balseiro Institute, 48
Bank of the South (BancoSur), 167
Becker, Gary, xiv, 14, 24, 37, 40, 101
Bendor, Jonathan, 31, 32
Binder, Martin, 44
biodiversity, 22, 25, 118, 121, 123, 134, 136, 193
Brazil, xi, xii, 3, 4, 6, 10, 18, 19, 21, 23, 26, 27, 28, 33, 55, 56, 57, 59, 60, 62, 63, 64, 65, 66, 68, 69, 70, 71, 72, 79, 82, 87, 91, 106, 134, 163, 166, 167, 168, 181, 182
Brazilian-Argentine Agency for Accounting and Control of Nuclear Materials (ABACC), 71
BRICS, 158, 166
  Development Bank, 167
Budgets
  of state agencies, 5, 7, 9, 10, 18, 29, 30, 36, 66, 83, 97, 115, 120, 121, 176
Bureaucracies, 4, 7, 9, 14, 17, 20, 22, 24, 31, 34, 35, 41, 66, 101, 157, 183, 184, 186, 187
  Appointive, 34
  Autonomy, 5, 30, 33, 43, 45, 53, 57, 60, 68, 119, 182, 186, 187
  Expertise, 6, 8, 31, 33, 48, 76, 183
bureaucrat
  environmental, 12, 21, 28, 120, 122, 124, 125, 128, 157
  expert, xiii, xiv, 1, 5, 10, 12, 16, 21, 23, 29, 32, 35, 37, 47, 56, 62, 67, 76, 97, 98, 99, 105, 116, 125, 139, 141, 158, 159, 170, 182
  nuclear, xii, xiii, xvi, 1, 48, 51, 62, 82, 93, 182
  skill investment, xv
  Weberian, 31, 32–34
Bureaucratic autonomy. *See* Bureaucracies

Canada Deuterium Uranium-Candu, 51
Carasales, Julio C., 52

Carlos Saúl Menem
President of Argentina, 66, 120
Carpenter, Daniel, 9, 43, 186, 187
Chile, 82, 83
China, 21, 55, 58, 77, 79, 91, 131, 134, 158, 163, 164, 168
China and the 2000 Commodity Boom, 163–165
Climate Change, 5, 10, 22, 25, 31, 99, 118, 121, 123, 124, 129, 136, 189, 194, 195, 199
CNEA, 47, 49, 60, 66, 181, 187
CNEN, 23, 47, 56, 66, 68, 181, 187
Coll, Jorge A., 50
commodity boom, 158, 165, 167
Common System of Accounting and Control of Nuclear Materials (SCCC), 71
Convention on Biological Diversity (CBD), 122
Cooperation, 109, 140
Agreements, 106, 111
Bureaucrats, 121
Environmental, 130, 134, 139, 153, 156, 171
GEF, 122, 130, 144, 145, 154
Green, 131, 155
Inter-Agency, 95, 97, 98, 99, 101, 109, 115, 116, 117, 118, 128, 132, 136, 139, 140, 141, 144, 145, 155, 156, 158, 159, 160, 167, 170, 174, 177, 178, 182
International, 115, 117, 118, 119, 130, 140, 142, 143, 157, 158, 178, 180
Inter-state, 142, 179
Measure, 99, 125
NEST, 116, 136
Network, 116, 175
Regional, 128
South–South, 166, 167
State-agencies, 154, 174
Technical, 106, 108, 141, 142, 146, 155, 157, 160
Theory, 108
Transgovernmental, 99, 155, 167
Cooperation, 142, 147
Cross-National Projects
Definition, 5
Crowdsourcing, 176
Cruz, Brito, 15

Deforestation, 22, 118
Degussa–Leybold, 50
Delegation
Bureaucratic, 14–15
Democracy, xi, 46, 55, 65, 106, 108, 112, 178, 181, 185
Democratization, xi, xii, 14, 15, 47, 64, 65, 66, 77
Department of Technical Cooperation
IAEA, 84
Developmental
State, 33, 56
Discretion
bureaucratic, 31, 43, 119

Earth Summit, 1992, 119
El Guaraní, 6, 22, 26, 128
Aquifer, 3–4
Embalse, 51, 52, 70
Emerging markets, 28, 117, 158, 166, 184
Emma Perez Ferreira
President of CNEA, 55, 67, 70
Environmental Protection Agency (EPA), 185
epistemic communities, 15, 16, 17, 43, 191
EURATOM, 83
European Space Agency, 75
Evangelista, Matthew, 6
Evans, Peter, 18, 19, 24, 32, 33, 158, 187
Exponential Random Graph Models, 23

Fernando Collor de Mello
President of Brazil, 66, 70
foreign debt crisis, 9, 64, 77, 163

GEF. *See* Global Environmental Facility
Gender, 188–189
Gender mainstreaming in public policy, 189
Germany, 34, 53, 58, 62, 63, 64
Nuclear Supplier, 63
Global Environment Facility, xi, xiv, 4, 5, 21, 44, 116, 122, 133, 139, 159, 175, 192, 202
Globalization, 14
governance, 6, 26, 180, 183

Haas, Peter M., 6, 15, 43
Heavy water, 51, 52, 54
Huber, John D., 31

Human Capital, xiv, 7, 17, 19, 24, 37, 40, 41

IAEA. *See* International Atomic Energy Agency
IBGE, 9
IBSA Dialogue Forum, 167
India, 19, 33, 51, 61, 77, 79, 91, 94, 131, 134, 158, 166, 168, 181, 184
INEGI
  National Bureau of Statistics and Geography in Mexico, 9
Information age, xvi, 10, 14, 20, 67, 179, 180, 183, 187
International Atomic Energy Agency, xi, xii, xiv, 5, 20, 21, 28, 29, 38, 44, 48, 54, 58, 60, 73, 76, 84, 100, 116
International Inter-Agency Networks, 25, 86, 100, 136
International Monetary Fund (IMF), 10, 66, 166
International Space Station (ISS), 74
International waters, 22, 116, 122, 124
INVAP, 52

Japan, 58, 75, 77, 79, 91, 121
JAXA, 75

Kapstein, Ethan B., 6, 16
Kenya, 91, 93, 129, 131, 134, 160
Keohane, Robert, 5

Labor market, 34
Light water, 51

Market-oriented reforms. *See* Neoliberal reforms
Meirowitz, Adam, 31, 32
Menem, Carlos Saúl
  President of Argentina, 66
Mexico, 9, 21, 36, 64, 65, 79, 82, 93, 134
Minamata Convention on Mercury, 122

National Aeronautics and Space Administration (NASA), 9, 53, 75
National Commission for Atomic Energy. *See* CNEA
National Commission for Nuclear Energy. *See* CNEN
National Council Research of Brazil, 57
National Institute of Public Administration, 7
Neoliberal reforms, xvi, 10, 66, 157, 163
NEST, 20, 21, 22, 23, 25, 26, 27, 28, 29, 41, 45, 48, 49, 52, 54, 55, 57, 70, 72, 73, 74, 76, 77, 79, 80, 81, 85, 95, 97, 102, 103, 105, 108, 116, 117, 118, 125, 127, 156, 159, 160, 162, 181, 182, 186, 188
  Agencies, 92, 93, 115
  Bureaucrats, 78, 105, 117
  Cooperation, 77
  Data, 98, 101, 142
  Experts, 79
  Networks, 77, 80, 84, 86, 92, 94, 95, 99, 102, 103, 108, 117, 125, 145, 177
  Policy, 101
  Programs, 93
  Projects, 8, 80, 83, 95, 98, 100, 101, 102, 105, 106, 108
  State managers, 16
Networks
  Bifurcated, 95
  Collaborative, 2, 40, 41, 76, 85, 94, 97, 143, 160, 177
  Defined, 38
  Homophily in, 12, 22, 23, 24, 41, 42, 72, 82, 91, 98, 104, 109, 113, 115, 142, 143, 147, 153, 154, 159
  Knowledge, 13
  Professional, 8, 38, 188, 189
Neves, Tancredo, 65
Nicaragua, 8
Niskanen, William, 5
Non-Proliferation Treaty (NPT), 1, 52, 71, 181
Nuclear
  Energy producers, 79, 87, 91, 93
Nuclear Safety, 78–79, 98
Nuclebras (Brazilian Nuclear Enterprises), 62
Nye, Joseph S., 5

Oceania, 123, 134, 146, 153
Organisation for Economic Co-operation and Development (OECD), 5, 9, 31, 34, 76, 77, 91, 122, 166, 183, 184, 185, 186
Ornstein, Roberto, 52

Pakistan, 67, 77, 79, 82, 91, 181
Paraguay, 3, 6, 21, 26, 87, 124, 128, 167
Parallel Nuclear Program of Brazil, 63
Paraná River, 51
Perón, Juan Domingo, 48, 49
Peru, 50
Pielke, Roger A., 11
Pierre Auger International Cosmic Ray Observatory, 74
Plata River, 127, 162
Portugal, 15
Project Huemul, 48
Projects
  in Human health, xiii, 73, 75, 78, 79
  in Public health. *See* in Human health
  in Water, 3, 22, 25, 73, 116, 124, 136
  Multi-focal areas, 124
  Regional vs. global, 22
Public goods, 25, 180

Quihillalt, Oscar A., Admiral
  President of CNEA, 49

Radiation Safety, xii, 8, 69, 73, 76
Regional Co-operative Agreement for Research, Development and Training Related to Nuclear Science and Technology for Asia and the Pacific (RCA), 76
Regional Cooperative Arrangement for the Promotion of Nuclear Science and Technology in Latin America and the Caribbean (ARCAL), 76
Ricardo Raúl Alfonsín
  President of Argentina, 55
Richter, Ronald, 48
Río de la Plata. *See* Plate River
RKA, 75
Rueschemeyer, Dietrich, 14, 187
Russia, 158, 166

SAG
  Projects, 21
Sarney, Jose, 65
Schneider, Ben Ross, 14, 17, 18, 24, 32, 33, 56, 157, 187
Scientific and Technical Advisory Panel (STAP), GEF, 130
Secretariat for the Environment and Sustainable Development of Argentina (SAyDS), 119–121
Shipan, Charles R., 31
Siemens A.G., 51
Sikkink, Kathryn, 14, 17, 20, 24, 25, 32, 33
Skills
  Gap, 37
  Gap in Millenials, 185
  Gap in the United States, 184
  Gender Inequality in, 188–189
  General and Specific, 40–41
  Research and Development (R&D), 2, 9, 82, 115, 176
  Upgrading, xv, 2, 12, 13, 17, 18, 23, 24, 28, 31, 34, 40, 44, 46, 71, 73, 78, 117, 140, 177, 178, 183, 184
Skocpol, Theda, 14, 187
Slaughter, Anne Marie, 6, 26, 42, 43, 86, 180, 181, 183
Small island states, 124, 125
South Africa, 8, 21, 27, 36, 81, 87, 91, 166, 167
State expertise. *See* Bureaucracies
STEM, 19
Stockholm Convention on Persistent Organic Pollutants (POPs), 122
Streeck, Wolfgang, 10, 14, 37, 101

Tanzania, 19, 91, 93, 129, 160
Technology Transfer Agreement (TTA), 51
The Lost Decade
  of Development (1980s), 64
Thurner, Paul W., 44
Transboundary Diagnostic Analysis (TDA), 128
Transboundary water. *See* international waters
transgovernmentalism, 42, 43, 74, 180
  definition, 4
Treaty of Tlatelolco, 71

UN Convention to Combat Desertification (UNCCD), 122
UNEP. *See* United Nations Environmental Program
Union of South American Nations (UNASUR), 167
United Nations Environmental Program, 29, 38, 116, 130
United Nations Framework Convention on Climate Change, 44, 117, 122, 162

United States, 9, 31, 51, 52, 54, 55, 57, 58, 59, 61, 166, 176, 184, 186
United States nuclear policy, 58
Uruguay, 3, 4, 6, 21, 26, 79, 87, 120, 124, 127, 128, 134, 162

Venezuela, 3, 77, 167
Vinhas, Laercio, 18

Water Security, 5, 31
Weber, Max, 2, 30, 32, 33
Women bureaucrats. *See* Gender